GRAHAM GREENE'S CONRADIAN MASTERPLOT

Graham Greene's Conradian Masterplot

The Arabesques of Influence

Robert Pendleton

First published in Great Britain 1996 by
MACMILLAN PRESS LTD
Houndmills, Basingstoke, Hampshire RG21 6XS
and London
Companies and representatives
throughout the world

A catalogue record for this book is available
from the British Library.

ISBN 0-333-62888-8

First published in the United States of America 1996 by
ST. MARTIN'S PRESS, INC.,
Scholarly and Reference Division,
175 Fifth Avenue,
New York, N.Y. 10010

ISBN 0-312-12571-2

Library of Congress Cataloging-in-Publication Data
Pendleton, Robert.
Graham Greene's Conradian masterplot: the arabesques of influence
/ Robert Pendleton.
p. cm.
Includes bibliographical references (p.) and index.
ISBN 0-312-12571-2
1. Greene, Graham, 1904-91—Knowledge—Literature. 2. Greene,
Graham, 1904-91—Stories, plots etc. 3. Conrad, Joseph,
1857-1924—Influence. 4. English fiction—Stories, plots, etc.
5. Influence (Literary, artistic, etc.) I. Title.
PR6013.R44Z6578 1996
823'.912—dc20 94-44448
CIP

---

10 9 8 7 6 5 4 3 2 1
05 04 03 02 01 00 99 98 97 96

Printed in Great Britain by
Ipswich Book Co Ltd, Ipswich, Suffolk

Contents

For G.S. and F.D.M.

Acknowledgements

I am grateful to the Harry Ransom Humanities Research Center for allowing me to inspect Greene's letters, manuscripts and diaries. Appreciative thanks are also extended to Porter Abbott, Bettina Barrett, Bishop George Barrett, Eloise Hay, Joss Marsh, Evelyn B. Pendleton, Donna Rudolph and Cedric Watts for their helpful commentaries on the manuscript at various stages of its completion.

Introduction

Literary influence comes easily and dies hard. Graham Greene seems, at least from his undergraduate years, to have experienced an almost fatal attraction for Joseph Conrad. At Balliol, for example, Greene wrote a poem which asserted that 'no Browne brings me such pleasure, / As my loved Barrie, Conrad, Bernard Shaw' (129), and in a letter to his fiancée in 1925, he told her 'I love you more than John Donne . . . and Joseph Conrad and wet laurels' (219).[1] While it remains unclear if the eventual failure of their marriage can be attributed to Greene's penchant for such comparisons, his own testimony in the travel journal *In Search of a Character* (1962) blames Conrad's 'too great and too disastrous' influence (31) for the failure of his second novel, *Rumour at Nightfall* (1931). In the autobiographical work, *A Sort of Life* (1972), Greene reflects that 'There is no spark in *The Name of Action* or *Rumour at Nightfall* because there was nothing of myself in them. . . . All that was left in the heavy pages of the second was the distorted ghost of Conrad' (*A Sort of Life* 206). He castigates *Rumour at Nightfall* as 'romantic and derivative' (211), describing its prose in *Ways of Escape* (1982) as 'flat and stilted and pretentious' and its characterisation as 'non-existent', explaining that 'the young writer had obviously been reading again and alas! admiring Conrad's worst novel, *The Arrow of Gold*' (*Ways* 16–17).

However, Greene's assertion that this influence was mainly stylistic obscures the generic similarity of his novels to Conrad's. Both writers show a common tendency to merge different kinds of narrative, producing what E.D. Hirsch Jr defines as an 'intrinsic genre'.[2] Hirsch argues that 'the growth of new genres depends upon an imaginative leap [by which] the old is assimilated to the new and something genuinely new is realised' (Hirsch 105), a process which may occur through 'two old types [being] *amalgamated* . . . or an existing type . . . *extended*' (105). I wish to argue that both Conrad's and Greene's novels join the adventure story of Robert Louis Stevenson, Rider Haggard and John Buchan, on the one hand, with the more realistic political novel defined by Flaubert, Turgenev and

Maupassant, and the intricate depiction of human interiority by Henry James, on the other. The result is the creation of a unique type of political adventure story dramatised by psychological motivation.

While many critics have noted comparisons between Greene and Conrad, they usually concentrate their attention upon theme rather than genre.[3] It seems more profitable, however, to examine Conrad's and Greene's fictions in terms of the way they fuse different types of story, in order to convey thematic concerns at a more profound level. The dramatisation of such a dilemma between faith and betrayal in *Under Western Eyes* and *The Quiet American*, for example, reveals interiority of character in the form of Fowler's and Razumov's personal guilt and remorse. Psychological revelation actually structures the adventure plot, the conspiratorial machinations of which enmesh these protagonists in a more than physical way, so that finally the individual's dilemma microcosmically embodies the larger imperialistic oppression which the novels seek to interrogate.

Recent studies move towards a consensus that there is a complex interaction between genres. John G. Cawelti and Robert Scholes suggest that we need to be flexible in defining the 'popular' and the 'serious'. Cawelti distinguishes 'formulaic' works, which 'necessarily stress intense and immediate kinds of excitement and gratification' from 'mimetic' ones characterised by 'more complex and ambiguous analyses of character and motivation' (Cawelti 14), seeing these genres as 'two poles that most literary works lie somewhere between' (13). Similarly, Robert Scholes describes 'a continuum of possibilities, along which superior linguistic competence enables readers to derive entertainment from increasingly complex works' (Scholes 59). Winifred Fluck goes further, attempting to complicate the view which sees popular culture as formulaic and stereotypical 'because it does not dare or does not want to disturb existing patterns of perception' (Fluck 53). He argues that we cannot take for granted that this 'mere affirmation' which is hypothetically to be found in formulaic literature 'should provide pleasure to such an unusual degree that it is consistently sought' (53). He thinks that 'only if the text provides a certain amount of genuinely felt anxiety and disturbance will the reader become engaged' (53–6). Rejecting the distinction between modernism and mass culture which separates 'the conventional use of signs on the one side and the model of an unexpected new and semantically disruptive combination of signs on the other' (56), Fluck argues that 'each medium and genre within popular culture obviously has its own cycle of innovation and conventionalization' (56). Popular texts can be innovative, he thinks, by mediating between 'a conventional use of signs and its disturbance in ways that may not endanger its own readability', whereas the experimental text 'cannot entirely dissolve convention if it wants to retain a last remnant of accessibility' (57). Fluck concludes that it is necessary to develop 'a perspective in which the popular text . . . is not merely the "low" or debased version of established cultural forms, but emerges as a "third" model of aesthetic function besides those of realism and modernism' (62).

Peter Rabinowitz shifts the argument further towards reception theory to view the notions of 'popular' and 'serious' literature merely as ready-made 'strategies' for reading, which can be narrower or broader, depending on how many and which 'rules' the reader applies (Rabinowitz 176–8). Rabinowitz argues that in popular literature, which is metonymic and plot-oriented, the reader usually emphasises 'rules of configuration' (185), 'a knowledge of patterns [whereby] we can . . . develop expectations and experience a sense of completion' (44). In this way, we tend to consider an element which is brought to our attention in a work of popular fiction 'in terms of what it may tell us about plot outcome, rather than in terms of what it may reveal about the inner states of the characters and the world of the book' (185).[4]

Conrad's and Greene's novels demand to be read with an awareness of these rules of notice, which apply both to plot-orientated fiction and to narratives which deal with 'inner states of the characters and the world of the book'. If, as Jerry Palmer suggests, the plot of the thriller 'is the process by which the hero averts [a] conspiracy' (Palmer 53), then the hero who averts this conspiracy in Greene's and Conrad's novels is often the conspirator himself. Marlow, the narrator of *Lord Jim*, for example, is as much concerned with the inner changes of the protagonist (and his own) as with Jim's external successes in Patusan; the narrative constantly interrogates Jim's inner failure in deserting the *Patna* pilgrims and his decision to face execution for unintentionally betraying his adopted people, 'the Bugis'. It is impossible finally to distinguish the external adventure from the interior one.

This mixed genre was not of course immaculately conceived by Conrad. His novels in many ways constitute a response to a division between the adventure formula and the interior narrative which began to make itself felt in the later part of the nineteenth century during the final stages of Dickens's career and after his death. While George Eliot, Meredith and Henry James came increasingly to insist on the novel as a developed art form that would reveal the details of character through assiduous linguistic and formal expression, such writers as Wilkie Collins, Rider Haggard, Anthony Hope, Stanley Weyman and Robert Louis Stevenson emphasise the romance and suspense of pure adventure formula, with less attention to the development of character and motive.

This division of sensibilities is due partly, as Q. D. Leavis concludes in her seminal study, *Fiction and the Reading Public* (1932), to the decreasing price of novels during the later part of the nineteenth century. Leavis argues that 'What saved the lower middle-class public for some time from a drug addiction to fiction was the simple fact of the exorbitant price of novels' although 'the turn of those who early in the century were . . . deprived of the novels of fashion came with Dickens and periodical publication' (Leavis 152). Leavis details the dramatic decrease in the price of fiction through the later nineteenth century, together with the increase in price of the three-volume novel, which 'made all the difference to the novelist with no popular appeal' because while 'a serious novelist could make a handsome living without surrendering anything' in George Eliot's time, 'this was no longer the case' when Conrad began to write (161). Leavis sees 'the sudden opening of the fiction market to the general public' as 'a blow to serious reading' because it divided 'highbrow' readers and writers from 'lowbrow' ones (161). For this she blames the influence of 'the experiments of Flaubert, Zola, Maupassant, Turgenev, Balzac, even of Victor Hugo' on 'a whole body of English novelists determined to write novels which should be works of art' (168). These 'highbrow' novelists, Leavis continues, 'unlike the merely serious novelists of the past', who aim, 'like George Eliot . . . at moral ends easily comprehended by the half-educated, set out to develop the possibilities of [their] medium for ends outside the understanding of the ordinary reader' (168). Although Dickens and George Eliot are 'near neighbours', Leavis identifies 'an unbridged and unpassable gulf between Marie Corelli and Henry James', concluding that in this way 'the great novelists of the age pass out of the common reader's field of vision' (169).

Leavis, however, chooses the most extreme example with which to illustrate her thesis. Even in this case, we might ask if the 'gulf' between Corelli and James is *absolutely* 'unbridged and unpassable'. James, after all, develops popular themes such as espionage in *The Princess Casamassima*, while Corelli – simplistically and sensationally admittedly – makes at least some attempt to reveal spirituality in her work. The situation is of course more ambiguous in the case of Conrad, whose role as a 'double agent' moving self-consciously – and perhaps self-servingly – between genres has come to be recognised by more recent critics in terms of what Hugh Kenner identifies as the general continuity between modernist and popular forms.[5] In his book *Joseph Conrad: A Literary Life* (1984), Cedric Watts shows that publishing history tends to confirm Conrad's mixed generic allegiances, commenting that when we see his work 'situated not in a collected edition on the library shelves but in the pages of a variegated magazine cheek by jowl with advertisements for whiskey, tobacco, and toothpaste, we may gain a healthy sense of the Conrad who, among other things, was an entertainer competing with entertainers, a communicator busily exploiting the first great era of mass communications' (Watts, *Literary Life* 133).

These conflicting strains of Conrad's and Greene's literary inheritance motivate them alternately to resist and to conform to opposing paradigms. They are able to use the tension between the adventure story and the interior narrative as an energising impetus for their fiction, as opportunities for self-consciousness, reflexivity, and innovation, while situating their work more strongly in Victorian realism than other 'high' modernist novelists such as James Joyce and Virginia Woolf. This duality in their work often takes the form of a discussion of genres within the fiction itself. Lord Jim's reading of light adventure stories and Rollo Martins's writing of formulaic westerns (in Greene's *The Third Man*), implicitly distinguish the intrinsic genres of these novels from the discrete subgenres which compose them, suggesting that the narratives make up a whole greater than the sum of their parts.

Greene may have realised that it was his generic affinities with Conrad that were partly responsible for 'the disastrous influence' on his own early work. In *A Sort of Life* (1972), he describes his early writing as an 'elaborate scaffolding built from an older writer's blueprint', which he had to 'write off as apprentice work' in order to 'begin again naked [with] an adventure story [*Stamboul Train*]' (*A Sort of Life* 212). The resulting novel suggests that Greene's method of remedying the situation was to abstract *one* of Conrad's subgenres from the otherwise elaborate scaffolding, in order to simplify his own work and play down within it the Conradian tendency for weighty meditations upon the interior self, romantic love and historical and political destiny.

The propitiatory function of Greene's vow 'never again' to 'read a novel of Conrad's', which he 'kept for more than a quarter of a century', seems initially to have been successful (*Sort* 212). *Stamboul Train* (1932), a fast-moving thriller set on the Orient Express, fragments the Conradian sub-genres and establishes the pattern for a series of 'entertainments', as Greene termed them in contrast to his 'novels'. During this period of his self-imposed abstinence, however, he does not so much deviate from Conrad as segregate the strains of different Conradian influences. While foregrounding action in the entertainments, he concentrates upon dilemmas of human interiority in his 'novels', displacing Conrad into two different narrative modes – that of the late nineteenth and early twentieth-century adventure genre of John Buchan in entertainments such as *Stamboul Train* (1932), *The Confidential Agent* (1939), and *The Ministry of Fear* (1942), and that of the Catholic fiction of Mauriac, Bernanos, and Waugh in works such as *Brighton Rock* (1939), *The Power and the Glory* (1944), and *The Heart of the Matter* (1948).

What appear to be operating, then, as 'deviations', eventually emerge as a series of 'displaced repetitions' of two discrete sub-genres of Conrad, the interior narrative and the thriller. Having made a brief appearance in early novels such as *It's a Battlefield* (1933), however, the political narrative is almost completely eclipsed during the first part of Greene's career, when he loses sight of the ideological concerns so prominent in *Heart of Darkness*, *Nostromo*, *The Secret Agent*, and *Under Western Eyes*. Although there are, of course, notable exceptions such as *The Power and the Glory* (1940), which treats the themes of faith and betrayal within a political plot, the narrative of interior revelation is generally detached between 1932 and 1955 from the sense of a wider Conradian political milieu. It is only after the end of the forties that Greene begins consistently to bind these deviations and to bring the repressed combination of Conradian influences fully to light in each successive work. He reaches the full extent of the deviation towards a Buchanesque thriller formula with the *film noir* screenplay of *The Third Man* (1947), while the Catholic 'detour' arrives at an impasse with the appropriately titled novel, *The End of the Affair* (1951). It is as though these two works provide a dual catharsis which allows Greene once more to invoke the political influence of Conrad in conjunction with his own development of the interiorised thriller.

With this model of a shared intrinsic genre in mind, let us now turn more specifically to the question of Conrad's influence on Greene. A systematic examination of Greene's and Conrad's intertextuality has been attempted by only one critic, David Leon Higdon, in an essay published in 1979. Higdon adopts the perspective of Harold Bloom's well-known study, *The Anxiety of Influence* (1974), suggesting that the close affinities between Conrad and Greene 'are . . . in the nature of an adversarial relationship' (Higdon 29) and that Conrad is Greene's 'ghostly adversary' (41). However, while this article helps to articulate some points of connection between the various phases of Greene's career and Conrad's novels, Bloom's six stages of influence seem too idiosyncratic to be applied systematically to the individual complexities of the case in hand.[6] Higdon himself, in fact, bears this out by mentioning Bloom's work only briefly and then concentrating his discussion upon a more specific comparison of the two novelists.

I would suggest that Peter Brooks's theory of plot can illuminate the question of Greene's and Conrad's intertextuality more closely and thoroughly than Bloom's theory of influence. Although Brooks addresses single narratives, his work may also be applied to Greene's total narrative *opus*, a term I will use in the sense of a writer's total work conceived as a meta-narrative. This is analogous to the way in which plots themselves are often modelled on the shape of a life or career. In *Reading for the Plot* (1984), Brooks adapts Freudian theory to explore the structure of narrative rather than to psychoanalyse the motivation of authors, as Bloom does, or of characters within narratives, in the way of earlier psychoanalytic critics. He believes that plots are motivated by an initial trauma, identifying a 'moment at which "story" . . . is stimulated from quiescence into a state of narratability, into a tension, a kind of irritation, which demands narration' (Brooks 103). The narrative then 'works through' this trauma, apparently by taking a series of detours from the repressed denouement. These detours, however, are in fact displaced repetitions of the 'secret' to be revealed at the end of the fiction. Eventually the meaning of the repressed material is 'bound' – organised and brought to light by means of the denouement – and the text achieves what Brooks describes as a 'serviceable [perceptible] discharge' (101).

Detours or deviations provide plots with 'ballast', preventing them from reaching their denouements too soon. Although inevitably 'the narrative must tend toward its end, seek illumination in its own death', Brooks stipulates that this must be 'the right death, the correct end', for 'there is a danger of short-circuit' – of 'reaching the end too quickly, of achieving the im-proper death' (104). To avoid this kind of premature conclusion, narratives are structured by a series of deviations from their main plots, 'arabesques', as he calls them in their more intricate form. Yet the end remains in view. Readers must feel that the plot is leading somewhere and that the given deviations are tending towards meaningful closure, even though the secret of the denouement is for the moment concealed.

Lord Jim's enterprise in Patusan is a good example of this deviation within a single text – a deviation which, in the manner of the 'eastern bride', veils for the present his 'opportunity' – his eventual end in self-sacrificial death. The Patusan deviation is central to the plot of *Lord Jim*. Jim's adventure in Patusan is the embodiment of his 'dream', the acting through of the shadowy fantasies of the earlier part of the book. As fictional character, Jim needs to be 'satisfied – quite' (*Lord Jim* 416), to follow the dream through to the end, *usque ad finem*, in the words of Stein (215). The reader also needs this deviation in order to feel 'satisfied' that the complete story of Jim has been told. In this way, the danger of short-circuit is avoided – the risk of creating an unsatisfactorily short, inadequate narrative such as Conrad felt 'Lord Jim: A Sketch' would have been. Moreover, 'short-circuit' is a danger Conrad himself was quite explicitly aware of, as he demonstrates in the 'Author's Note' to *Chance*, where defending himself against critics of the novel's lengthiness, he comments that '[n]o doubt . . . by selecting a certain method and taking great pains the whole story might have been written out on a cigarette paper', although '[f]or that matter the whole history of mankind could be written thus if only approached with sufficient detachment', concluding: 'But in the infinitely minute stories about men and women it is my lot on earth to narrate I am not capable of such detachment' (*Chance* x). The point is not weakened by the probability that *Chance* itself would have benefited by a few such short-circuits.

This Conradian genre of the interiorised political thriller constantly returns within Greene's narrative *opus*. It harks implicitly back to the trauma of his early failed novels – a trauma which served the useful purpose of fully 'arousing' his work and stimulating its development, causing him to shake off (or so he thought) his 'quiescent' acceptance of Conrad's influence. In fact, however, the generic and thematic detours Greene makes to avoid Conrad allow him to explore the various facets of this influence without again succumbing to it, enabling him eventually to manipulate and control it. The major direction of these detours is away from the political narrative; they take the form of displaced repetitions of the thriller formula and the psychological story, the two other major components of the Conradian masterplot.

My argument develops as follows. Chapter 1, '"The Proper Formula": Conrad's Transformed Adventure Story', argues that Conrad's major work develops a generic fusion between a psychological narrative and a political adventure story, uniting narrative modes dissociated in the late nineteenth-century English novel. Towards the end of his career, however, the romantic love story, with only a background of political intrigue, returns into his work. It is this sub-genre which Greene imitates in his earlier novels, falling under what he saw in the first instance as Conrad's 'disastrous' influence. Chapter 2, '"Writing off the Elaborate Scaffolding": Greene's Detour to Adventure', discusses the fragmenting effect of the Conradian love romance on the generic makeup of Greene's earlier work. Having produced in his earliest novels confused narratives which seek to negotiate among a number of Conradian subgenres, Greene increasingly suppresses the political narrative in the 'entertainments' of the thirties and forties. Blending the Conradian revelation of interiority with something resembling a Buchanesque thriller, he dramatises the protagonist's sense of existential isolation, eventually to rediscover the narrative structure of the observer–hero's search for the 'other'.

In parallel to the discussion of the thriller formula in Chapter 2, the third chapter, '"A Distant Memory of the Sanctus Bell": Greene's Catholic "Heart of Darkness"' traces Greene's creation of a Catholic version of Conrad's psychological narrative of faith and betrayal. These novels also repress a potential political plot, concentrating instead upon theological dilemmas. Gradually, however, Greene brings Catholic interiority together with an African setting, converting the psychological journey of *Heart of Darkness* into the documentary form of the travel narrative in *Journey without Maps* (1935). Although *The Heart of the Matter* (1948) evades its potential as a colonial novel in favour of a private dilemma of faith, *A Burnt-Out Case* (1960) integrates the interior drama of religious doubt with a more socially aware form of fiction.

Chapter 4, '"He Who Forms a Tie": The Conradian Protagonist in Greene's Later Novels', examines the return of the political emphasis into works following *The Quiet American* (1955). In *The Honorary Consul* (1973), Greene brings back the fully Catholic version of the inner quest, setting it in a generic and dramatic dialogue with the political plot. The final chapter, '"Dissolving into Laughter"', identifies a series of comic fictions constructed by a joining of ludic, post-modern forms of humorous fantasy with both the religious allegory and the political thriller. Through playing different kinds of narratives against each other, these works – especially *Monsignor Quixote* (1982) – embody Greene's translation of Conradian scepticism into a mode of Catholic agnosticism, constructing a vision of ontological openness. Embarking on the sea-changes of Greene's long and varied career, we are, then – in every sense Brooks can describe and more – 'reading for the plot'.

1

'The Proper Formula': Conrad's Transformed Adventure Story

I

In *A Personal Record,* Conrad reports that *Nicholas Nickleby* was his 'first introduction to English imaginative literature' (*Personal Record* 71), and confesses that he has 'such an intense and unreasoning affection' for *Bleak House,* 'dating from the days of [his] childhood, that its very weaknesses are more precious to [him] than the strengths of other men's work' (124). Conrad found Dickens attractive for his ability to combine a suspenseful plot with a revelation of character and atmosphere through structure, style, and imagery. In *Bleak House,* we can clearly see the combination of a formulaic detective plot with a wider tragic vision of English society, where a continuing self-examination by the protagonist Esther Summerson produces an interrogation of the self and that society at multiple levels. In this sense, Dickens's narrative technique becomes one of Conrad's principal inspirations.

Although Dickens is not the only nineteenth-century novelist to combine action and interiority, he was the last principal figure to do so in the older realistic tradition of Defoe, Fielding, Smollett, and Scott. However, as I have argued, this tradition becomes a divided one during the later nineteenth century, taking the form of Stevenson's and Haggard's essentially formulaic plots, on the one hand, and George Eliot's, George Meredith's, and Henry James's more complex revelations of human interiority, on the other. As an outsider, perhaps Conrad was able to maintain more critical distance than many of his contemporaries from these discrete subgenres, self-consciously manipulating and complicating them in his fiction. Various critics tend to emphasise the opposing ingredients of his work differently. While David Thorburn argues that Conrad's major work 'shows us the extent to which [his] major achievement is founded, often, on the recurring, even *defining* features of the traditional adventure story' (Thorburn 41), Elsa Nettels, by contrast, concentrates upon his important bond with Henry James, which she defines as 'their dedication to the art of fiction and their abiding interest in the method of rendering the inner life of characters and the inwardness of situations' (Nettels ix).

It would seem more accurate, however, to view these opposing currents as dynamic, changing qualities which interact differently in each of Conrad's novels. Conrad (and later also Greene) had an immense admiration for James, whom he perhaps used as a criterion with which to maintain his sense of the importance of the interiority of human character. In his essay 'Henry James: An Appreciation' (1905), Conrad contrasts, 'for the quickening of our maturer years', the 'fiercest excitements of a romance *de cape et d'épée*, the romance of yard-arm and boarding pike so dear to youth, whose knowledge of action (as of other things) is imperfect and limited' – with 'the tasks set . . . the difficulties presented, to the sense of truth, of necessity – before all, of conduct – of Mr Henry James's men and women' (85). Conrad goes on to compare unfavourably what he calls James's 'solution by rejection', which 'must always present a certain lack of finality', with 'the usual methods of solution by rewards and punishments', such as 'crowned love . . . fortune . . . a broken leg or . . . sudden death' (85). Although the reader's wish 'to be set at rest' is 'perhaps the only true desire of mankind, coming thus to light in its hours of leisure', Conrad disparages such 'light holiday literature', as he calls it in *Lord Jim* (5), concluding with approval that 'One is never set at rest by Mr Henry James's novels' (88).

Yet Conrad does not follow James all the way in this emphasis of the interior narrative. Although Marlow's 'inconclusive' tale in *Heart of Darkness* (11) denies the reader closure, Conrad frequently uses the 'usual methods of solution' he professes so to despise, even in the major work: for example in the 'sudden deaths' of Winnie or Nostromo. Furthermore, 'crowned love' often provides the denouement of his minor fiction, as in the final union of Captain Anthony and Flora de Barral in *Chance*, or of Lieutenant Réal and Arlette in *The Rover*.

Some of Conrad's plots, then, fulfil their 'potentially melodramatic' quality, as David Thorburn terms it, more completely than others. One of Conrad's most formulaic fictions is *Romance* (1903), written in collaboration with Ford Madox Ford. Thorburn argues that this novel most emphatically demonstrates Conrad's affinities with Stevenson's *Catriona* through 'being set in a past that is not too distant', and by focusing on 'the adventures of a young man fleeing his enemies across strange country in the company of the girl he loves and must protect' (Thorburn 33). Stevenson's hero, Thorburn notes, is 'a callow but strong-hearted conventionally reared young fellow with an acute sense of honour who seems in many ways the ancestor of the similarly presented hero of *Romance*'; each 'is also the narrator of his story', which is told 'ostensibly . . . many years after the events' (33), a 'potentially rich perspective' which, Thorburn concludes, 'neither Stevenson nor Conrad and Ford turn . . . to any serious use' (34).

Thorburn views *Romance* as leading into the major work and showing us the extent to which 'Conrad's major achievement is founded, often, on the recurring, even *defining* features of the traditional adventure story' (41). However, this paradigm of foundation and construction seems misleadingly and simplistically dualistic in the light of the more subtle integration and interplay of genres which Conrad brings to his more well-known novels. In this particular case, *Romance* is the exception which proves the rule. It is different in kind from the major work precisely because the adventure story genre is so conspicuously foregrounded, resulting in little more than an undeveloped Bildungsroman which traces John Kemp's circular progress from dangerous situation to fortunate escape and back to dangerous situation, until the timely arrival of *The Lion*, his rescue from the gallows and his reunion with Seraphina. Although Conrad asserts that the book 'is *not* a boy's story', he also 'hoped [it] would be a popular piece of romantic literature that could tap the audience for Stevenson, Anthony Hope, and Rider Haggard' (Karl, *Conrad: Three Lives* 438) and that with its 'easy style . . . action, romantic atmosphere and . . . happy ending after no end of real hair's breadth escapes', it held 'a promise of popular success' (Karl and Davies, *Letters* 2:366).

In the light of Conrad's considerably more complex fusions of the adventure story, interior narrative, and political theme, which were fully developed by 1904, *Romance* is better seen as a momentary lapse from Conrad's more significant work. In the novels from *Heart of Darkness* to *Under Western Eyes*, the adventure story genre is more usefully conceived not as an independent entity somehow 'there' in the fiction, but in terms of Rabinowitz's or Fluck's reception theory – as a loosely defined strategy for reading, the perception of an invitation towards one mode of interpretation working alongside other such invitations.[1] With Dickens's work as an infrastructural reference point, Conrad drew on a wide range of sources which contribute to the sub-genres of his novels, including the adventure stories of Haggard, Kipling, Stevenson, Marryat, and Cooper, the realistic political narratives of Flaubert, Turgenev, and Hugo, and the Polish Romantic and Positivist traditions.[2]

In this way, Conrad's own work follows a pattern of narrative deviation and return which anticipates that of Greene's *opus*. Conrad begins his career with a colonial adventure story, *Almayer's Folly* (1895), which concentrates upon the interiority of the protagonist as well as portraying the complex multi-cultural setting and the interaction of these at a generic level. However, in his next two novels, *An Outcast of the Islands* (1896) and *The Rescue* (1898, 1919), a narrative of romantic love tends to smother the political one. Again, in his final phase, the 'stealthy Nemesis' of the unadulterated love romance eventually overtakes Conrad's fiction once more. From *Chance* (1912) through the later novels, *The Arrow of Gold* (1919), *The Rover* (1924) and the unfinished *Suspense* (1925), this genre dominates the narrative structure, placing what remains of the interior, political and adventure narratives in an ambiguous and confusing light.

Following an overview of these later and earlier novels, I will concentrate upon the works from *Heart of Darkness* (1899) through *Lord Jim* (1900), *Nostromo* (1904), *The Secret Agent* (1907), *Under Western Eyes* (1911) and *Victory* (1915). In these works, Conrad reintroduces issues of wider social significance, orchestrating them with the other principal sub-genres of the adventure story – the revelation of the protagonist's interior psychology and the love romance. In this way, different generic strands resonate significantly with each other, creating the sense of a whole greater than the sum of its parts which characterises the Conradian masterplot.

II

An interior narrative is already working against a political adventure story in Conrad's earliest novel, *Almayer's Folly* (1895). The pursuit of Dain by the Dutch, together with his subsequent escape through a stratagem worthy of a Conan Doyle culprit, provides a conspiracy germane to the thriller form; however, this adventure story is subtly modified by Almayer's ironic delusion that he can fulfil the typical Haggardesque quest for treasure in the interior of the island. Traditional suspense is also subverted, as Allan H. Simmons shows, 'by an inscribed narrative ambiguity' (Simmons 14) brought about by narrative tensions which direct us towards '*process* rather than *product*' (15). This process reveals the significance of Almayer's interior narrative in a political sense as the betrayal of solidarity with the rest of mankind.[3] Almayer severs his links first with his own race by marrying a native woman, then with his beloved daughter when she chooses the Malay Dain as her lover, and finally loses any sense of human contact at the end of the novel. Both the development of Almayer's interiority and the adventure plot are intimately intermingled with an imperial narrative which dramatises the complex interaction of races.

The traditional 'treasure hunt' of the adventure story is deliberately confined to Almayer's deluded fantasies, which 'were often busy with gold . . . he had failed to secure . . . or gold he meant to secure yet' (*Almayer's Folly* 7). These are contrasted with the reality of his life, which is depicted in terms of what Greene would later call Conrad's 'drab Edwardian realism' (*Pleasure* 123): the 'dusty door' of Lingard & Co.'s office, with its 'general air of squalid neglect' (*Almayer's Folly* 16–17). Almayer is in many ways a typical 'seedy' Greenean exile who, recalling Mr Tench in *The Power and the Glory*, 'put[s] off his departure from year to year, always expecting some favourable turn of fortune' (ibid. 27). He is a colonialist in the worst possible position who can neither exploit the country he has come to live in as Lingard is able to do, nor relinquish enough of his white identity to find fulfilment in the native family he has raised.

Almayer's attitude to his Malay wife encapsulates in many ways the trend of the conquering race to plunder undeveloped countries for material resources while caring nothing for their inhabitants. It is a condition of Lingard's making Almayer his heir, that he will marry Lingard's adopted daughter, an undertaking which he accepts quite lightly, feeling only 'a confused consciousness of shame that he was a white man' (*Almayer's Folly* 12); this is backed up by a mental proviso that 'she may mercifully die' and 'a vague idea of shutting her up somewhere' (13). However, Almayer suffers a form of poetic justice for his unthinking relinquishment of human feeling through the loss of his daughter Nina's affection, a loss brought about by his inability to eschew fantasy in favour of a directly felt emotion. One of the most rending scenes of the novel is his rejection of Nina when she falls in love with Dain Maroola, an occasion exacerbated in its poignancy by Almayer's temptation to have the courage of his convictions and 'go native' in an authentic way, to 'suddenly take her to his heart, forget his shame, and pain, and anger, and follow her' (156).

However, the effectiveness of Almayer's internal development – or decline – is more a product of the narrative's concern with issues of a wider political significance than of the conflict between a father and a daughter. *Almayer's Folly* effectively plays against each other the different sub-genres of interior revelation, adventure story, love story and political narrative to create a complex depiction of conflicting cultures within a colonial setting. In his book *The Deceptive Text* (1984), Cedric Watts argues that this interaction adds an intricate sense of multicultural diversity to the novel's political dimension. Watts defines two plots in *Almayer's Folly*: an 'overt' one in which the ambush of Dain leads to his 'precipitated elopement' with Nina, bringing about Almayer's realisation that they have deceived him, and a 'covert' one which reveals that Dain was attacked as a result of the Arab trader Abdulla's treachery. Watts argues that the significance of this lies in 'the intensely ironic complex of racial, national and sexual revenge', whereby 'Arab betrays Balinese and European, as once European had prevented marriage of half-caste to Arab, and as once European had been thought to betray Arab [Reshid] into ambush' (Watts 51). To this we might add a mention of the reverse Darwinism that structures Almayer's decline. From a fantasised immersion in 'all the possibilities of an opulent existence' (*Almayer's Folly* 12), Almayer moves towards a reduced and almost constantly drugged state in which he seems 'taken complete charge of' by his pet monkey (164).

While the narrative of the love romance between Nina and Dain is controlled and contextualised by the relationship of father and daughter and by the issues of racial identification in *Almayer's Folly*, it tends virtually to take over in Conrad's second novel, *An Outcast of the Islands* (1896), just as the native girl Aïssa dominates the white protagonist's will. There is little of the assiduous charting of interior psychology that motivates Jocelyn Baines to describe Almayer as a kind of Eastern Madame Bovary (146), for Conrad's heaping all the blame for a white man's downfall on an irresistible erotic attraction to a primitive woman tends to obscure the complex political analysis of the first novel. George Orwell's remark that Greene's novel *The Heart of the Matter* 'might as well be happening in a London suburb' (Orwell 106) applies here also. In the same way, the relationships in

The Outcast of the Islands are localised, the property of characters whose purpose seems merely to embody abstract passions and who are isolated from a broader political context.

Unlike Almayer, the protagonist Willems is almost wholly unremarkable. Although, like his fictional forebear, he too becomes a 'man from nowhere' (*Outcast* 28), a man without a race, the erotic attraction which leads him to this pass is less analysed than merely asserted: 'while she was near there was nothing in the whole world – for that idle man – but her look and her smile. Nothing in the past, nothing in the future; and in the present only the luminous fact of her existence' (76–7). There is no attempt to place Willems's irresistible erotic attraction within a context which reveals the role of the white man in the east; similarly, there is little development of Aïssa's view of Willems: 'To her [he] appeared as remote, as brilliant, as terrible, as necessary, as the sun that gives life to these lands. . . . She had watched him . . . fascinated by love, fascinated by danger' (248). Interracial sexuality is elevated to the status of an ontological imperative, reducing the political ramifications of the conspiracy plot to mere background.

The Outcast of the Islands, then, is very much a 'sequel' to *Almayer's Folly*; what vestiges of political significance it appears to have are derived from the intertextuality the two novels share. Although the conspiracy plot whereby Abdulla gains knowledge of the route into Lingard's river has suggestions of the complex interaction of races in the East Indies at the time, it is finally pressed completely into the service of the erotic narrative, as is the revelation of psychological interiority. The result is a colonial rendering of the archetypal Samson and Delilah story to which all the conspiracies in the novel are subjugated: Babalatchi's plan 'to make use of Willems for the destruction of Lingard's influence' (60), as well as Almayer's scheme to use Willems's abandoned wife Joanna as a means for ridding himself of an unwanted competitor for Lingard's affections. Despite the apparent intimations of political and racial significance, the teleological impetus of the narrative is towards the conventional showdown of romantic melodrama when the archetypal erotic triangle of Willems, Aïssa, and Joanna is finally brought together and Aïssa shoots her lover.

Interestingly enough, the novel gains a more authentic Greene–Conrad quality in Carol Reed's film version (1952), starring Trevor Howard, Robert Morley, Ralph Richardson and Wilfred Hyde-White. In the scene where Almayer (Robert Morley) and Lingard (Ralph

Richardson) wear paper hats at Almayer's birthday party, the effect is to create a light-hearted atmosphere beneath the tense emotions. More reminiscent of Greene's black, sometimes surreal humour, the hats provide an incongruous foil to the deeper tensions underlying the men's relationships, while the poignancy of the isolated white colonialist is emphasised in another sequence in which Almayer encourages his young daughter to shout 'pig!' after Willems, recalling the small boy in the crowd in Reed's previous film of Greene's *The Third Man* (1949).[4] It would seem that if 'the inclusion of children as unwitting commentators on adult folly' is one of 'Reed's trademarks' (Moss 202), this is a motif Reed developed together with Greene, who worked on the screenplays of Reed's two previous films of his fictions, *The Third Man* and *The Fallen Idol* (1948). Most importantly, however, Reed evokes in *The Outcast of the Islands* a more definite sense of the Conrad–Greene political milieu by means of a number of impressive *tableaux* which show the native inhabitants looking on at the white men's pitiful folly. All in all, through drawing on the potential rather than the actuality of Conrad's novel, the film serves to clarify that the precise point of contact between the two writers lies in the 'political-interior-adventure story' which constitutes a sympathetic but unflinchingly ironic appraisal of a degenerate European *Zeitgeist* within a colonial context.

By avoiding the emphasis on the love romance in *The Outcast of the Islands*, Conrad's next short novel, *The Nigger of the Narcissus* (1897), seems similar to Greene's own later attempt to 'begin again naked' (*A Sort of Life* 212). Conrad restricts himself to the almost feudal society on board ship, dramatising the danger caused that society when one of its members refuses to co-operate with the rest. The result is a taut adventure story combined with a rather simplistic political allegory casting Captain Allistoun as the ruler of this microcosmic kingdom against the socialist Donkin, who represents a threat to its solidarity. The comparative isolation of the sea-adventure genre, which we find also in 'Youth', 'The End of the Tether', and 'Typhoon', suggests a parallel detour to the love romance. These contrasting departures are comparable to Greene's own early excursions into the thriller and religious novel.

Neither of these, however, are genres to which Conrad wishes permanently to confine himself. The interior processes of a protagonist involved in an act of political betrayal, which he had first explored in *Almayer's Folly*, represent a repressed factor of the Conradian masterplot in Conrad's own case, as well as Greene's.

This element partially returns in *The Rescue*, which was begun in 1898 but abandoned and not finished till 1919. The novel's theme of a white man's betrayal of natives because of the return of his past world suggests a trial run for *Lord Jim*; however, this is confused by the final unbalanced emphasis upon the love narrative. Eloise Hay notes that while Lingard is a pure politician 'subverted by unrecognised erotic impulses' (Hay 97), the emphasis remains on these erotic impulses rather than on the political past. In this way, 'the whole point of the political fable is weakened out of existence', because it is 'Venus in Victorian drapery' that is 'the dealer of the tragic blow' rather than 'Lingard's forgotten western past as Wyndham had predicted it would be [in the manuscript version]' (Hay 105). Hay suggests that the unfortunate result of this is that 'the sacrifice of Hassim and Immada dumbfounds us as a bloody holocaust, a dreadful mistake rather than the inevitable reversal of Lingard's politically criminal irresolution' (105). Altogether, *The Rescue* teeters uncomfortably between externalised adventure formula (relayed here by the political conspiracy) and an interior narrative. This becomes further confused with a love story which seeks to reveal the memory of Lingard's white past but succeeds only in excavating an erotic attraction for Mrs Travers.

This profound ambiguity of genre may partially explain Conrad's inability to finish the novel in 1898. (It was later completed in 1919 at a time when he was in the process of a final deviation into romance. In one letter he told Edward Garnett: 'I can't write a word. . . . I want to make [*The Rescue*] a kind of glorified book for boys – You know. No analysis. No damned mouthing. Pictures – pictures – pictures. That's what I want to do. And I can do that. Can't I?' (Karl and Davies, *Collected Letters* 1:392). Obviously he couldn't, for as he comments in the 1919 'Author's Note' to *The Rescue*, he had turned aside in 1898 to the more pressing concerns of 'Youth', *Heart of Darkness*, and *Lord Jim* because he had 'lost . . . the sense of the proper formula of expression, the only formula that would suit' (*Rescue* x).

This tendency to diverge towards either a straightforward version of the love romance or the adventure story characterises both Conrad's very early and his very late work. Thomas Moser, in his well-known study *Joseph Conrad: Achievement and Decline* (1957), judges the later novels to be dominated by the ascendant theme of love, 'the lowest common denominator of the apprentice work' (Moser 3). These fictions tend to displace the narratives of inner psychology and political dilemma into depictions of romantic experiences undergone by the protagonist in isolation. It seems extremely difficult for Conrad to keep his critical and sceptical guard up when dealing with such powerful emotions without falling into tried and clichéd formulas. While the love romance figures in much of the major work – in the love relationships of Jewel and Jim in *Lord Jim*, Martin Decoud and Antonia Avellanos in *Nostromo* and the possible one between Razumov and Natalia in *Under Western Eyes* – there is an important distinction to be made. In these cases it is controlled by different generic strands within the narrative, which portray other aspects of human experience such as political relationships and more varied ontological perspectives. These different sub-genres work against each other to form a more polyvalent narrative.

It seems appropriate here, then, to delay discussion of Conrad's 'major' novels and move ahead to his final period. After 1912, the romantic love story heightened by an adventure story returns into his narrative *opus* to become the element which first attracts Greene. In *Chance* (1912), narrated by a Marlow aptly diagnosed as senile by Alan Warren Friedman, the detective plot is almost completely subordinate to the triumph of young love. *Chance* represents an almost Jamesian *tour-de-force* performed on the stock theme of romantic love and its trials. Nor are the literary influences limited to James, whose preternaturally evil governess Conrad has surely borrowed from *The Turn of the Screw*: Conrad also fuses the sea-adventure with a family romance drawn from Dickens's *Little Dorrit*, whereby a selfish ex-convict father attempts to block the romantic fulfilment of a devoted daughter.

To complicate matters even further, *Chance* is characterised by a considerable generic uneasiness which entails Conrad apparently undercutting this romantic theme. The self-consciously titled part divisions, 'The Damsel' and 'The Knight', together with Marlow's defensive comment that '[w]e are the creatures of our light literature much more than is generally suspected' (*Chance* 288) and his protest that 'It is not exactly a story for boys' (311), indicate a deliberate and artificial attempt to qualify the love romance. Conrad employs several other such devious stratagems to this end, such as the contrived counterpointing of Marlow's constant misogyny against the anonymous narrator's protests. There is also the tendency to fall into light farces of misunderstanding, as when Marlow initially interprets Mrs Fynes's comment that Anthony and Flora 'are so unutterly unsuited to each other' (143) as applying to Fyne and his dog. All these appear to indicate a fundamental uneasiness with the foregrounding of the love romance.

This appears also to be the case in Conrad's elaborate Jamesian investigation into the interior motivations behind the human relationships in *Chance*. With multiple narrators deployed to create a psychological detective story which reveals the rather slight circumstances of Anthony's and Flora's romance, the fiction comes to seem like the narrative equivalent of the 'straw man' fallacy. Similarly, Marlow devotes a great deal of effort to synthesise his own role in the story with the tale gleaned from the unimaginative Powell, from whom 'the inwardness of what was passing before his eyes was hidden' (426). At the best, his report captures some of the atmosphere of suppressed emotions of hatred, jealousy and uneasiness centred around the Captain's domestic circumstances aboard *The Ferndale*; at the worst, it reads like a parodic display of virtuosity which rewrites *Little Dorrit* in the style of *The Wings of the Dove*.

Finally, *Chance* is so unlike mainstream Conrad that it suggests the emergence of a repressed Victorian narrative in the midst of his work, a trend which develops further at the end of his career. All in all, the novel seems trivial; there is no real significance demonstrated in the rescue of the victimised and exploited Flora. 'Literature' with a capital 'L' is placed at the service of light entertainment, a duality which is further reflected by the contrast between the detailed psychological analysis of characters' motivation and the almost frivolous quality of the frequent insistence on 'chance' as the etiological root of the plot.

Apart from *Victory*, which I will discuss later, Conrad's later work never returns to portray character within a fully political narrative. In *The Arrow of Gold* (1919), the account of Monsieur George's infatuation with Rita, together with a minute depiction of his interior processes, comes to obscure almost completely the political adventure story drawn from Conrad's gun-running days in Marseilles. Daphna Erdinast-Vulcan sees the novel's failure as 'a reflection of an unresolved generic ambiguity' which entails the constant undermining and violation of the generic conventions of romance 'by a process of 'defamiliarisation' due to the narrative frame, the anti-climactic denouement and M. George's disillusionment' ('Double-Edged' 215–22). Erdinast-Vulcan sees this hesitation as deriving from the conflict between romance and irony, two genres which are better managed in major novels such as *Nostromo* and *Lord Jim*. I wish to argue, however, that the ambiguity of *The Arrow of Gold* is the result of the novel's uncertainty whether to be a political adventure story or a romantic love narrative.

Although the narrator declares directly in his 'First Note' that '[h]istory has nothing to do with this tale' (*Arrow* 4), and his thinly disguised fictional counterpart, Monsieur George, similarly declares his lack of interest in Don Carlos's 'fight for a kingdom' (8), the effect is misleading. The narrative as a whole teeters constantly between political and erotic intrigue. Monsieur George continues to play down the political significance of his involvement with the Legitimist cause as 'commonplace' (8), attempting to substitute the 'psychoanalytic detective' motif of *Heart of Darkness*, whereby the protagonist attempts to interpret a photograph or picture of or by his political 'secret sharer'. While George dismisses Don Carlos, who is pictured on the front page of an illustrated paper, as 'picturesque enough, seated on a boulder . . . all around him a landscape of savage mountains' (8), it also 'arrest[s his] attention' (8). To all intents and purposes though, surely, we see Don Carlos as inseparable from his cause; however, our curiosity to hear more of the political dimension of George's involvement with the Carlists is never satisfied.

Instead, Conrad concentrates his narrative powers on the more elusive oral presentation of Rita, whom Monsieur George hears of first in a conversation between Blunt and Mills. The parallel between Monsieur George's and the reader's first apprehension of Rita defines her as the centrepiece of the narrative: these men 'had *seen* her, while to [George] she was being "presented," elusively, in vanishing words, in the shifting tones of an unfamiliar voice' (31). Monsieur George's concern is to portray 'romance', almost in the abstract, not concrete political relationships. The narrative shows his development from being interested in 'the adventures and fortunes of a man' (31) to his initiation in the experience of romantic love. The function of the political theme diminishes into providing melodramatic background to his love affair with Rita, but not without considerably confusing us on the way. This confusion is augmented by the condensation of the conspiracies, pursuits and setbacks of the gun-running adventure into a few summaries which crop up from time to time in the narrative.

Conrad's main concern is to recount a romantic and chivalrous love story in which a hero battles 'monsters' in order to free a heroine and unite with her. As usual, there are helpers and advisers: Rita's servant Rose plays the part of a 'go-between', while Dominic

Cervoni and Madame Léonore, a more mature, almost parental couple, advise the narrator. The love story is finally brought together with the adventure story in the latter stages of the novel, but too late to save it. The gun-running plot, which had in any case merely provided atmosphere, now sinks completely into oblivion together with Dominic's boat, while a new conspiracy plot emerges with José Ortega's arrival. The detailed dramatisation of George's discovery of Ortega's identity slows down and modifies the melodramatic plot, as does the minutely particularised rendering of the scene in which Ortega rattles the door handle of Rita's room while she slowly explodes into uncontrollable laughter. These episodes represent isolated *tours de force*, however; overall, *The Arrow of Gold* is marred by an unresolved confusion between the genres of political adventure story and love romance.

In his last works, *The Rover* (1924) and the unfinished novel *Suspense* (1925), Conrad attempts to create wider-ranging fictions in which a love story is displaced into a historical narrative of imperialism and revolution set in the Napoleonic era. This apparently new integration of sub-genres, however, represents what Peter Brooks would call in the context of a single narrative a return to 'quiescence'.[5]

In *The Rover* (1924), Conrad brings the sea-adventure together with an interior narrative, a political context and a love story to create a fiction which celebrates the awakening in the protagonist Peyrol of primary emotional sympathies after a lifetime of scorn and indifference. The different generic strands are seamlessly integrated, but the final effect remains unsatisfactorily sentimental through the elevation of romantic love into an absolute quality held capable of redeeming even the most serious of childhood traumas. The rover Peyrol discovers a different kind of adventure, together with a different reason for conspiracy from the more conventional Stevensonian ones which had characterised his long and violent life, which 'had put a drop of universal scorn, a wonderful sedative into [his] soul' (*Rover* 25). However, the 'lovable creature' Arlette produces on him 'the effect of a child' and arouses 'a kind of intimate emotion which he had not known before to exist by itself in a man' (88). His growing parental feeling towards her also has the effect of psychologically regenerating Arlette's own withdrawn personality traumatised by her bloody childhood experiences with the *sans-culottes* of the Revolution: 'from the first moment', Peyrol has 'the power to soothe her aimless unrest' (146).

Peyrol is also 'the first human being to break through that schooled reserve which the precariousness of all things had forced upon' the 'self-contained' Lieutenant Réal, another isolated 'orphan of the revolution' (71). From a feeling of a 'mistrustful liking mixed with some contempt of a purely doctrinaire kind' (71), Réal progresses to his final declaration that the rover had 'a great heart' (286). His association with Peyrol, together with the 'complete change from the odious town' he enjoys during his visits to Escampobar (209), results in a lowering of his emotional defences which makes him vulnerable enough to fall violently in love with Arlette. He is one of those 'Natures schooled into insensibility [which] when once overcome by a mastering passion are like vanquished giants ready for despair' (224).

Réal's discovery of his primary emotional ties with humanity, however, comes into immediate conflict with his official mission, which is to deceive the English navy with military disinformation. To resolve this conflict, the ending of *The Rover* undergoes a sentimental reversal of *Lord Jim*: instead of Réal's finding it necessary to abandon Arlette in favour of his duty, he is saved by Peyrol's development of an ingenious conspiracy whereby Peyrol himself will undertake the mission in Réal's place. At the same time fortuitous events neatly dispose of the blocker figure Scevola, whose mad jealousy of Arlette provides one of the principal obstacles to her union with Réal.

In spite of its apparent engagement with history, then, *The Rover* finally elevates to pre-eminence the genre of the romantic love story. As in early Greene, which as we shall see alternately foregrounds the adventure story and a Catholic form of interiority, the subgenre which nearly always suffers most in this case is the political narrative. Although an adventure story is combined with a romantic plot in these novels, the narrative depiction of a wider society functions nearly exclusively to provide background atmosphere. Although there is an implicit kind of Dickensian disapproval of the French Revolutionary terror, the only explicit declaration of this is the English Captain Vincent's assertion that he hates France's 'political principles and the characters of their public men' (Conrad, *Rover* 275). Even then this is qualified by a homage to individual qualities which transcend ideology, a hope that his 'lordship will admit that for courage and determination we could not have found worthier adversaries anywhere on the globe' (275). The episode seems like a throwback to *The Nigger of the Narcissus*, in contrast to the concentrated political analysis of *Heart of Darkness*, *Nostromo*, or *Under Western Eyes* which it might have become.

It is likely that the final result of Conrad's unfinished novel *Suspense* (1925), also set in Napoleonic times, would have been similar, even though the narrative seems occasionally to hint of a deeper sense of history, as in the remarks about Napoleon's 'idea' (*Suspense* 182), or the 'sense of the moving force in his genius' (38). Although the novel's setting in Genoa in an atmosphere of anti-Austrian ferment might suggest that Conrad's artistic plan was to create a broad historical and political canvas which would place individual characters in the context of their times, the uncompleted manuscript emphasises the familiar genre of the romantic love story with only a background of political adventure. It seems that eventually *Suspense* would have concentrated upon Cosmo's developing love for his childhood friend Adèle. While this strand of the plot is given a certain *frisson* in the style of Dumas's *Count of Monte Cristo* when Adèle's husband Count Héloise conspires to remove him, the adventure story finally remains at the service of the love narrative. Though it is perhaps unwise to speculate upon Conrad's intentions, the generic direction of the existing text indicates that the story would probably have concluded with Cosmo's and Arlette's union. In this way, the 'usual solution' of 'crowned love' denigrated by Conrad in his essay on Henry James[6] would be the culmination of the hero's adventures. At the conclusion of his work, the subgenres of Conrad's masterplot remain literally in suspense.

III

The middle years of Conrad's work, from the abandonment of *The Rescue* in 1898 until the publication of *Victory* in 1915, contrast greatly with the fragmented beginning and end of his career. The novels of this period weave together political, interior and adventure narratives in a dialogic and dynamic interplay. Discussing the relationship between *Heart of Darkness* and *The Rescue*, Eloise Hay concludes that 'Conrad needed to write as much as he did of *The Rescue* before 1898 . . . in order to see what the Travers team really meant to him, in order to release for his full view all the phantoms in command of his mind' (Hay 107). She comments that in *Heart of Darkness* the 'yacht people' fulfil the potential they had shown in *The Rescue* to become 'images of European men and women whose history has passed on to them a torch of illusion which they carry into "backward" territories' (107). In *Heart of Darkness*, Conrad finds what he later calls 'the proper formula of expression' in the 'Author's Note' to *The Rescue*, a formula he thought he had lost (*Rescue* xi). This 'proper formula' is fundamentally generic, locating the protagonist's inner narrative within an account of political destiny. *Heart of Darkness*, *Nostromo* and *The Secret Agent* portray public and private facets of reality as inextricably united while in similar fashion *Lord Jim*, *Victory* and *Under Western Eyes* represent dilemmas between faith and betrayal in ways which reveal the larger political and colonial milieux of the fiction.

The reader interprets the political adventure narrative of *Heart of Darkness* through decoding the intricate ambiguities of Marlow's alternate narrative revelations and self-veilings. On the one hand, Marlow condemns the taking away of the earth 'from those who have a different complexion or slightly flatter noses than ourselves' as 'not a pretty thing when you look into it too much' (Conrad, *Heart* 10), yet implicitly defends the modern British version of imperialism as redeemed 'by the idea . . . at the back of it' (10). However, when he defines this 'idea' as something 'you can set up, and bow down before, and offer a sacrifice to' (10), we recall that this is exactly what Kurtz himself has done. We reach an understanding of the ideology of imperialism through the movements of Marlow's interiority, a process which is complicated by his lie at the end of the novel.

The reader's deciphering of Marlow's narrative also works at the level of genre. Along with imperialism, the other principal object of Conrad's irony in *Heart of Darkness* is the late nineteenth-century adventure genre itself, particularly as exemplified by Rider Haggard, whom Conrad once said he found 'too horrible for words'.[7] Although it would be ungenerous to suppose that his opinion was influenced in any way by Allan Quatermain's uncomplimentary remarks about sailors in *King Solomon's Mines* (1885) – for example their 'fatal amorous propensities' (249) – the many parallels between Haggard's novel and *Heart of Darkness* encourage us to view *King Solomon's Mines* as a criterion of the adventure plot which Conrad transmuted, as in Hugh Kenner's formula for modernism, into 'something rich and strange' (Kenner 109).

Many critics have commented in recent years upon Conrad's manipulation of the nineteenth-century adventure story. Murray Pittock draws a number of detailed parallels between *She* and *Heart of Darkness*, as do Gilbert and Gubar in their analysis of the *femme fatale*, where they note that Haggard's Ayesha makes a 'brief but dramatic appearance' as the savage African woman (Gilbert and Gubar 45). These studies seem singularly inconclusive, however, compared with Richard Ruppel's analysis of the close parallels between *Heart of Darkness* and other 'exotic' stories of the nineties, especially C. J. Hutcliffe-Hynes's 'The Transfer' (1896). Ruppel concludes that 'no other contemporary exotic story, except perhaps Conrad's own "The Outpost of Progress," provides such a sweeping attack on colonial trade, and few question, the way *Heart of Darkness* appears to question, whether European civilisation will ultimately benefit the natives in the colonies' (Ruppel 13). Similarly, David H. Stewart, comparing Kipling's 'The Man Who Would Be King' (1888) with *Heart of Darkness*, argues that despite the many similarities between them Kipling finally 'acquiesced to, if he did not wholly condone, colonialism' (Stewart 198); he concludes that Conrad, however, 'provides one of its most damaging *exposés*, if not straight repudiations' (199).

Moreover, there is a further dimension in which the reader's generic expectations become an active ingredient in the ideological structure of Conrad's narratives. These fictions satirise colonialism through manipulating the adventure story, which Martin Green calls its principal 'energising myth' (Green xi). The anti-imperialist political dimension of the major novels transmutes the late nineteenth-century tale of blood and thunder, normally so acquiescent to imperialism, into a different type of narrative. A comparison of *Heart of Darkness* and *King Solomon's Mines* demonstrates this.

Dennis Butts, in his introduction to a recent edition of Haggard's novel, defines the adventure story as usually beginning 'with a minor crisis, perhaps the death of a relative, before the hero leaves home in search of his fortune, accompanied by some faithful friend or servant' (xi). The adventure draws to a close, Butts observes, when 'the hero encounters a great crisis, usually performing courageously, before he returns home triumphant and often loaded with riches' (xi). In general, *King Solomon's Mines* sticks quite closely to this formula. Allan Quatermain meets Sir Henry Curtis and Captain John Good after a spell of bad luck on a hunting trip (10), agreeing to go with them to find Sir Henry's missing brother and to seek out a treasure by means of an ancient map, as in Stevenson's *Treasure Island*, Haggard's *She* and many other such stories. There is also the hint of a conspiracy within their party in the mystery surrounding the identity of Umbopa, together with various crises along the way: their near death from thirst in the middle of the desert, the attack of the natives, the great battle between Ignosi's and Twala's forces and their final imprisonment and escape from the treasure chamber. They must overcome these obstacles before they 'return home triumphant and laden with riches' (Haggard, *King* xi).

The interaction of the British heroes and the natives is also characterised by what Butts calls the usual 'unquestioning assumption of British superiority over all foreigners' (vii). Indeed, Quatermain and his companions become quite seriously engaged in a civilising mission to 'wean', as Marlow's aunt puts it in *Heart of Darkness,* 'those ignorant millions from their horrid ways' (*Heart* 16). They determine to fight against the arbitrary justice and cruelty of Twala, the ruler, and extract a promise from Ignosi – really the pretender Umbopa with whom they wish to replace Twala – that when he comes to power, 'the witch-hunters shall hunt no more, nor shall any man die the death without judgement' (176). *King Solomon's Mines* depicts the confirming stereotypes of empire seen so often in the late nineteenth-century adventure story: there are 'bad' natives who need civilising and 'good' ones compliant with European mores who will carry out this process. Particularly poignant in the light of Conrad's treatment of imperialism is Ignosi's unironic avowal that 'English gentlemen tell no lies' (176).

In *Heart of Darkness,* Conrad transmutes these qualities in quite specific ways. Marlow's tale presents a fundamentally different conception of narrative which contrasts with Allan Quatermain's belief 'that a true story, however strange it may be, does not require to be decked out in fine words' (Haggard, *King Solomon's Mines* 6). Quatermain begins his narrative in a colloquial, apparently spontaneous, *ex tempore* tone somewhat anticipatory of Marlow's – 'It is a curious thing that at my age – fifty-five last birthday – I should find myself taking up a pen to try and write a history' (7). He exhibits some degree of self-consciousness in his perplexity as to 'why [he is] going to write this book' (7), but quickly comes up with several reasons so definite he can tabulate them numerically, the more quickly to get on with the conventional unfolding of plot. The principal motive is that he is 'going to tell the strangest tale that [he knows] of' (8), which amounts to a more or less tacit acceptance of the adventure story's function of providing vicarious excitement for its readers through exotic, heightened settings, plots and themes.

By contrast, the narrator of *Heart of Darkness* describes the meaning of Marlow's tale as being 'not inside like a kernel, but outside, enveloping the tale which brought it out only as a glow brings out a haze' (*Heart* 9). Marlow doesn't want to bother his listeners with 'what happened to [him] personally', deliberately disappointing the narrator and others like him in search of a yarn by seeming 'unaware of what their audience would best like to hear' (11). Marlow describes the effect of the Congo experience on himself only in vague terms: 'It seemed somehow to throw a kind of light on everything about me – and into my thoughts. It was . . . not extraordinary in any way – not very clear either. No. Not very clear. And yet it seemed to throw a kind of light' (11).

Conrad's transformation of the adventure story by means of a more detailed examination of the characterological interiority and a more sceptical interrogation of imperialism takes on an extra dimension through the publishing history of the novel. When *Heart of Darkness* first appeared in *Blackwood's Magazine*, the expectations of readers based on the periodical's usual content would have prepared them for an adventure story which confirmed the ideological tenets of empire. These expectations are encouraged by the beginning of *Heart of Darkness*, where Marlow constantly gives signals that this is the kind of tale he will be telling. The initial stages of the journey to Africa seem bound up with dark and sinister forebodings of conspiracy and danger. When Marlow arrives in the Congo, there are apparently a number of attempts on the part of the manager and his cronies to delay the journey up the river to visit Kurtz: they sink the riverboat and remain visibly reluctant to tell Marlow much about the mysterious agent. The scene in which Marlow finds himself eavesdropping on the manager's and his uncle's discussion of Kurtz also utilises a typical thriller motif, closely recalling the episode in Robert Louis Stevenson's *Treasure Island* in which the boy protagonist Jim Hawkins overhears from within the apple barrel the mutinous plots hatched by Long John Silver and his fellow pirates. While Jim is saved from discovery by the timely sighting of their destination, Marlow gives himself away by standing up in astonishment; rather than overpowering him and throwing him in the water, though, as a well-tried reader of cloak and dagger tales would expect, the two villains merely walk away as if nothing had happened, not deigning to notice him.

This 'fizzling out', as it were, of the adventure formula is symptomatic of what Conrad gradually does throughout the remainder of the novel. The fact that the manager and his cronies conspire to delay the rescue journey, therefore making it more likely that Kurtz will perish in the jungle, is singularly unimportant compared with Marlow's interior journey towards Kurtz. Through discovering that this emissary of light and civilisation has succumbed to a barbarism comparable in every way to Twala's in *King Solomon's Mines*, Marlow discovers the inherent savagery in the 'idea' of imperialism and finally, through his involvement with Kurtz, the corruption and falsehood in which he himself is implicated.

Conrad presses his transformation of Haggard's novel even further when he shows Kurtz using similar methods of subduing the natives to those devised by the adventurers in *King Solomon's Mines*. Good's removal of his false teeth, the display of his 'beautiful white legs', Quatermain's demonstration of firearms and the prediction of the eclipse humorously confirm the adventurers' claim that they are extraterrestrial, semi-divine beings. However, Kurtz's use of Western technology to establish his absolute power leads to his finally indulging in 'abominable rites' with the natives himself rather than exerting the civilising influence he had originally intended. Sartorial rituals are also a way of sustaining European mores in the wild. In *King Solomon's Mines*, we view Good's elaborate toilet (109–10) – and likewise his donning of full Royal Naval uniform in *Allan Quatermain* (1887) – with a sympathetic humour. Through mocking civilised dress codes, the narrative in fact appreciatively condones civilisation. Good is a stainless heroic adventurer rendered only more sympathetic by the quirks of his personality; he is 'one of us', if, that is, we happen to be late nineteenth-century adventure buffs. In *Heart of Darkness*, by contrast, Marlow seems to sense that the Chief Accountant, who keeps himself so immaculate in 'the demoralisation of the land', rather absurdly resembles a 'hairdresser's dummy' (*Heart* 21); yet at the same time Marlow curiously asserts that he 'respects' him (21). The effect on the reader here is one of a marked incongruity whose irony reflects back on Marlow as well as on the accountant, an irony that might undermine the contemporary reader's certainty that the accountant is someone to be respected and yet simultaneously allows this response if its opposite proves too threatening. Either way, the effect introduced is one of acute uneasiness.

Heart of Darkness is a complex fusion of different narrative modes which spur, even tease, the reader with enigmas of interpretation. Again, Conrad develops the method initiated in his early fiction of uniting the love story with the political adventure narrative and so to chart the personal and ideological significance of both. Often the presence of women in the male adventure story is either non-existent, decorative or sinister. In *King Solomon's Mines*, Quatermain advises us that, although his tale is the 'strangest' one he knows of, 'there is no woman in it, except Foulata [and] Gagool, if she was a woman and not a fiend' (9). Haggard portrays women in a way that defines them merely as an accessory part of the male adventurer's quest into the unknown, a background element compared with the adventure proper. Foulata and Gagool are two contrasting female archetypes, the 'good mother' and the 'demonic' mother. Foulata poses a threat to the travellers by falling in love with Good – her decision to follow him wherever he goes, Quatermain thinks, 'will be rather awkward if [they] ever get out of this' (261) – while Gagool is explicitly bent on the white men's destruction. Just as Kurtz's African mistress attempts to persuade Kurtz to murder the Russian Harlequin (*Heart of Darkness* 61), Gagool aligns herself with a powerful and cruel king, Twala, through whom she wields power. By a fortunate accident which keeps the male-dominated form of the adventure-story genre intact, both Gagool and Foulata destroy each other when Foulata attempts to prevent Gagool from trapping her and the white men inside the treasure chamber.

By contrast, Conrad extends the political adventure story from one involving action and physical conflict to create one which shows its intrinsic connection with individual psychology and the political relations between men and women. Marlow seems to echo the general attitude of the male adventurer when he asserts that 'the women . . . should be out of it' and that '[w]e must help them to stay in that beautiful world of their own lest ours gets worse' (*Heart* 49). Yet finally his comments reverberate ironically through the text and return to haunt him, showing that the contemporary state of relations between men and women is intrinsically related to the continuation of the abuses of imperialism. In *Heart of Darkness*, the darker and lighter sides of the female – Foulata and Gagool – are brought together and complicated in the figures of Kurtz's African mistress and his European 'Intended'. Though neither figures so prominently in the plot of the novel as Foulata and Gagool in *King Solomon's Mines*, they are significant in ways which reveal the theme of imperialism. We are led to believe initially that Kurtz's African mistress – the 'wild and gorgeous apparition of a woman . . . draped in striped and fringed cloths . . . [with] bizarre things, charms, gifts of witch-men' (60) – is a kind of darker double of the white fiancée. Yet they are finally merged in the fiction in a way that does not negate their cultural difference, as does Quatermain's cavalier statement that 'Women are women, all the world over, whatever their colour' (246). The Intended and the African woman are both victims of Kurtz's abandonment: there is no neat solution for the tragic solitude of the 'wild and gorgeous apparition' when Kurtz is taken away on the riverboat. As is frequently noted, the African's gesture of 'open[ing] her bare arms and [throwing] them up rigid above her head' (*Heart* 60) in a gesture of farewell links her to the Intended's similar action at the end of the novel.

Kurtz's abandonment of mistress and fiancée, together with Marlow's figurative abandonment of the Intended in her 'own world' through his lie, points to the conclusion implicit in *Heart of Darkness* that European men have abandoned women in general and for this reason the men's world is in fact 'getting worse'. Through not knowing the realities of the Belgian Congo and what Kurtz has turned into there, influential European women such as Kurtz's Intended and Marlow's aunt are able to idealise the 'White Man's Burden'. The narrative all along has been leading us to see, in Peter Hyland's words, that 'The concept of woman that controls [Marlow's] dealings with the Intended is fundamental to his concept of civilisation' (Hyland 7). The 'heart of darkness', then, is located not in 'the dark continent' but in civilisation itself, within the 'sepulchral city' driven by its material interests, to be sure, but most importantly within the Jamesian movements of individual consciousness and their manifestations in the daily interactions of individuals. *Heart of Darkness* embodies a crisis in late nineteenth-century European culture brought about by Europe's influential women not knowing what its male colonialists were up to. By fusing the male adventure story with an interior narrative more germane to the domestic novel of the nineteenth century and allowing them to reverberate ironically against each other, Conrad establishes a generic programme for the major novels which follow.

IV

In his book *Dreams of Adventure, Deeds of Empire* (1979), Martin Green distinguishes between the adventure story and romance in terms of the adventure story's stronger relations with the modern world, imperialism and technology. The 'patriotic and chivalrous romanticism' which Conrad inherited from his Polish background, Green argues, 'was an important element in [his] situation as a writer', because 'it set a standard of extreme idealism, and a model of heroic temperament' which, in contrast to the more pragmatic qualities of 'adventure', dominated his imagination (Green 300). This leads, Green argues, to an ambivalence, a lack of clarity in Conrad's fiction. He suggests that *Lord Jim* (1900) 'demonstrates the effort it cost Conrad to make a full-scale, full-weight artistic form for his adventure material' (313) and thinks that he 'offers us an ironic view of [the adventure] genre', while also 'affirm[ing] its value' (314). Green concludes that the prevailing ideology of anti-imperialism in the twenties and thirties has tended unwarrantably to over-value Conrad and place him in the centre of the canon, when in fact he was not completely in control of what he was doing: 'he set the two sides of his temperament fighting, and backed them both equally' (316).

However, Green's argument tends to ascribe literary success almost wholly to the ideological machinations of the critical establishment. While academic approval such as F. R. Leavis's may have had some influence on the rise of Conrad's fiction to its present position of prominence, it is extremely doubtful whether attractive packaging can cover up faulty contents indefinitely. An alternative – and to my mind preferable – explanation of the generic tension in *Lord Jim* is that the opposition between romance and adventure is subjected to a controlled and ironic treatment which provides the sustaining quality of the fiction.

Conrad explores the relations between adventure and romance through a close psychological examination of Jim. The novel asks whether it is possible to retain the ideals of the romantic adventure story in a modern world characterised by commercial enterprise. *Lord Jim* dramatises a number of responses to modern imperialism, simultaneously lamenting and accepting the necessity for the passing of the romantic adventurer from the twentieth-century spirit of commerce and technology. Broadly speaking, the genre of *Lord Jim* is that of romantic tragedy in the form of prose fiction. Jim seems to approximate the familiar paradigm of the tragic hero in terms of the Aristotelian demise of a good but flawed protagonist who fails through a combination of excess and a series of logical circumstances.

As in *Heart of Darkness*, Conrad also blends in elements of new genres, such as the detective story and the Jamesian narrative of interiority. *Lord Jim* continues Marlow's investigation of empire through the scrutiny of a protagonist who seems to embody one of its central dilemmas. Jim represents for Marlow a psychological mystery: Marlow thinks that 'he looked as genuine as a new sovereign but there was some infernal alloy in his metal' (*Lord Jim* 45). While he 'would have trusted the deck to [him] on the strength of a single glance', he finds 'depths of horror' in the thought that 'it wouldn't have been safe' (45). As in *Heart of Darkness*, Marlow, through investigating Jim's role in the Patna affair, is also investigating himself: he has 'a distinct notion [he] wished to find . . . some profound and redeeming cause, some merciful explanation, some convincing shadow of an excuse' in order to lay 'the most obstinate ghost of man's creation . . . the doubt of the sovereign power enthroned in a fixed standard of conduct' (50).

The narrative structure of Marlow's sleuthing develops the metaphorical search in *Heart of Darkness* whereby an observer–narrator 'seeks' an obscure protagonist. A device also used by Greene in his first-person narratives, *The Quiet American*, *The End of the Affair* and *The Third Man*, this hermeneutic investigation manipulates the literal and conventional 'search for the missing relative' in the more formulaic version of the adventure genre. Marlow elicits the story in the manner of a hybrid psychoanalyst–detective from Jim and other characters. In the first part, he tries to solve the mystery of Jim by interviewing various people connected with the *Patna* episode. However, he can get no satisfactory explanation from the 'priest-like' French Lieutenant, who although initially sympathetic finds it impossible to deviate from his strict ideal of honour. He is equally unsuccessful with the 'complacent soul' of the apparently flawless 'Big Brierly', who is unable to live with 'the verdict . . . of unmitigated guilt' Marlow imagines that he must have pronounced upon himself after 'holding silent enquiry into his own case' (*Lord Jim* 58).

Even more than *Heart of Darkness*, *Lord Jim* interrogates imperialism through self-consciously manipulating 'romance', in Green's sense of the word. Jim's guiding fantasy is to be the hero of such a story. He becomes conscious of his 'vocation for the sea', when after 'a course of light holiday literature' (6) his thoughts are 'full of valorous deeds' (20). Later, he thinks that his journey into the unknown, bearing Stein's ring as a token, is 'like something you read of in books' (233–4). It is only when Marlow visits Stein that he begins to make some sense of Jim, for Stein himself could be the hero of one of Jim's romances. With his experience of heroic endeavours, brushes with danger and fortunate escapes, Stein acts as a kind of mythical guide for Jim towards the full realisation of his own romantic fantasies, confirming Ralph Rader's observation that the structure of *Lord Jim* 'is closely akin to popular adventure stories in which the hero fails in a first attempt and is redeemed in a second' (230).

Green's supposition that Conrad loses his balance when he experiments with popular forms seems derived from Fredric Jameson's well-known commentary in his book, *The Political Unconscious* (1981). Having suggested that Conrad's place is 'still unstable, undecidable, and his work unclassifiable, spilling out of high literature into light reading and romance' (206), Jameson denigrates the second part of *Lord Jim* as 'a diminution of narrative intensity from 'the intricate and proto-textual search for the "truth" of the scandal of the abandoned ship, to that more lineal account of Jim's later career in Patusan, which, a virtual paradigm of romance as such, comes before us as the prototype of the various "degraded" sub-genres into which mass culture will be articulated' (207).

However, Jameson's critique, like Green's, bases its initial premise on a lack of artistic coherence, when it is just as reasonable to suppose that the unresolvable tension between the conflicting genres of romantic adventure formula and ironic hermeneutic scrutiny provides the very foundation of Conrad's aesthetic. To see the Patusan episode isolated from its disastrous ending as almost pure Haggardesque adventure is to miss the point, for its status as formulaic fiction is itself aimed at the reader's generic expectations. Jim journeys into a strange and unknown country to seek his fortune and initially becomes embroiled in a conflict between local contestants for power. He makes a heroic escape from the Rajah's compound and finds succour with the other local magnate Doramin, whose wife, one of those consolingly familiar natives so frequently encountered in Haggard's novels, takes 'a motherly fancy' to our hero, making 'a to-do [over him] as if [he] had been her own son' (*Lord Jim* 255). Dain Waris, another member of this happy native family, also seems easily to slip into the Umbopa-role of the noble savage friend to the European adventurer, with 'something excessive, almost fanatical, in his devotion to his "white lord"' (270).

With the aid of these congenial helpers, Jim makes his way to the position of the God-like European familiar in Haggard's work. He is 'gifted with supernatural powers' (266). The popular legend is that 'with the touch of one finger [he] had thrown down the gate' (270), while 'a story was travelling slowly down the coast about a white man in Patusan who had got hold of an extraordinary gem . . . partly by the exercise of his wonderful strength and partly by cunning' (280). When established in power, Jim takes up the white man's burden with a will and proves very successful at sorting out native thefts and marital disputes – at least in comparison with more prosaic colonists like Almayer, or Greene's Major Scobie. True again to Haggard, Jim becomes romantically involved with a young native woman – an affair which, like Sir Henry Curtis's love for Nypheta in *Allan Quatermain*, begins in the midst of intrigue and danger when factions of the natives influenced by her father are conspiring against Jim's life.

It is the outcome of Jim's enterprise which decisively transforms this potentially Haggardesque adventure into a form that both mocks and celebrates it. Jewel has a similar apprehension to Foulata's in *King Solomon's Mines* that a love affair between a white adventurer and a native woman is destined to end unhappily when the white man returns to his own people. Sure enough, Jim's world does come to claim him back, but the 'return' of this particular 'repressed' is itself bound up with Jim's own previous failure, taking the form of his guilt over the Patna episode, which is reinvoked with such black serendipity by Gentleman Brown. Jim's consequent responsibility for Dain Waris's death – reversing the motif of white man/native comrades – leads to his former protector Doramin becoming his executioner, a fate accepted in this case by 'the man who would be king'.

It is not only these variations in plot which suggest that the narrative is in control of its more formulaic sub-genre. Linda Shires suggests that to connect with Stein the anonymous man to whom Marlow sends the manuscript version of the end of Jim's story allows 'a reader [to] see Conrad balancing his own attraction to and reservations about romanticism' (Shires 20). Shires contrasts Stein with this 'privileged' reader, arguing that the latter 'is potentially the best reader of the novel', because 'unlike Stein, he is keen to know Jim as more than a stereotype or self-reflection' and 'does not share Jim's sense of self-involvement' (26). She concludes that 'Conrad's implied reader . . . corresponds to no single figure but owns qualities of both these men', embodying 'the very fluctuation between knowing and not knowing which is the subject of the novel' (28).

In terms of the present discussion of genre, this metafictional dialogue between the two figures of Stein, the mythical guide, and the anonymous narratee of the novel's final section introduces a further dimension of the conflict between the romantic and commercial spirits of adventure. Even though Stein has seen many places in the Archipelago 'in the original dusk of their being before light (and even electric light) had been carried into them for the sake of better morality and . . . the greater profit, too' (*Lord Jim* 219), this day has passed in favour of the privileged reader's, who thinks, Marlow explains, '"that giving your life up to them" (*them* meaning all of mankind with skins brown, yellow, or black in colour) "was like selling your soul to a brute"' (339). The anonymous gentleman 'contend[s] that "that kind of thing" was only endurable and enduring when based on a firm conviction in the truth of ideas racially our own, in whose name are established the order, the morality of an ethical progress' (339). He wants the strength of this conviction 'at our backs', because 'without it the sacrifice is only forgetfulness, the way of offering is only perdition' (339). *Lord Jim* guides the contemporary reader away from a wholesale rejection or acceptance of Jim's romantic imperialism, by both celebrating its high-flown spirit, while also tragically accepting its inevitable superannuation.

V

Nostromo (1904) continues the investigation of imperialism with the central question as to whether genuinely philanthropic intentions can alleviate suffering and improve the quality of life in developing countries. If Jim's romantic imagination is at odds with the modern technological and commercial spirit of colonial enterprise, can Gould, by contrast, succeed through significantly lacking a romantic disposition, compensating for this through the corporate backing and material interests which *Lord Jim*'s 'privileged reader' stipulates to be necessary for modern imperialism? It seems, though, that eventually these well-intentioned material interests become detached from the altruistic ends they had begun to work towards. As Dr Monygham tells Mrs Gould towards the end of the novel, 'the material interests will not let you jeopardise their development for a mere idea of pity and justice' because 'their law . . . is founded on expediency, and is inhuman . . . without rectitude, without the continuity and the force that can be found only in a moral principle' (*Nostromo* 418). Indeed, his conjecture that 'the time approaches when all that the Gould concession stands for shall weigh as heavily upon the people as the barbarism, cruelty, and misrule of a few years back' (418–19) seems already implicit in the San Tomé mine's guards, dogs and barricades (96).

Material interests become divorced from the interests of humanity because they are without a 'moral principle'. Gould's inner motives are finally not to better the country but to compensate for the weakness which his father revealed to him in childhood, 'another form of enchantment' deriving from the San Tomé mine 'into whose magic formula there entered hope, vigour, and self-confidence, instead of weary indignation and despair' (60–61). Just as Conrad delicately advances us to the conclusion in *Heart of Darkness* that even imperialists with an 'idea' are to be classified with the loot-scramblers, he shows in *Nostromo* that Gould, in spite of his air of high rectitude and imperturbable Englishness, is finally an 'equal' with the bandit Hernandez 'before the lawlessness of the land' (300). Gould has become so almost in spite of himself, through using immoral means such as bribery and political manoeuvring towards the worthy end of political stability. He realises this, but is caught up in his mental obsession with the mine, making psychological arrangements with himself worthy of a James protagonist. Rationalising to his wife his subtle corruption by material interests, he feels for a moment 'as if the silver mine, which had killed his father, had decoyed him further than he meant to go'; despite this, he simultaneously intuits 'with roundabout logic of emotions . . . that the worthiness of his life was bound up with success' (81–2).

However, *Nostromo* by no means focuses exclusively upon one character. In contrast to the conservatively Eurocentric vision identified by Marxist critics such as Fredric Jameson and Edward Said,[8] the novel represents a vision of Latin America through the combination of multiple perspectives. Nostromo's romantic mirroring of Gould shows that an impoverished relation with one's inner self may be a transcultural phenomenon. The ex-sailor Nostromo's ability to lead men and carry through a practical undertaking suggests that Conrad has set up an experiment to investigate the possibility of living out on shore the quasi-feudal values of *The Nigger of the Narcissus*. Nevertheless, if such values are sustained only by the confirmation of others, they will founder amid the complexities of imperialistic endeavour. After his flight with the silver, Nostromo feels that 'the necessity of living concealed' makes the splendid reputation he has built up 'seem vain and foolish, like a flattering dream come suddenly to an end' (342). When he finds that Decoud has taken four ingots to weigh himself down in his suicide attempt, he decides to steal the treasure, rationalising his action through a process similar to Gould's.

Like Gould, Nostromo feels he has gone so far on a self-destructive road that he does not have the will to turn back. His motives for stealing the silver are an obscure blending of social resentment, inner despair and pride in his reputation. It is almost a desperate gesture of guilt arising from his refusal to get a priest for the dying Teresa Viola. Her 'lost soul' and the 'vanished life' of Martin Decoud have 'paid for' the 'accursed treasure' (412), he thinks, and his 'blank stillness of awe' before this fact is 'succeeded by a gust of immense pride' (412). This prompts his sense that '[t]here was no one in the world but Gian' Battista Fidanza, Capataz de Cargadores, the incorruptible and faithful Nostromo, to pay such a price' (412). As yet another justification, he builds up resentment against the 'San Tomé mine, which appeared to him hateful and immense, lording it by its vast wealth over the valour, the toil, the fidelity of the poor' (413). Described as a 'victim of the disenchanted vanity which is the reward of audacious action' (412), Nostromo is sustained by little consciousness of his inner motives.

As in *Heart of Darkness* and *Lord Jim,* the dissociation of action and interiority dramatises how a developed inner life, such as that reputedly enjoyed by many late Victorian and early modern middle and upper-class women, lacks the political power to spread its benefits among a wider society. Conrad uses the plight of Mrs Gould to complicate the opposition established in *Heart of Darkness* between male and female versions of imperialism. Although Mrs Gould is 'guided by an alert perception of values' and is 'highly gifted in the art of human intercourse which consists in delicate shades of self-forgetfulness' (50), the effect is almost as if Kurtz's Intended, well briefed by Marlow's aunt, had accompanied him to the Congo. Mr and Mrs Gould's separate conceptions of Western civilisation's role in the third world increasingly make communication between them impossible. Conrad treats with a sympathetic irony Mrs Gould's self-deception when she lets Charles give 'a vast shape to the vagueness of her unselfish ambitions' to alleviate the sufferings of the local inhabitants (81). That her well-intentioned liberal humanism and Dickensian ideology of charitable works will not provide the answer to Costaguana's problems is confirmed by her comparison to 'a good fairy, weary with a long career of well-doing, touched by the withering suspicion of the uselessness of her powers' (427).

The relationship of Mr and Mrs Gould dramatises the schism between private values and political opportunism. There are few dialogues in Conrad's novels which show more his drawing on Henry James's delicate rendering of conversational rhythm and personal gesture than the following, in which a revelation of inner feelings and impulses – especially those of Mrs Gould – combines with an allusive, almost fragmentary, dialogue. The prose cadences seem always to be moving towards a dying fall, suggesting the distance between Mr Gould's uneasy compromise with his material obsessions and Mrs Gould's horrified knowledge of the straits into which these material interests have brought them:

> 'Ah, if only one knew how far you mean to go,' said his wife inwardly trembling, but in an almost playful tone.
>
> 'Any distance, any length, of course,' was the answer, in a matter-of-fact tone, which caused Mrs Gould to make another effort to repress a shudder.
>
> She stood up, smiling graciously, and her little figure seemed to be diminished still more by the heavy mass of her hair. . . .
>
> 'But always to success,' she said, persuasively.
>
> Charles Gould, enveloping her in the steely blue glance of his attentive eyes, answered without hesitation:
>
> 'Oh, there is no alternative.'
>
> He put an immense assurance into his tone. As to the words, this was all that his conscience would allow him to say.
>
> Mrs Gould's smile remained a shade too long upon her lips. She murmured:
>
> 'I will leave you; I've a slight headache. . . .' (179)

If a self-aware interiority is separated in this way from the world of action in *Nostromo*, distorted inner motives and political decisions are by contrast intricately connected throughout the novel. This ironic interweaving emphasises that policy is developed not at the conference table but by means of delicate interpersonal manoeuvres, often in more informal settings. Martin Decoud explains to Mrs Gould that he sets in motion the movement towards the separation of the Occidental Province from the rest of Costaguana simply because Antonia 'won't leave Sulaco for [his] sake, [and] therefore Sulaco must leave the rest of the Republic to its fate' (185).

The exchange between Decoud and Mrs Gould, which lasts the good part of a chapter, is characterised by a series of subtle manipulations. Decoud has returned after Gould's departure under the pretext of looking for Antonia's fan, but really to buttonhole Mrs Gould alone on the subject and unfold his plan to her. His policy seems to consist of the shock tactics of a brutal honesty, in the course of which he apparently tells her a few home truths about her husband, asking her if she is 'aware to what point he has idealised the existence, the worth, the meaning of the San Tomé mine', and asserting that Gould 'could not believe his own motives if he did not make them first a part of some fairy tale' (185). However, his own method here is quite Machiavellian for, as he later writes in the letter to his sister, he realises that Mrs Gould is 'a good ally' because she 'has understood her husband's dangerous passion [and] seizes upon all [Decoud's] suggestions with a sure instinct that in the end they make for the safety of the Gould concession' (207). Decoud vies with the narrator for insight when he sees that Gould defers to his wife 'as if he wished to make up for . . . that sentimental unfaithfulness which surrenders her happiness, her life to the seduction of an idea' (207).

Nevertheless, although Decoud shares much of the narrator's insight and ironic perspective, the novel does not allow his stance to become an absolute one. In this way, *Nostromo* consists of multiple, refracted narrative perspectives, the effect of which suggests that its world is not 'finished' but available to change in terms of policies not controlled by 'material interests'. Just as W. B. Yeats later chose finally to 'mock mockers' in his poem *Nineteen Hundred and Nineteen* (236), Decoud becomes merely the mirror image of the idealists, romantics and deluded visionaries who people the pages of *Nostromo*: they deconstruct each other. Decoud is a moral nihilist who 'had pushed the habit of universal raillery to a point where it blinded him to the genuine impulses of his own nature' (*Nostromo* 135); he admits that he is 'no more of a patriot than the Capataz of the Sulaco Cargadores' (165). It is indeed fitting that he is paired with Nostromo in the mission to remove the silver, for both experience a moral death when removed from the sustaining company of society.

Alone on the Great Isabel, Decoud comes to behold the universe 'as a succession of incomprehensible images' and dies, the narrator comments, 'from solitude and want of faith in himself and others' (408). These 'images' could almost refer to the disrupted narrative structure of *Nostromo* itself, whose prismatic narratives most profoundly alter the form of the late nineteenth-century adventure story. If world events are the ironic outcome of obscure inner motives and action itself 'consolatory' or 'a drug' which compensates for an impoverished inner life (*Nostromo* 66), then the experience of reading the fiction denies us vicarious participation in the lineal sequence of events which characterises the adventure genre. Any suspense is short-circuited even more quickly than in *Heart of Darkness*, first by the breaking of chronological narration throughout the novel and then by its parody in the form of Captain Mitchell's banal account of the climax and aftermath of the revolution to the 'privileged' yet considerably confused passenger (390). Mitchell's story comes precisely at the point of greatest potential adventure: where Nostromo is about to undertake his heroic ride to Cayta. Among Conrad's novels, it is perhaps *Nostromo* which most demands active interpretation in order to unravel the complex portrayal by different narrative perspectives of a tragic though well-intentioned imperialism.

VI

With *The Secret Agent* (1907), Conrad moves his attention from the late nineteenth-century adventure story to a subverted version of a detective/espionage thriller. As James Walton notes, *The Secret Agent* 'extends a tradition established by *Bleak House*' by the use of a 'detective motif to implement a comprehensive and intricate social satire' (Walton 456). In this way, Conrad artistically manipulates the elements of conspiracy, suspense, investigation and revelation more characteristic of formulaic literature to develop a type of nineteenth-century political narrative dealing with anarchism and revolution which had been established by such novels as Dostoevsky's *The Possessed* (1871–2), Turgenev's *Virgin Soil* (1877), James's *The Princess Casamassima* (1886) and Stevenson's *The Dynamiter* (1885).

A genre dealing more strictly with espionage, however, was in its embryonic stage in the early years of the twentieth century. Generally taking the form of 'invasion literature', these narratives exploit contemporary fears of the growing might of Germany. In the more well-known ones – Sir Arthur Conan Doyle's 'The Adventure of the Bruce Partingdon Plans' (1917) and Erskine Childers' *The Riddle of the Sands* (1903) for instance – the emphasis is upon the penetration of an espionage conspiracy which takes for granted that the implied reader's political sympathies are with the British. Yet these fictions do not fully engage with history, for the ideological sympathies they rely on do not demand reflection and might in given circumstances be quite adaptable. John G. Cawelti observes that '[m]ost audiences would appear to be capable of temporarily tolerating a wide range of political and social ideologies for the sake of enjoying a good yarn' (32). Invasion narratives encourage the reader not to draw political conclusions, but to become caught up in the metonymic process of plot, reversal and denouement. As in the case of the adventure story, the litmus test of whether a spy novel transcends its genre is the extent to which it interacts with a number of other types of narrative – especially a political one – to render a fuller representation of the myriad 'genres' of human life.

Conrad saw *The Secret Agent* as 'a new departure in *genre* and . . . a sustained effort in ironical treatment of a melodramatic subject' (*Letters to Cunninghame Graham*, ed. C. T. Watts 160). As such he uses melodrama to embody the complex mechanisms of urban society and to convert 'certain typical melodramatic conventions to a fresh use', as Zdzislaw Najder observes (161). More importantly, however, he employs formulaic devices to communicate the intricacy of his theme at the level of the reader's generic expectations. Like *Heart of Darkness* and *Nostromo*, *The Secret Agent* is what we might call a 'thriller interruptus', in which the promise of melodrama proper is held out, only eventually to be withdrawn. Rather than ingeniously weaving an instant solution to the crime from observing Stevie's clothes, as Sherlock Holmes would be able to do, Heat is lucky enough to have Stevie's name and address handed straight to him – one might almost say on a shovel. Both Heat's and the Assistant Commissioner's confrontations with Verloc occur offstage, emphasising the problematic human relations centred around the crime rather than the bare processes of law enforcement. *The Secret Agent* plays with our expectations derived from formulaic literature that a 'good' detective will pursue a 'bad' criminal, by distancing us from *all* the characters. Concentrating upon a realistic depiction of the milieu in which the 'crime' takes place, it probes the unstable nature of modern political reality through a detached, ironic examination of psychological motivation.

Even more than *Nostromo*, however, *The Secret Agent* emphasises its political plot over the interior revelation of character. It is the one of Conrad's novels most noticeably influenced by a thesis: blindness and partial vision distinguish in differing degrees the spectrum of its characters, who seem to be summed up by the narrator's comment that 'the way of even the most justifiable revolutions is prepared for by personal impulses disguised into creeds' (*Secret Agent* 102). Winnie, with her belief that 'things don't bear looking into very much' (175), and Stevie's impulsive and violent excitement at social injustice – 'Bad world for poor people' (168) – form an ironic accompaniment to the short-sighted Wurmt's and the deranged Mr Vladimir's philosophy of bomb-throwing, as well as to the weak-eyed Sir Ethelred's dislike of details. The clash of 'blind' egos which structures the plot of the novel, together with its ironic outcome and even the multiple genres which constitute it, are figuratively represented in Stevie's drawing of 'innumerable circles, concentric, eccentric; a corruscating whirl . . . that by their tangled multitude of repeated curves, uniformity of form, and confusion of intersecting lines suggested a rendering a cosmic chaos, the symbolism of a mad art attempting the inconceivable' (76).

The interlocking contrasts of character and the complex irony of *The Secret Agent* complicate this abstract quality to leave us with a series of paradoxical relationships between inner motives and practical results. Winnie's self-sacrifice finally results in Stevie's death, while the Assistant Commissioner's self-seeking plan not to upset his wife's friendship with Michaelis's Lady Patroness makes possible the discomfiture of Mr Vladimir. Nevertheless, the impersonal quality of the novel is responsible for its being the least consoling of Conrad's fictions, while the lack of a central protagonist weakens the force of the values of family and community it attempts to convey. We care in the abstract for the deaths of Winnie and Stevie, as we sympathise in a detached way with the tormented guilt of Winnie's betrayer, Comrade Ossipon, but there is nothing as powerfully or completely rendered as the plight of Mrs Gould in *Nostromo* or the revelation of Razumov's tormented interiority in *Under Western Eyes*, because interiority of character is not so greatly emphasised. *The Secret Agent* bases its political vision in the uninspiring masses' potential for resistance (or possibly inertia) and in the Professor's corresponding fears that 'the mass of mankind mighty in its numbers' may be 'impervious . . . to terror' (103). It is not a thought conducive to solidarity.

VII

In contrast to *The Secret Agent*, the greater integration of the thriller formula with an interior narrative, a potential love story and a political plot identify *Under Western Eyes* (1911) and *Victory* (1915) as the novels which most closely define the Conradian masterplot, along with *Heart of Darkness*. It is now possible to translate the generic makeup of this masterplot into more specifically narrative terms as follows. An uncommitted protagonist initially feeling no ties nor commitments to any other person or political creed – 'uninvolved' like Conrad's Marlow in *Heart of Darkness*, Razumov in *Under Western Eyes*, Heyst in *Victory* – is caught up through circumstances with 'the community of mankind' (*Lord Jim* 157). In the course of events, he may betray another character through attempting to remain an uncommitted bystander. At various points he may be confronted with a father-confessor figure who has some insight into his plight and who encourages him to confess and redeem himself. (This he may or may not do: Marlow confesses only to his listeners in *Heart of Darkness*.) Whatever the outcome, however, Conrad (and later Greene) attempt to chart twentieth-century consciousness in its individual and political modes through manipulating and fusing literary genres commonly associated with individual consciousness, on the one hand, and with the political world, on the other.

Under Western Eyes returns to Conrad's continuing preoccupation with an individual protagonist caught up in a dilemma between faith and betrayal within a political context, a theme present in *The Secret Agent* only in the attenuated form of Ossipon's guilt at the end of the novel over his betrayal of Winnie. Razumov's betrayal of Haldin, however, is intricately linked with their political situation as Russians. They are both 'secret sharers' of a common political destiny, the tragic standoff between revolution and 'the decrepit, old, hundred years old spectre of Russian might', as Conrad describes it in his essay 'Autocracy and War' (89). Razumov and Haldin are representatives of the political deadlock of contemporary Russia: Razumov aligns himself with an autocratic ideology, while Haldin just as mistakenly identifies with a revolutionary one. Both these ideologies are doomed, however, because neither recognises the principle of legality, although Razumov eventually comes to understand the tragic situation in which he and Haldin are involved and is able to affirm solidarity even with those he considers deluded revolutionaries.

Razumov's interior adventure intricately unfolds, at the level both of plot and of reader expectations. We are shuttled between an adventure and psychological narrative in a process which formally dramatises his dilemma between political commitment and non-involvement – whether to remain a private individual or to become involved in a programme of wider social change – a recurring problem for the twentieth-century Western intellectual which Greene also probes. Like a typical spy, Razumov fears discovery but he also experiences a guilty but repressed wish to have everything out in the open. The reader is similarly ambivalent, wishing both for his concealment and for his discovery.

At a structural level too, the novel manipulates our expectations of a spy thriller. The disrupted chronology of the Professor's narration emphasises the psychological effects of Razumov's isolation in Geneva before we are shown its causes and antecedents in the form of more 'conspiratorial' motifs such as the recruiting and 'running' of an agent (*Under Western Eyes* 292–3), briefing sessions at the 'safe house' of the oculist's shop (289), the 'maildrop' in Vienna (299) and the planting of disinformation in order to establish Razumov's credentials with the revolutionaries (293). In this way, the central focus of the novel is established in Razumov, the private individual *par excellence*, 'as lonely in the world as a man swimming in the deep sea' (61). When Haldin threatens his goal of peacefully making his way in the academic world, Razumov deceives himself that he can solve the problem by projecting his vision of organic conservatism onto the autocratic Russian state.

Razumov distances Haldin as 'the withered member which must be cut off' (81), asking: 'by what bond of common faith, of common conviction, am I obliged to let that fanatical idiot drag me down with him?' (82). What he overlooks is the necessary connection of individual existence with its political context; 'living in a period of mental and political unrest', he 'forgot the dangers menacing the stability of the institutions which give rewards and appointments' (60–61). The novel charts Razumov's unsuccessful attempt to amputate the political dimension of his narrative from its interior aspects, which leads ironically to his growing sense of identity with Haldin as a fellow Russian and human being. Razumov has, in a figurative sense, died at the same time as Haldin and become a 'phantom' himself. From the evening of the betrayal when he has an hallucination of Haldin lying in the snow (81) until his recurring idea of his figure still lying on the bed (97, 106–07), his obsession grows as Haldin becomes 'a moral spectre infinitely more effective than any visible apparition of the dead' (286). This increasing mental preoccupation leads to his agonised confrontations with Natalia

Haldin in Geneva, when 'every word uttered by Haldin lived in Razumov's memory . . . like haunting shapes [which] could not be exorcised' (183).

In this way, Razumov's identity gradually but relentlessly converges with Haldin's, defining a more authentic political narrative which takes account also of the individual. Razumov envies 'the other' the 'repose' he has attained and his 'continu[ing] to exist in the affection of that mourning old woman [Mrs Haldin]' (317); indeed, he finds it 'impossible to get rid of him', concluding that it is himself whom he has 'given up to destruction' (318). His fear of giving himself away becomes identical with his guilt over giving Haldin away. Speaking for the first time with the teacher of languages, he feels 'a sort of apprehension as if for another, for someone he knew without being able to put a name to the personality' (208); on a different occasion, it is 'as though another self, an independent sharer of his mind, had been able to view his whole person very distinctly indeed' (232). This is the culmination of a process which began with Razumov's missing the one chance offered him to leave behind his loneliness, when on the way to Prince K.'s he 'embrace[s] for a whole minute the delirious purpose of rushing to his lodgings and flinging himself on his knees by the side of the bed . . . to pour out a full confession . . . that would end in embraces and tears; in an incredible fellowship of souls' (83).

It is too early, however, for such an apotheosis. Although Razumov guiltily hallucinates the torture of Haldin in the form of 'his own brain suffering on the rack', he fails to see the face of this 'long, pale figure' (121). Razumov is caught up in a phantom-like, dissociated existence; divorced from political and social ties with the community of mankind, he falls into 'a dream, minutely followed, wearing one into harsh laughter, to fury, to death – with the fear of awakening at the end . . .' (298). This is a recurring motif in Conrad's work (later taken up by Greene) which shows an uncommitted man enmeshed by circumstances in a terrifying series of events at odds with his hitherto ordinary existence, a motif which links and complicates the psychological, political, and melodramatic levels of the novel's mixed genre. Razumov's repressed but urgent desire to confess is projected through the multiple senses in which 'betrayal' is used. He initially protests that '[a]ll a man can betray is his conscience' (82) and that in any case Haldin 'had done all that was necessary to betray himself' (108). Throughout his dangerous interviews with the other revolutionaries, Razumov is aware that he is 'a conspirator everlastingly on his guard against *self*-betrayal in a world of secret spies' (my emphasis; 199). This situation extends until the awakening of 'that side of our emotional life to which his solitary existence had been a stranger' – the contact with Natalia Haldin – finally causes him to 'betray [him]self back', as he puts it in his journal, 'into truth and peace' (331), when he declares: 'it was myself whom I have betrayed most basely' (333).

As well as meeting and merging within Razumov's consciousness, interior psychology and political thriller come together at the level of external plot. As in *Heart of Darkness*, *Lord Jim* and *The Secret Agent*, the protagonist fences verbally with his antagonists. Razumov is a double agent in rather an intricate sense of the term. In the conventional sense of the spy story he pretends allegiances both to the Tzarist government and to the Genevan revolutionaries, yet his concealed sympathy for Haldin complicates this more simplistic dilemma. While he must 'be very prudent' in his interviews with Councillor Mikulin (120) to conceal his initial attempt to help Haldin escape, his major problem lies not in avoiding detection but in his dangerous discovery that he can not in fact turn Haldin into the alien caricature as he had attempted, nor can he despise all the other revolutionaries to the same extent as he does General T. and Peter Ivanovitch. Although he attempts to maintain an attitude of mockery, 'kidding on the level' with Haldin that his interview with Ziemianitch 'was satisfactory in a sense' and that he 'came away from it much relieved' (96), he is in fact mocking his own guilt by dicing with danger. He attempts to evade his own interiority by remaining at the level of the thriller plot.

Under Western Eyes constantly returns, then, to the interior psychological narrative centred upon Razumov. Encounters with other people are a constant source of disturbance to him: he is 'profoundly troubled' by Mikulin's 'mild gaze', which was 'not curious, not inquisitive – certainly not suspicious' (120). With his 'passionless persistence' and 'something resembling sympathy' (120), Mikulin is a doubling of detective and father-confessor such as we find in Porphyry in Dostoevsky's *Crime and Punishment* and later in Inspector Vigot in Greene's *The Quiet American*. Although his desire to acquire a secret agent rather than a concern for Razumov's soul inspires Mikulin's insidious enquiry as to where he intends to retire (130), the question preys constantly upon Razumov's thoughts, provoking an impulse to confess comparable to Castle's interview with Boris in Greene's *The Human Factor*. Razumov wishes to confess to Mikulin because he fancies that the official 'was, perhaps, the only man in the world able to understand his conduct' (284).

The drama of Razumov's 'contaminat[ed] . . . soul' (280) defines *Under Western Eyes's* mixed genre of the interior thriller. Instead of concentrating merely on 'the hunt for the mole', the narrative seeks to interpret the intrinsically political *and* spiritual disease to which its protagonist has succumbed. Greene later develops this 'hermeneutic' type of spy/detective narrative, even using the specific terms of disease and infection in *The Quiet American* and *A Burnt-Out Case*. First Razumov likens the presence of Haldin in his rooms to 'harbouring a pestilential disease . . . a subtle pest that would convert earth into hell' (77). Then in Geneva, as Razumov's identity blends with Haldin's, the narrator surmises that Razumov treats the journal he is writing 'as a threatened man may look fearfully at his own face in the glass, formulating to himself reassuring excuses for his appearance marked by the taint of some insidious *hereditary* disease' (my emphasis; 220). Finally, in his interview with Sophia Antonovna, Razumov thinks that 'all day long he had been saying the wrong things' because of a 'disease of perversity overcoming his will' (250). A closely related image which adapts the thriller form to a psychopathological narrative (one also seen in Greene's *The End of the Affair* and *A Burnt-Out Case*) is the figurative use of poison to express an inner mental state: 'the bitterness accumulated' in Tekla's heart, which 'had got into her veins and, like some subtle poison, had decomposed her fidelity' to Peter Ivanovitch and Madame de S. (236).

Again anticipating Greene, a further merging of interiority with formulaic suspense contrasts the protagonist's heightened mental state with the routine banalities of life. This is furthered by the largely uncomprehending attitude of the narrator. Razumov's mental agony beyond the pale of ordinary human experience is set against the casual curiosity of 'a specimen of early tourist in knickerbockers' who hangs about 'scenting something unusual' (262) in the scene where Razumov harangues Sophia Antonovna. 'Ah!' comments the narrator, as usual scenting melodramatic potential, 'If [the tourist] had only known what the chance of commonplace travelling had suddenly put in his way!' (262). However, the narrator is reading only at the level of the exotic espionage genre and has little more insight than the tourist himself.

The generic affinities between *Under Western Eyes* and much of Greene's work also make themselves felt in a variety of tonal and stylistic similarities, parallels which point towards a fundamental sympathy of vision, religious orientation and world view. In an apparently deliberate displacement of the title, Greene wrote in a review that all Conrad retained of Catholicism was 'the ironic sense of an omniscience and of the final unimportance of human life under the watching eyes' (*Essays* 184). This seems to capture the detached, weary, yet sympathetic tone which characterises much of Greene's and Conrad's prose, especially in the passage discussed above in which Razumov regards his writing 'as a man looks at himself in a mirror . . . formulating to himself reassuring excuses' (*Under Western Eyes* 220). Third-person interior revelation conveys sympathy in so far as Razumov's feelings are respectfully entered into, yet at the same time introduces a detachment which might have been bridged through free indirect discourse. A similar passage from Greene's *A Burnt-Out Case* also embodies the isolation of the alienated protagonist Querry, who 'wonder[s] when it was that he had first begun to detest laughter like a bad smell' (*Burnt-Out Case* 15). Again, the format in which the narrator interprets the character's experience with sympathetic detachment conveys a central alienation, metatextually capturing the 'foreign language' of Querry's mental state. The natives 'were not laughing at him, they were laughing with each other, and he was abandoned . . . to his own region where laughter was like the unknown syllables of an enemy tongue' (15).

What Greene identifies as Conrad's quasi-Catholic narrative stance also extends into the theme of *Under Western Eyes*, suggesting that in this novel Conrad comes nearest to expressing something resembling Greene's religious sense. As implied author, Conrad often seems to take on Greene's paradoxical stance of a 'catholic agnostic' who has ceased to embrace the faith wholeheartedly in all its ritualistic manifestations but still uses its paradigms to interpret experience. Razumov is ironically doubled with both Haldin and 'the devil', between whom he eventually has to choose. When Sophia Antonovna reports that 'in the last weeks of his life [Ziemianitch] suffered from the notion that he had been beaten by the devil' (*Under Western Eyes* 272), Razumov uses the myth to interpret the bewildering circumstances of his mental agony: 'It was *as if* the devil himself were playing a game with all of them in turn' (272). Later he seems even to identify with 'the devil', when he confesses in his journal that his intention was 'to steal Natalia's soul' (331), finally admitting that he has 'the greatest difficulty in saving [him]self from the superstition of an active Providence', the alternative to which 'would be the personal Devil of our simple ancestors' (325). In this way, Conrad and Greene salvage from Christian mythology motifs which interpret human interiority while also retaining their accessibility to the agnostic reader.

Like Haldin and Natalia herself, then, Razumov has become in the very minimal Conradian and Greenean sense of the word 'a believer'. The religious overtone is also clear in the 'post-mortem' which Sophia Antonovna pronounces upon him, a motif which characterises many of Greene's Catholic novels, whereby a character – often a priest – makes a tentative summing up of the protagonist. Conrad leaves the judgement rather more open than Greene usually does, however, for while Sophia Antonovna asserts that 'There are evil moments in every life' and asks 'how many . . . would deliver themselves up deliberately to perdition . . . rather than go on living, secretly debased in their own eyes' (347), she also undermines this apparent authoritativeness with the dubious closing comment that 'Peter Ivanovitch is an inspired man' (349). Conrad represents a more flexible dialogue between religion and agnosticism than is to be found, at least in Greene's strictly 'Catholic' novels, by using belief less obtrusively to embody a less conclusive vision of the political *status quo* in individual human characters.

VIII

This 'ironic . . . omniscience' is also present in *Victory* (1915). Although the novel may appear initially to regress to Conrad's early romanticism, *Victory* is a fully political work in which a variety of sub-genres together represent a many-faceted modern world.[9] The political implications of the aloof moral nihilist Heyst merge with the love story and adventure plot to create exactly the kind of ironically comic narrative of Europe in contact with the developing world which Greene's work continues. Indeed, Greene singles *Victory* out as one of the 'great English novels of the last fifty years' (*Essays* 184), later choosing as an epilogue for *The Human Factor* (1978) one of Heyst's most self-revealing speeches: 'I only know that he who forms a tie is lost. The germ of corruption has entered into his soul' (199–200).

Heyst is perhaps Conrad's most 'Greenean' protagonist, whose 'persistent inertia' (*Victory* 3) and non-involvement with the rest of humanity brings down disaster on his own and others' heads. With 'a taste for silence', he has no intention of ever leaving the islands because 'Not a single soul belonging to him lived anywhere on earth' (66). Like Anthony Farrant in Greene's *England Made Me* (1936) or Brown in *The Comedians* (1964), Heyst is a kind of beachcomber character who has 'perceived the means of passing through life without suffering and almost without a single care in the world – invulnerable because elusive' (90). His youthful intention had been 'to drift altogether and literally, body and soul, like a detached leaf . . . without ever catching on to anything' (92); as Terry Collits notes, he is 'the veritable antithesis of the collective life of the polis' (310). Recalling Major Scobie in Greene's *The Heart of the Matter* (1948), Heyst 'cultivate[s] that form of contempt which is called pity' (174), although Scobie does not use Heyst's method of playful courtesy and 'consummate politeness' to remain detached. Heyst's incapacity for human relationships is derived from his father, recalling other Conrad figures such as Charles Gould in *Nostromo*, as well as protagonists of Greene whose paternal relationships seem to have cursed them with a similar inability to relate to others: Andrews in *The Man Within*, Anthony Farrant in *England Made Me* and Eduardo Plarr in *The Honorary Consul*, for example.

Heyst's detachment, however, is ironically and inevitably imperfect. One of '[t]hose dreamy spectators of the world's agitation [who] are terrible once the desire to act gets hold of them' (77), he becomes caught up almost in spite of himself with Morrison and Lena, unwittingly releasing hostile forces such as the frustrated resentment of Schomberg, the ferocity of which he has no conception. Such people, comments the narrator, 'lower their head and charge a wall with an amazing serenity which nothing but an indisciplined imagination can give' (77). The result of Heyst's 'indisciplined imagination' is that although Lena 'capture[s] his awakened faculty of observation' and gives him 'the sensation of a new experience' (71), she cannot overcome his moral and spiritual isolation. He is solitary European malehood in but not of the 'paradisal' Pacific island. Significantly, their stay in this exotic location turns out to be a Jamesian variation of interpersonal gaps and silences upon R. M. Ballantyne's boys' adventure story, *The Coral Island* (1856). Lena tells Heyst: 'sometimes it seems to me that you can never love me for myself, only for myself, as people do love each other when it is for ever' (221), anticipating similarly frustrated female protagonists depicted by Greene in an expatriate setting: Louise in *The Heart of the Matter*, Martha in *The Comedians* or Sylvie in *The Honorary Consul*.

Resisting Ricardo with the 'force of instinct which is the true source of every great display of energy' (292), Lena's capability of shouldering responsibility in the face of danger to protect a weaker male protagonist also demonstrates her greater 'connectedness' to the world. Again one thinks of Greene's heroines, especially Anne Crowder in *A Gun For Sale* (1936), who might also have declared that 'A girl can always put up a fight' (*Victory* 85). In this way, Lena's closer involvement both with Heyst's psychology and in the conspiracy plot avoids a formulaic love story. The love relationship is portrayed as one theme among others within a multi-faceted narrative centred around the contrasting characters of Heyst and Lena in an early twentieth-century colonial setting. The love and adventure plots are closely woven into one single political narrative through their clear and consistent focus on Heyst's flawed, aloof character, which combined with external events such as the death of Morrison and the dangerous problem of Mr Jones and his followers sets in motion Schomberg's conspiracy.

As in many of Conrad's and Greene's novels, 'the personal interview' scene dramatises the clashing character motivations behind the plot, bringing Jamesian psychological analysis together with the 'romance *de cape et d'épée*'. There is in fact very little action of the swashbuckling kind in the novel; rather, a gradual but ineluctable tension is developed through confrontations between varying combinations of Heyst, Lena, Schomberg, Ricardo, Jones and Wang, until the denouement is brought about in two parallel interviews between Heyst and Jones and between Lena and Ricardo.

In the course of these encounters, *Victory* emerges as the novel to which Conrad brings most fully his sense of incongruous ironic comedy. The reversal undergone by Mr Jones's allegiances provides a satiric depiction of the decaying English upper class such as Greene himself would have relished: 'I tell you', explodes Jones to Heyst on hearing of Ricardo's deception, 'a gentleman is no match for the common herd. And yet one must make use of the brutes' (388). In this way, Conrad transforms the ideological *complaisance* of Haggard's farcical celebrations of lovable colonialists, so that the bored, upper-class (probably homosexual) card-sharping outcast Mr Jones becomes the ultimate variation on Sir Henry Curtis's questing adventurer and the bloodthirsty cockney henchman Ricardo, the 'faithful servant' figure who accompanies him: 'Are you likely to get bored?' Ricardo asks his master with sinister undertones, 'I know them fits come on you suddenly. . . . I am quite content . . . I mean as long as you don't get bored. It wouldn't do, sir' (277). Jones and Ricardo transform and particularise the plot's stock melodramatic potential by satirising the class relations upon which colonial power relies for its displays of force when literally scrambling for loot in the developing world. Ricardo – and also Schomberg – dismiss the danger of native interference with the projected journey to Heyst's island, looking on native life as 'a mere play of shadows' and believing that 'the dominant race could walk through unaffected and disregarded in the pursuit of its incomprehensible aims and needs' (167).

Yet Heyst too is blind to the realities of the imperial order. He embodies the contemporary European *Zeitgeist* in the form of the 'habit of profound reflection . . . the most pernicious of all the habits formed by civilised man' (x–xi), which Conrad castigates in his preface. The factor which neither Heyst nor the villains take into account is the Chinese servant Wang, who represents the antithesis of these qualities. Though initially appearing as one of the invisible native multitude communicating in pidgin English and playing the subservient domestic materialising at need, Wang, whose thought processes are untramelled by 'any notions of romantic honour or tender conscience' (307), emerges finally as having a ruthlessly rational view of the dangers of white civilisation. He is a complete foil to Heyst. Seeing the struggle of Lena and Ricardo, he immediately '[makes] up his mind to give up all connection with Number One, a man not only disarmed but already half vanquished' (291). Although having no ties in the world apart from his Alfuro woman, he forms his decision 'according to the plain reason of things, such as it appeared to him in the light of his simple feeling for self-preservation' (307).

Wang's full role is complex and never becomes fully explicit. However, his shooting of Pedro makes it seem altogether likely that if Mr Jones, 'tumbled into the water . . . perhaps not by accident' (411), it was Wang who helped him on his way. We are also perhaps invited to conclude that Wang shot Heyst before setting the house on fire himself.[10] This is suggested by Wang's self-protective attitude regarding whites, of which Davidson is unaware, as well as by his being 'very pleased' to discover Jones in the water; declaring 'that made everything safe', he goes 'at once over the hill to fetch his Alfuro woman back to the hut' (411).

Collits argues that 'Wang is transformed before our eyes from a stage Chinaman into an active participant in the real world', going on to note that 'just enough of his life is revealed to point up the drastic and fatal limitation of the Heystian world-view, while the world thus opened up is represented as significantly unavailable for complete assimilation' (319).[11] The implicit opposition of Wang and Heyst emphasises the primary form of solidarity with one's immediate family, which Wang affirms but Heyst neglects. Wang is an oriental version of Mrs Schomberg and Lena, as well as recalling Winnie Verloc's loyalty to Stevie in *The Secret Agent*. He is in fact the missing political link in *Victory* which the reader must decode to understand the full political import of the fiction. The combination of Wang and Heyst defines a political adventure story based upon psychological motivation, which makes *Victory*, along with *Under Western Eyes*, a climactic point of Conrad's work. Both novels define a type of protagonist who will become the centrepiece of Greene's post-colonial novels.

2

'Writing off the Elaborate Scaffolding': Greene's Detour to Adventure

I

During his first years of writing, Greene was, as he later confessed, 'reading again and alas! admiring Conrad's worst novel *The Arrow of Gold*' (*Ways of Escape* 17). Yet it is not so much what he called the 'romantic[ism] and derivative[ness]' of this novel's theme that mars his early fiction, but the confusion of its generic makeup. Like Conrad, Greene seems unsure what *kind* of novel he is attempting to write. *The Man Within* (1929) teeters uneasily between interior revelation and boys' smuggling adventure. Similarly, *The Name of Action* (1930) is unsure whether to be a spy story or a tale of erotic intrigue, while *Rumour at Nightfall* (1931) is an almost unintelligible interior drama which seethes with romantic rivalry. Complicated by a series of *Doppelgänger*s and multiple betrayals, it is even set during the Carlist revolution, Conrad's personal stamping ground. Greene's novels from *The Man Within* to *It's a Battlefield* (1933) represent the period of quiescence or narrative non-being that Peter Brooks describes in terms of Freudian theory as preceding the beginning and end of single narrative plots.

Greene later describes his early writing in *A Sort of Life* (1972) as 'an elaborate scaffolding built from an older writer's blueprint' which he 'had to write off as apprentice work' (212). It is only in 1932, when he determines to '[begin] again naked . . . with an adventure story [*Stamboul Train*]' (*Sort* 212), that he deviates significantly from Conrad. This process of 'stripping down', however, results in little more than a more straightforward version of a thriller formula borrowed from John Buchan, a displacement of one particular Conradian sub-genre. Although *Stamboul Train* (1932), *England Made Me* (1935), *A Gun for Sale* (1936), and *The Confidential Agent* (1939) attempt to integrate interior revelation, political narrative, thriller formula and love romance, the tendency to emphasise a psychological thriller combined with a love story while playing down the political narrative increases in the later entertainments, especially in *The Ministry of Fear* (1943) and *The Third Man* (1947). In these novels, politics becomes almost completely eclipsed by psychological revelation of the protagonist's dilemma within the structure of a thriller plot.

The six entertainments of the thirties and forties seem to take the form of two trilogies. The first consists of *Stamboul Train* (1932), *A Gun for Sale* (1935) and *England Made Me* (1936), while the second comprises *The Confidential Agent* (1939), *The Ministry of Fear* (1943) and *The Third Man* (1947). The first of these groups is more fragmented, with Greene drawing considerably on a story of emotional betrayal, as seen in Conrad's *Victory*, as well as on the wider political concerns of *The Secret Agent*, features which he largely relinquishes in the second cycle.

When Greene takes the interior thriller formula to its logical conclusion and writes a *film noir* screenplay, *The Third Man* (1947), the result surprisingly reveals the hitherto suppressed narrative structure of *Heart of Darkness*, the interpretive search by an observer–hero for a metaphysically evil 'other'. However, this is displaced into the cinematic style of Fritz Lang. It is as though Greene has gone through a process of enlarging particular sub-genres of Conrad's work during his early work, immersing them in other influences such as Buchan, *film noir* or the Catholic novel. In spite of a temporary regression to Conrad in *The Tenth Man* (1948, 1985), *The Third Man*'s reworking of *Heart of Darkness* finally enables Greene to see these sub-genres more clearly in preparation for a return to the full Conradian masterplot complete with the political narrative in *The Quiet American* (1955).

II

In the 'Author's Note' to *The Man Within* (1929), the older and apparently wiser Greene describes his attempts to revise the novel, confessing that the story nevertheless 'remained just as embarrassingly romantic, the style as derivative'. However, even in this first published novel, Greene is already experimenting with the mixed genre of the interior thriller and moreover showing a tendency to emphasise the thriller element to a greater degree than Conrad.

While the protagonist's dilemma between faith and betrayal recalls Razumov's in *Under Western Eyes, The Man Within* is not a political novel but a Conradian interior thriller with definite shades of Conrad's most marked excursion into the nineteenth-century boys' adventure story, *Romance*. Psychological and romantic pursuit motifs are foregrounded in preference to political material. Andrews takes refuge from Carlyon, the smuggler friend whom he has betrayed to the law, with an ambiguous woman helper whom he is unsure whether to trust. Indeed, the interest of the narrative tends to focus more and more upon this relationship, allowing the issues of smuggling and the law to recede into the background. Like *The Arrow of Gold, The Man Within* moves from what might have been a historical adventure story with social and political interest to become one which details the protagonist's inner struggle in terms of romantic love.

Similarly, Andrews's betrayals are personal rather than political. He gives away his smuggler companions for similar reasons to those for which Razumov does Haldin – to satisfy a desire for peace and legality. The motive behind this is largely to 'kill' the memory of his late father – also a smuggler – who represented for him 'the sneers, the racket, that infernal sea' (*Man Within* 85). This is Razumov on a purely individual plane. There are continual references to Andrews's 'other self', or his 'inner critic', which seems to be an internalised version of his father. He is 'made up of two persons, the sentimental, bullying, desiring child and another more stern critic. . . . Always while one part of him spoke, another part stood on one side and wondered, "Is this I who am speaking? Can I really exist like this?"' (24). His process of inner education is very much that of the divided Conrad hero, but is centred upon the individual rather than society. Although, like Lord Jim, he wishes to 'shut [his] eyes and leap' into being, to do a 'foolish thoughtless thing' (138), this is for the sake of his own inner peace rather than a conscious 'return to the ranks'.

Recalling Charles Gould in *Nostromo* and Axel Heyst in *Victory*, the question is whether Andrews can develop from identification with a blocking father-figure to a more equal relationship. The stand-off between his allegiances to Carlyon and to his father is duplicated by his hesitancy between Elizabeth and Lucy. Like Natalia Haldin in *Under Western Eyes*, Elizabeth represents for Andrews a redemptive inspiration to overcome his sense of doubleness. Andrews, however, betrays her through his infidelity with Lucy, the 'whore' counterpart of Elizabeth's 'madonna', whose 'smile, which promised fun' banishes Andrews's 'temporary homesickness for Elizabeth's cottage' (112). In this way, a more explicitly erotic element combines with the romantic dimension of Conradian betrayal, which simplifies the terms of Andrews's competing loyalties into 'harlot versus virgin'. While Elizabeth differs from the purely idealised female heroine through her sense of humour, which anticipates some of the women in later Greene novels such as *The Comedians* (1964) or *Travels with My Aunt* (1969), the narrative still does not manage to complicate Andrews's elevated view of her to a quasi-religious figure, an embodiment of 'wisdom and . . . sanity' (221).

Generically foregrounding the love story in Andrews's process of self-realisation, *The Man Within* closely follows *The Arrow of Gold*. In a larger political context, the issue of smuggling seems trivial, the stock subject of the boys' adventure story; neither is there any significant historical grounding apart from the Bow Street Runners' pointing vaguely to the early nineteenth century. Although Andrews's self-imposed verdict and sentence when he confesses that he is responsible for Elizabeth's murder recalls Lord Jim's delivering himself up to Doramin, the difference lies in *Lord Jim*'s tragic admittance that the romantic form of colonialism has finally been superannuated. The motives behind Andrews's self-deliverance are limited to the personal psychology of his split personality, on the one hand, or to the widely abstract issues of 'good faith' and 'courage', on the other. Its significance lies only in uniting his individual personality so that 'he need no longer be torn in two between that spirit and the stern unresting critic'. His 'sense of . . . exhilaration' upon discovering that he is 'that critic' (220) merely represents an attempt to excavate the emphatic closural mode of the nineteenth-century *bildungsroman*, a debased form of which Conrad also drew on in the intertext *Romance*. Rather than the complex social portrayals of an aspiring middle class hero or heroine represented by the high *bildungsromans* of Eliot and Dickens, *The Man Within* is an uneasy attempt to combine the psychology of adolescence – the development of a young man through the experience of the higher and lower forms of love – with the exotic modes of the late nineteenth-century adventure story.[1]

The Name of Action (1930) is a more recognisably Greenean transposition of the adventure story into the genre of the espionage thriller. The purer element of suspense is most visible when Chant and Weber are smuggling arms into Trier through the canal, a melodramatic episode which emphasises the familiar suspense pattern of escape and pursuit. Like many similar scenes from Buchan, such as the pursued Richard Hannay in *The Thirty-Nine Steps* forced into the role of pretending to be the 'radical candidate' at a local political meeting, the occasion is fused with a comic element which relies for its effect upon an incongruous blending of the melodramatic and the banal. The Anglophile customs officer wishes to discuss the Tottenham Court Road, thus obstructing his companion officer Muller's acceptance of the usual bribe. The comic incongruity of the banally familiar with the heightened and melodramatic, paradoxically increases the excitement of the scene but has little more significance than the creation of suspense.

There is a hint of a potentially larger political context when Muller finally consents to let the cargo through – precisely *because* he has an inkling of what it is. Weber explains this as Muller's 'always want[ing] to be on the winning side' (*Name of Action* 217). In like vein, the brief flashback at the beginning of the novel to Chant's attempt to resist Kurtz's proffered mission recalls the Conradian protagonist caught up in a revolution against his will.[2] This has a similar effect to the way in which the disrupted chronology of *Under Western Eyes* gradually reveals the process of political decision. Indeed, the political narrative seems to gain a foothold in the first part of Greene's novel through the various portrayals of political decisions and events as they are enacted in individual confrontations. For example, the dictator Demassener discourses to Chant on the virtues of autocracy, avowing that he 'hate[s] freedom' because it means 'freedom for the animal in man', when he by contrast 'would bind men in clean chains' (71). Recalling Conrad's *The Secret Agent*, Greene also depicts a spectrum covering various kinds of revolutionaries, such as Kurtz, who Demassener says 'was infinitely better than the men he tried to lead' (73), the dependable Weber and the unsympathetic Kapper, who lampoons the Demasseners with his obscene rhymes.

As I have indicated, however, the novel momentarily picks up such strands of a political narrative, only to let them fall once more. One explanation of this may be found in similar biographical episodes shared by each writer. Greene's youthful involvement as a spy for the German Embassy in the French-occupied Palatinate results in a generically fragmented novel comparable to *The Arrow of Gold*, which Conrad also based on an early experience of revolutionary activity. Both writers had been interested in these affairs as much for the sake of an escapade as to engage with a political endeavour. Greene confesses in *A Sort of Life* that, as well as being 'easily aroused to indignation by cruelties not [his] own', he was motivated to approach the Germans by 'the idea of experiencing a little danger' (139). This corroborates the unclear political basis of the narrative and its eventual eclipse by a romantic, interiorised thriller. Politics and much of the psychological interest give way to Chant's love for Madame Demassener, just as 'the possession of that jewel had driven from [Chant's] memory all thought of his mission and all remembrance that he was her husband's enemy' (79). Generic uncertainty is responsible for a series of contrived incidents in the plot, coincidences unprepared for by detailed circumstances or motivation of character such as the chance meetings between Chant and Anne-Marie Demassener which occur twice – almost farcically – on the occasion of a car crash. Indeed, on Chant's very first evening in Trier, Madame Demassener crashes her car outside the cobbler's shop which happens to be the centre of revolutionary activity. Again, later in the smuggling operation, Chant causes what he thinks to be a police car to crash but inevitably finds the person that he 'certainly . . . did not expect to [Anne-Marie Demassener] . . . upright in the driver's seat' (229).

As if this is not enough, Greene introduces a further generic ambiguity in the form of an ironic vein which confusingly undercuts the love story. Having told himself that '[a]ll [Anne-Marie's] sensibilities were finer than his' and that her 'tremulous fingers . . . would have shown, he was certain, the same exquisite awareness to silk, to a stone, to a feather gathered from the grass' (235), Chant eventually finds that her feelings towards him are based purely on sexual desire. Her husband is impotent and although she's been faithful to him, 'faithful to nothing' as she puts it 'for five years', she 'can't stand it any longer' (246). Chant, however, wants marriage, and although he has sex with her he hates himself, as the tired cliché goes, in the morning. Here, as in *The Man Within*, Greene attempts to portray the typical Bildungsroman development of a young man through the experience of contrasting kinds of love. The lesson, however, finally seems to counsel an ambiguous rejection of romance while still yearning ambivalently for the shunned experience.

Altogether, *The Name of Action* starts too many generic hares, none of which it succeeds in catching. What initially seems to be an interior political narrative modulates into a thriller involving gun-running and then into an ironised love romance, so that in the end these different sub-genres run out of control and must be violently yoked together by the melodramatic showdown in Demassener's office. When Kapper takes advantage of Chant's love affair with Madame Demassener and her revelation of her husband's impotence in order to bring about a political scandal, Chant judges himself guilty of betraying her; for this reason, he attempts to deliver himself up for execution in the grand style of Lord Jim. Saved at the last moment by Kapper, he leaves Trier in disillusionment with the wounded Demassener, accompanied by the ironic chorus of an American journalist who seems to have strayed from the pages of Evelyn Waugh: 'Lord, what a scoop' (311). In a famous essay on *Hamlet*, T. S. Eliot thinks Shakespeare attempts to join together earlier versions of the story which stressed discrete sub-genres of the revenge plot. It is a final irony that Greene's novel also loses the name of action through fragmenting into so many different kinds of narrative which are not reintegrated at the thematic level as an overt problem (as in Hamlet) concerning the hero's choice of a proper plot.

The tendency of this aggregation of Conradian sub-genres to eclipse a potentially strong political plot reaches its most extreme point in *Rumour at Nightfall* (1931). The novel chooses exactly the same period of the Carlist wars as Conrad in *The Arrow of Gold*, likewise centring upon a foreign protagonist who becomes enmeshed with a beautiful and mysterious woman near to the centre of a revolutionary conspiracy. Not content with this high-flown romantic theme, however, Greene also develops a series of *Doppelgänger*s which enact the Conradian search by the English journalist Chase for a mysterious 'other', the revolutionary chief Caveda, together with a rapidly complicating series of betrayals, counter-betrayals, confessions, and redemptions. As in *The Name of Action*, Greene is finally driven to bring these together in a contrived, if not desperate, resolution.

Recalling Conrad's most famous exploitation of the *Doppelgänger* motif in 'The Secret Sharer' (1912), Greene plays with the idea – only finally to let it go – that Caveda represents Chase's inner self, even perhaps to the extent of lacking an objective reality. Near the beginning of the novel, Chase finds that not only do Caveda's gloves fit him exactly but he and his counterpart also look alike from a distance. He 'amuse[s] himself with the fancy' as to whether 'the man exist[s] at all': although he has 'the gloves in his pocket . . . they had never felt the touch of Caveda's finger' (*Rumour* 45). There are a number of similarly inconsequential experimentations with this Conradian motif, which is drawn primarily from *Heart of Darkness*. Recalling Marlow's meditation on Kurtz's painting of the sinister woman, Chase attempts to gain an insight into Caveda through studying a picture of Caveda's lover, Señorita Monti. This attempt is rather unsuccessful, however, for he is 'a little daunted by the face and a little amazed that it should have any interest for a man like Caveda' (20).

Surprisingly, though, these expectations of a *Doppelgänger*-based plot are never satisfied, giving only an abstract rather than a specific sense of interior character. Developed so clearly and effectively by Conrad in *Heart of Darkness*, 'The Secret Sharer' and *Under Western Eyes*, the *Doppelgänger* motif becomes endlessly complicated and confused through its uncontrolled spawning of paired sets of characters. Chase has yet another double, his English friend Crane, whose 'nervous attentive eyes and . . . lips' he sees 'in the mirror of rain before him, where if there had been any reflection it should have been that of his own face' (39). To make matters worse, this doubling of Chase and Crane crosses over somehow into the pairing of Chase and Caveda, in the process of which Crane's and Caveda's identities also become merged!

The Conradian themes of personal, romantic, and political betrayal cut across and further confuse the *Doppelgänger* motif throughout *Rumour at Nightfall*. Señorita Monti unintentionally betrays her one-time lover Caveda to Chase, who is working with the Alphonsist militia (90). Then Crane, who has fallen in love with her, betrays his friend Chase by telling her the truth about Chase's motives (96–7). Crane then confesses to Chase (115), but this redemptive act does not finally prevent Chase from betraying Crane to the Alphonsists together with Caveda's planned uprising. As if this is not enough, Greene introduces Catholicism into the process. As well as being the 'outsider' or 'foreigner' of the existential adventure story, Chase is also the 'heretic', the figure alienated from the Catholic religion who cannot understand the soldiers' wish to disturb a dying man with confession (8). Crane, by contrast, embraces Señorita Monti's religion when they confess their sins to each other in a dubious blending of romantic and religious interiority (213), later coercing a priest to marry them.

Despite these multiple thematic levels, the purpose of the *Doppelgänger* motif finally and rather anticlimactically turns out to lie in Chase's personal bildung – his quest for self-discovery. This has the effect of reducing to individualised proportions what had promised to be a wider political narrative with the quasi-metaphysical dimensions of *Heart of Darkness*. While Caveda is the absent factor throughout the novel, the blank identity waiting to be filled, Greene introduces a deliberately pragmatic mode of realism into the potentially epiphanic scene in which Chase apprehends the features of his double for the first time. When Señorita Monti drops a picture of Caveda onto the face of the dead Crane, whom Chase has betrayed, it 'usurp[s] the function of life, so that the body stretched there was kindled into a deceitful vitality, and a living man looked up at him from the ground with handsome plausible features' (297). The intention is obviously to cut through the convoluted psychologies of romanticism to a level of simplicity which exposes the brutality of Chase's act, for the face makes Chase feel 'the first ungrudging pain, the first unqualified humility' (298). The final premium, however, seems slight against the effort needed to decode the narrative entanglements of the work as a whole.

Like Conrad in *The Arrow of Gold*, then, Greene leads us initially to believe that *Rumour at Nightfall* will combine a narrative search for interiority with a story of political intrigue and revolution, but fails to deliver on this promise. The psychological revelation of the protagonists, together with the development of the love romance, quickly diminishes the Carlist wars to the status of an exotic backdrop, while the historical particularities of the situation are subsumed by 'the great, the fundamental things, Liberalism, the poor, freedom' (44). The quadrangular series of betrayals among Crane, Chase, Caveda and Señorita Monti is eventually resolved only by what appears to be an act of narrative desperation – the 'sad union' of Chase and Señorita Monti after Chase has betrayed Crane to his death (299). This ploy almost burlesques the ending of *Heart of Darkness*, where Marlow's betrayal of Kurtz's memory and of the truth about imperialism is enacted in the triangular relationship established between himself, Kurtz, and Kurtz's Intended. Now the surviving male is himself betrothed to the deceased's wife and all the political and psychological doublings are revealed to have been directed towards a decayed version of the traditional Victorian ending in happy marriage.

III

Despite Greene's assertion that after *Rumour at Nightfall* he began again 'naked' with *Stamboul Train* (1932), the process of disentanglement from the confused relation to Conrad in his earlier work takes place more gradually. For this reason, I have chosen to depart temporarily from chronology and move ahead to *It's a Battlefield* (1933) before returning to *Stamboul Train*, a novel which though not quite the radical transformation Greene later represented it as, certainly represents a significant departure from his early treatment of the Conradian masterplot.

It's a Battlefield still belongs clearly within the period of the 'Greene–Conrad plot' which I have defined in terms of Peter Brooks's narrative theory as that of quiescence or non-being, the sense of inertia that antedates the beginning of plots in a single narrative. Critics have often noted the close similarities with *The Secret Agent*, although more often than not largely confining themselves to matters of technique. Kenneth Allott and Miriam Farris, for example, comment on the similar use of irony in the two novels 'as a technique of presentation' (78), while Lynne Cheney makes a close investigation of structure, finding that both novels 'are the arrangements of an effect of an event, and in both cases the actions presented, unlike the actions themselves, happen offstage' (122–3). Leon Higdon develops this question of parallel technique further, suggesting that 'Greene deliberately calls attention to [the similarities] . . . as when he creates his own Assistant Commissioner and gives him a background remarkably close to Conrad's Assistant Commissioner' (37). Higdon also identifies Verloc's counterpart as Mr Surrogate and that of the influential society matron protecting Michaelis as Caroline Bury, going on to note that '[m]ore significantly, Greene expertly adapted certain technical features of *The Secret Agent* and exploited them fully without slavishly imitating them'. Higdon finds this to be 'especially evident in [Greene's] use of spatial form, juxtaposition of fragments, barrier time moments, and the penetrating irony' (37–8).

Intriguingly, Higdon suggests that *It's a Battlefield* represents a very explicit attempt by Greene to throw off the domination of Conrad, even to the point of committing a kind of artistic murder of a fictional Conradian surrogate. In this way, the running down of Conrad Drover, who was named after 'a seaman who had once lodged in [his parents'] house' (*Battlefield* 122),[3] represents a metatextual form of exorcism. However, while Higdon views *It's a Battlefield* as representing the beginning of a second period in Greene's relationship with Conrad, one in which he 'learned technique from Conrad while escaping his style and romantic settings' (Higdon 38), I believe the work to be more transitional in nature.

What Greene does is to substitute the more contemporary-minded, ironic Conrad for the florid and exotically historical writer of *The Arrow of Gold* and similar novels. He notes in his 'Diaries' for 26 July 1932 that he found Conrad's *Rover*, which he was reading at the time, 'a little blown out, scattered with high sounding clichés, the characters a little over-romantic, in fact one of Conrad's worst novels'.[4] Greene seems to have forgotten his vow to deny himself Conrad's fiction, for he was also re-reading *The Secret Agent* this summer while *It's a Battlefield* was 'fermenting' (Greene, 'Diaries' 29 June). Attracted now to the realistic – indeed seedy – atmosphere of the Conradian thriller, he notes that he 'admired more than ever the triumphant still life of the opening, the picture of the dingy stationers' and thinks 'the whole book wonderful material for a film' ('Diaries' 28 June). Two months later, on the other hand, it seems to be the thriller pursuit motif that is uppermost in his thoughts: 'the new novel grew in the mind. . . . The Commissioner's walk through the London streets, followed and conscious of being followed; & the end of the pursuit on Lady Ottoline's doorstep' ('Diaries' 28 August).

The hesitation is not without significance. As in the early fiction, the sub-genres of the Conradian masterplot remain largely dispersed and fragmented. Greene teeters between the thriller with romantic undertones and the political narrative, choosing now to opt for the latter. The shadowing of the Assistant Commissioner by Conrad Drover with his recently acquired revolver occupies only a very small portion of the novel's final stages, while the love affairs such as they are between Conrad and Milly and Jules and Kay are demoted from the sublime position previously given them and set firmly in the context of family betrayal and the social problems of poverty. Greene attempts to recreate Conrad's vision of modern urban society. Recalling Stevie's 'drawing of innumerable circles, concentric, eccentric' in *The Secret Agent* (76), he chooses an epigraph from A. W. Kinglake's *History of the War in the Crimea* which describes a battlefield 'made up of . . . small numberless circlets commensurate with such ranges of vision as the mist might allow' where 'each separate gathering of the English soldiery went on fighting its own little battle in happy and advantageous ignorance of the general state of the action'.

The urban vision of *It's a Battlefield* resembles very closely the impersonal, uncaring and uncomprehending society of *The Secret Agent*, controlled by the vagaries of individual impulse and the unpredictable outcomes of interpersonal interviews. Indeed, Stevie himself has a counterpart in Jim Drover, the central but absent protagonist who has landed in the condemned cell through stabbing a policeman about to hit Mrs Drover at a demonstration. Like Stevie's literally self-destructive involvement in Verloc's bombing plot, Drover's action is also motivated by the 'heart' rather than by the 'head'; neither of these characters understands the machinations of the *Realpolitik* which each narrative is at pains to reveal.

Like *The Secret Agent*, *It's a Battlefield* sympathises with the suffering caused by poverty and an oppressive social system, yet remains sceptical of the revolutionary organs which profess to counter the system. Greene avoids becoming explicitly ideological through depicting a communist party whose leaders are indifferent to the plight of individual members such as Drover, who 'doesn't matter', in comparison with the 'big job' they've 'got on now' (45). Recalling the society lady's friendship with Michaelis in *The Secret Agent*, Greene also shows complicity between the aristocracy and the revolutionaries in the friendship of Mr Surrogate, the upper-class communist and Caroline Drover, his late wife's friend.

It is in the characters of the Commissioner and Mr Surrogate, however, that Greene first grasps a more central feature of the Conradian masterplot which he will continue to develop throughout his career: that of the more private motivations behind an individual's political actions. Mr Surrogate's involvement with the communists is compensatory: '[p]ersonalities . . . had always betrayed him' whereas '[i]n a cause was exhilaration, a sense of freedom' (44). He prefers to 'live in a world of religions, of political parties and economic creeds', thinking that 'he would go mad rubbing shoulders at every turn with poor saviours, politicians, poor people begging bread' (44). The Assistant Commissioner, by contrast, is more conscious of the similar inclination he feels to take refuge in institutions: he has an uneasy conscience about 'upholding a system in which he had no interest, thinking of himself as 'a mercenary' and realising that 'it was only when he was tired or depressed that he dreamed of an organisation which could enlist his fidelity because of its inherent justice' (129–30).

Here, then, is a palpable sign of the incipient interest Greene feels at this stage of his career for a character's interior dilemma between conscience and political expediency. In the finale of the novel, moreover, this motif takes on a religious dimension when the Assistant Commissioner talks with the prison chaplain, who 'can't stand' the 'arbitrariness' and 'incomprehensibility' of human justice any longer (199) and is resigning from his post because of the cruelty of condemning Drover to eighteen years in prison. The passage almost epiphanically reveals the direction of Greene's later career in these two characters' reflection of the contrasting modes into which his work will later split, with the chaplain's meditation upon the nature of divine justice signalling the narrative expedition into Catholicism and the Assistant Commissioner's sudden insight into another crime indicating the parallel detour to the thriller genre.

IV

Greene's development in these early years proceeds by fits and starts. Published the year before *It's a Battlefield*, *Stamboul Train* (1932) is generally agreed to signal a radical departure from the romantic and narratively ornate quality of his early fiction. In one of the first major critical works on the novelist, *The Art of Graham Greene* (1963), Kenneth Allott and Miriam Farris conclude that '[n]o two books [*Stamboul Train* and *Rumour at Nightfall*] are more different' (75); however, they see this development as arising from the disappearance of 'the divided mind', when it seems clear that the protagonist in conflict with himself is still firmly present in most of the other 'entertainments'. Nor can Greene's sea-change be explained in terms of his finally rejecting 'an historical background', together with the determination 'to express himself through stories set in the present' (75–6). Rather, *Stamboul Train* represents the beginning of a process of generic simplification, a 'writing off' of Conrad's 'elaborate scaffolding' (*A Sort of Life* 212), by means of a more concentrated fusion of the interior narrative with a tautly constructed thriller formula.

This, however, is a gradual process, which is more observable in the later entertainments. In *Stamboul Train*, the complex concatenation of genres remains present in the form of a variety of different types of narrative drawn from the Conradian masterplot. For example, Dr Czinner is the protagonist of a political narrative of the type defined in *Under Western Eyes*. A communist who relinquishes his safe exile in England in order to return to Belgrade and instigate a proletarian revolution, he recalls with this act of self-sacrifice Razumov's courageous confession. Dr Czinner's heroism throws into relief the sordid and egotistic motives of the other passengers who, like the gallery of grotesques in *The Secret Agent*, present a microcosm of contemporary society. The Jewish businessman Myatt is at the centre of this satiric narrative, which counterpoints the attraction he feels towards the dancer Coral Musker with his professional self-interest, in this way blending in a story of romantic betrayal reminiscent of Conrad's *Victory*.

Greene ties these multiple Conradian plots together by setting them on a moving train, adapting a device used by John Buchan in *The Thirty-Nine Steps*. The consequent potential for introducing a number of random and fleeting encounters, as well as exciting pursuits and escapes by and from border guards and police, subjects the novel to a pressured unity of place, time and action. However, this artificial means of linking narratives is one that could not be consistently employed. Greene has not yet managed to unite the stories of his two major Conradian characters: the political protagonist, Czinner, and the uncommitted bystander, Myatt, who is guilty of betrayal. This results in a novel which centres alternately upon each figure, vacillating between the plot structures of *Under Western Eyes* and *Victory* while also evoking the atmosphere of a realistic thriller made up of a cross between *The Secret Agent* and *The Thirty-Nine Steps*.

Myatt is an updated version of Axel Heyst in *Victory*, temporarily rescuing the dancer Coral Musker from a downmarket showbusiness job, only eventually to abandon her, as Heyst does Lena. Misunderstanding seems built into their relations from the start, when they each declare that they 'seem to know' each other, an apparently romantic insinuation whose underside reminds Coral of 'the long stairs, the agent's door and the young friendly Jew, explaining gently and without interest that he had nothing to offer her' (*Stamboul Train* 49). Like Lena, Coral falls in love with Myatt out of gratitude, while he responds only with a 'painful pity' (26) reminiscent of Heyst. When Coral declares her love for him, Myatt appears to develop a corresponding feeling – 'she is dear and sweet, I should like to do things for her' (121) – yet like Heyst he cannot fully commit himself, rationalising the transfer of his affection by telling himself 'that she had already reason for gratitude' (121). Coral, on the other hand, experiences Lena's more primitive urge towards self-preservation, asserting her emotional rights when their separation seems inevitable: 'Why shouldn't I write to him? He might like it; he might want me still, and if he doesn't, why shouldn't I put up a fight?' (187)

The betrayal plot of *Under Western Eyes* also crosses over into the depiction of Myatt, a cold professional who attempts to remain uninvolved in the human world like Razumov: '[t]he night before he had tried in vain to work; the girl's face had come between him and the figures; now she was relegated to her proper place' (153). Although he attempts to rescue Coral when she is arrested with Dr Czinner at Subotica, he does so only from a half-hearted sense of duty. When the ticket clerk denies having seen her, 'Myatt knew suddenly that he would not be sorry to take [his] word and end his search; he would have done all that lay in his power, and he would be free' (173–4). Unlike Razumov, Myatt experiences no remorse. When he arrives in Istanbul, he feels 'that the whole unexplained incident at Subotica was unreal' and that '[v]ery soon he would have forgotten it because it was isolated from ordinary life and because it had no explanation' (200). Sure enough, at the end of the novel, he '[can] not remember her features', telling himself that he has 'done all [he] can for her' and that they 'should have said goodbye in any case in a few weeks' (215–16). Myatt experiences extreme 'happiness at being back with figures, with something that he could understand and that had no feelings' (200). For him there is no Conradian martyrdom and redemption; he quickly decides to marry Janet Pardoe for advantageous business and racial reasons, 'feeling quite at ease now that he knew her mother was Jewish and that her uncle was in his pocket' (210).

It is as though the Razumov prototype has been split into two characters in *Stamboul Train*. In direct contrast to Myatt stands the idealised political exile, Dr Czinner, who relinquishes his post at the safe but banal English boarding school to return to Belgrade and start a revolution. This is Razumov at the culmination of his quest when he decides to face the music. Although the journalist Mabel Warren thinks of him as 'a quixotic fool' (42), Czinner feels that he is 'alive again because [he is] conscious of death as a future possibility' (73). Moreover, Czinner is Greene's first displacement of the political protagonist into the mode of an agnostic Catholic Marxism. Paradoxically, his faith in each ideology is sustained by a necessary doubt, as when thinking of 'his duty to God' he corrects himself by substituting a 'two-faced god, a deity who comforted the poor in their distress... and a deity who persuaded them, for the sake of a doubtful future to endure their pain' (112). Yet the Christian element remains to qualify this. Czinner cannot wholly disbelieve, sometimes feeling 'an unreasoning resentment against those who nowadays were born without religious sense' (112–13). He is the first of Greene's protagonists reluctantly to retain a vestige of faith, while at the same time professing a Marxism he is not quite convinced of, at least in the abstract form it takes in his own final speech.

England Made Me (1935) more effectively unites a narrative revealing a divided protagonist with a political adventure plot. Anthony Farrant is a 'seedy adventurer' (27) who drifts constantly, resigning from post after post, 'at home in the one-night hotels, in the basement offices, among the small crooked flotations of transient businesses' (12). Anthony is 'fear, despair, disgrace . . . everything except success' (15), a hollow character behind whose 'firm hand-clasp and . . . easy joke, lay a deep nihilism' (51). Like his main Conradian prototype, Heyst, he cannot enter into a close relationship with another human being, attracting hostile and destructive forces towards himself through his inevitable inconsistency in attempting to remain apart. Recalling Heyst's playful courtesy, Anthony is outwardly full of charm but incapable of any real emotion, always playing a part; he also exists in the shadow of his father. His sister Kate thinks that their father 'beating [Anthony] in the nursery... to keep a stiff upper lip' has resulted in his self-repressed 'learning to love with moderation' and becoming 'farther away from [her] than he had ever been' (63–4).

Kate tells Anthony that he'd 'think it indecent to say [he] loved [her]' (185) and on one occasion '[drives] at his fingers with a pen-knife', telling him, 'This is how I love you, Anthony' (185). Anthony is the vacillating, divided protagonist in the face of urgent and threatening demands on his attention, while Kate recalls Lena's attitude in the face of danger, her greater degree of practical awareness, together with fewer scruples. Kate sees Anthony as 'incorrigibly conventional... hopelessly innocent' and 'frightened by his superficiality', thinks he 'need[s] protection' (143). As Lena with Ricardo, Kate tries unsuccessfully to use her influence to protect Anthony against Fred Hall's predatory violence. Just as Heyst embodies an enervated, nineteenth-century European sensibility, in him the colonialist's moral ambivalence between being a loot-scrambler or an emissary of light reaches its logical conclusion in a petty crookedness combined with a fatally inconsistent view that Krogh's swindle is not 'respectable'. England certainly did make Anthony.

Krogh, the 'insider dealer', represents the ruthless modern business world against which Anthony's superannuated virtues are unable to stand. It is the down-at-heel Minty who analyses Krogh's social and economic effect most satisfactorily: '[a]ll the money goes to Krogh and he doesn't employ half the men who were employed in the old cut-throat days' (126). Recalling Stevie's inarticulate ideas of social justice in *The Secret Agent*, the not very bright 'young Andersson' makes the long journey on foot to protest to Krogh about his father's dismissal, thinking 'with astonishment' that 'it's not right', an 'idea [which] had never occurred to him before' (148). The political narrative is set on a very effective collision course with the plot centred around Anthony's flawed psychology. Young Andersson acts as a catalyst who speeds the reversal in Anthony's apparently amicable relationship with Krogh. When Anthony refuses to throw Andersson out of the restaurant, Krogh's vicious bodyguard Fred Hall takes over. Although Anthony has a similar reluctance to deal with Krogh and Hall to Axel Heyst regarding Jones and Ricardo, his code of honour forbids him to countenance Krogh's dishonesty.

In this way, Anthony is a 'seedy' version of Conrad's Jim, who leaves behind after his martyrdom a 'living woman' (Kate), a sacrifice to his idea of what is right. In many other respects also, *England Made Me* displaces Conrad's romantic tragedy into a low mimetic mode. Anthony's father is a kind of debased version of Jim's, who transforms the parson's 'round of little thoughts about faith and virtue' (*Lord Jim* 341) into banal maxims such as '[h]onour the dead . . . a little bit of England . . . be chaste, prudent, pay your debts, and do not love immoderately' (*England Made Me* 63). The conclusions of both novels evoke similar responses: on the one hand admiration of martyrdom for the sake of a belief; on the other appalled regret at the protagonist's inability to survive.

England Made Me represents a crossroads within Greene's early work, where we find the different sub-genres of the interior narrative, modified love romance, conspiracy, and political story working together in ways which show, as Conrad's fiction does, the intrinsic connections between the inner and social modes of being. At the same time, we see Greene experimenting with other possible displacements of these Conradian elements. Some of these he later discards, such as the rendering of interiority through a Joycean stream-of-consciousness technique, but others he retains and develops, such as the 'seedy' Catholic exile Minty, who provides a kind of moral foil to the corrupt political world found later in characters like Dominguez in *The Quiet American*. Together, Minty and Anthony are the first of Greene's characters to embody a state of 'exile from [their] country and . . . class' (180). Neither is 'optimistic enough . . . to believe in peace, co-operation, the dignity of labour, or if they believed in them they were not young enough to work for them' (180). They are low-life versions of Razumov, 'neither one thing nor the other', only 'momentarily convinced by wine they couldn't afford that they believed in something; in the old country, in the king' (180). However, like many of Greene's uncommitted characters, if they do not adhere to a political or religious faith, neither have they sold out like Krogh or Hall.

England Made Me is constructed from setting both a political and an interior narrative within a thriller plot. The entertainments which follow, however, develop a purer form of melodrama, a direction perhaps encouraged by Greene's interest in the cinema and his writing of film reviews for *The Spectator* and *Night and Day*. Although he generally despised Alfred Hitchcock's films for consisting only 'of a series of small "amusing" melodramatic situations' (*Pleasure* 75), he nevertheless admired Hitchcock's translation of Conrad's *Secret Agent* into a formulaic thriller, *Sabotage* (1935). In this film, Verloc becomes a sinister figure of melodrama and his conspiracy merely a weakening of public morale by foreign agents. While Verloc is intensified, Stevie is softened, becoming what is supposed to be a charming young boy with an Eton accent; Winnie is similarly typecast as a conventional heroine who can later be rescued from the charge of murder by Hitchcock's chivalrous conflation of Inspector Heat and Comrade Ossipon into the young police officer, Ted. Greene's surprisingly charitable review of the film suggests that to some extent Hitchcock confirmed his own reading of the novel as a blend of realism and melodrama. Although he admits in his review that '*Sabotage* is not, of course, Conrad's *The Secret Agent*', and that the novel's 'dark drab passionate side of Edwardian London could never find its place in the popular cinema', he concludes that the 'melodrama' is 'convincingly realistic', despite the difficulties of transferring the novel's 'peculiar qualities – of madness and despair in four-wheelers and backstreets – to the screen' (*Pleasure* 123).

Nevertheless, Hitchcock's film perhaps reminds Greene of the potential of the 'dark drab passionate side' of Conrad's novel for translation into the realistic melodrama he now wishes to write himself. In the same year, he wrote *A Gun for Sale* quite consciously as 'a shocker' (Sherry, *Life* 577), a Buchanesque thriller complete with train pursuit on a Scottish express. Taking its cue from a plethora of contemporary invasion literature like *The Secret Agent*, *A Gun for Sale* portrays a conspiracy at a high level of authority and influence, with Sir Marcus the armaments manufacturer plotting to provoke a war in order to drum up business.[5] Greene does not lose sight of human interiority, however, for the conspiracy plot is constructed around Raven's emotional awakening to the real significance of the political conspiracy in which he is caught up.

The real interest of the novel, then, lies in the way Greene sets the narratives of interiority and conspiracy against each other. Marc Silverstein argues that 'Greene deliberately sets out to challenge – if not frustrate – reader expectations by either departing from the basic conventions of the formulaic narrative world or else utilising these conventions in such a way as to blur the line separating formulaic from mimetic fiction' (Silverstein 24). In this way, *A Gun for Sale* treads a very thin line between these two genres, invoking what Peter Rabinowitz calls 'different rules of notice'. Inviting us to read a melodramatic narrative complete with a neat consolatory closure, the novel gives contradictory signals that we are also reading something approximating an existential dramatisation of the 'terror of life', so easily lent expression, as Silverstein observes, 'through the genre of the spy thriller' (28). In this way, *A Gun for Sale* plays a 'Buchanesque' version of *Under Western Eyes* against what Allott and Farris call 'the underlying serious view of life' which they think is to be found in Greene's entertainments in contrast to 'the ordinary thriller' (126).

A Gun for Sale probes both the milieu and the psychology of its villains. Cholmondoley with his sinister emerald ring represents the typical 'emblem' motif of the Buchanesque thriller – the man with the missing finger in *The Thirty-Nine Steps* for example – although this cringing, sweet-toothed character also invokes the low-life banality of Verloc in *The Secret Agent*. Indeed, he even has an accommodation address at a shop that could be Mr Verloc's, selling 'postcards from Paris in sealed envelopes, American and French magazines, and books on flagellation in paper jackets for which the pimply youth and his sister . . . charged twenty shillings' (*Gun for Sale* 30). Raven, a psychopathic Razumov, is an emotionally isolated orphan who 'had never felt the least tenderness for anyone', whose 'mother had borne him when his father was in gaol' and had later 'cut her own throat with a kitchen knife' (66). Like Razumov too, Raven is eventually awakened to confession and remorse by a female protagonist, Anne, when 'something sharp and cold . . . breaking in his heart with great pain' leads him to confess his murder of the old minister (46). Similarly, Sir Marcus's isolation from the community of mankind is an important factor behind his indifference to the human suffering which would be caused by a war, which would amount to somewhat simplistic psychology were it not for the quite different character of Sir Marcus's boyhood companion in the home, the minister whom he has murdered.

The political narrative of *A Gun for Sale* also draws on *The Secret Agent*'s representation of political decisions as based ultimately on the interactions and conflicts of the individual characters making them. These interactions are dramatised in the form of what Aaron Fögel defines in his book on Conrad, *Coercion to Speak* (1985), as a 'forced dialogue,' an 'instrumental practice, conceived on a model of physical events, involving the application of force between persons, which like force in work can be creative or annihilating' (Fögel 6). As Sir Marcus tries painfully to extract an agreement from the Chief Constable to have the besieged Raven summarily shot, the ebb and flow of two personalities that fail to understand each other translate the conflict of policeman and villain into a drama of veiled insinuation and threat. In reply to Sir Marcus's question as to whether he hasn't any influence, the Chief Constable's evasively ambiguous answer – 'I'd like to please you' – provokes Sir Marcus to try and force him to the point with a concrete imperative, 'There's the telephone.' The Chief Constable's further attempt to retreat into generalities and perhaps intentionally fail to understand the drift of Sir Marcus's meaning – 'They are a good lot of boys. . . . You needn't be afraid' – forces Sir Marcus in frustration to declare himself – 'But he has got to be dead' (*Gun for Sale* 114). This kind of 'forced interview . . . in the . . . political world', as Fögel calls it (15), ends in deadlock with 'the gloom and indecision' of the Chief Constable (*Gun for Sale* 114); however, the result the next day is the shooting of Sir Marcus as well as of Raven, translating into a more specifically melodramatic form the explosive outcome of the verbal stalemate between Mr and Mrs Verloc.

The political narrative of *A Gun for Sale*, however, is subordinated to the interior drama and modified love narrative in which

Anne Crowder is a major protagonist in her own right, unlike the somewhat idealised figure of Conrad's Natalia Haldin. Anne's role is complicated by the fact that, caught up in the terror of isolation, she herself undergoes a major dilemma between faith and betrayal and is trapped between the law on one side in the form of Mathers, her policeman fiancé, and the menaces of the conspirators on the other. When Raven confesses, this double allegiance is given a further twist by Anne's sympathies undergoing a sharp reversal regarding him, which then change back at the end of the novel when she thinks of her betrayal of him and of her failure to keep alive his 'ghost': 'Only a shade of disquiet remained, a fading spectre of Raven . . . this sense of failure would never die from her brain' (184–5). A further development in Anne's feelings occurs when she translates this 'failure' (which the unimaginative Mathers interprets as a modest disavowal of her heroic action) into a further 'failing to atone' (185) for the initial betrayal.

This final revelation of Anne's interior processes completely subverts the typically affirmative closure of melodrama. The apparent sentimentality of the last paragraph's depiction of a 'cosy' English Christmas reinvokes Raven's bitterness at the hypocritical Christianity he was taught through his childhood in the orphan's home. Moreover, the recapitulation of the 'home' motif stresses the self-cancelling irony of that term as it is used throughout the novel and creates an uneasy, ambivalent ending. Like Anne, we are tempted to accept the uncomplicated ethical dualities of a thriller plot with a happy ending: 'she [sheltered] the ghost for a very short while longer, "I did fail"' (185). Although Anne forgets 'it . . . completely when the train drew into London', where she sees 'the sweet shops . . . full of white gauze stockings crammed with cheap gifts' (185), the 'unshadowed happiness' with which she sighs 'we're home' (186) is a suspect emotion. As we shall see more clearly in *The Ministry of Fear,* the uneasy tension between her doubt and relief expresses the generic tension between formulaic plot and existential realism at the level of character portrayal. Greene appears to console us with the stock configurations of Buchanesque invasion melodrama in which the lowly individual averts a war, yet finally undermines that comfort, leaving the sub-genres of existential drama and formulaic thriller in a state of irresolution. This indeterminacy suggests that to keep faith with political allegiances and personal conscience may involve the betrayal of one or the other. Throughout Greene's fiction, the personal is played constantly against the political and social in a way that suggests that the two modes of being are open to change and reinterpretation, just as are the genres of interior narrative and political adventure plot which structure their fictional expression.

V

In her book *The Dangerous Edge* (1990), Judith Adamson argues that Greene avoids a political solution to the breakdown of liberal humanism in the thirties. While Adamson suggests that he compensates for this by immersing the fiction in intricate visual detail (37), it is surely the concentration during this period upon the individual's existential terror and isolation which represses the political narrative. This tendency increases in the second 'trilogy' of entertainments – *The Confidential Agent* (1939), *The Ministry of Fear* (1943) and *The Third Man* (1947) – where Greene follows through as completely as possible with his detour from Conrad towards existential melodrama. The protagonists of these works, D., Arthur Rowe and Holly Martins, all experience a dilemma similar in some respects to Razumov's in *Under Western Eyes*. However, while a choice between faith and betrayal dramatises their inner psychology, it is a thriller plot concentrated upon the isolated protagonist rather than a specifically political set of circumstances, which structures the narrative of personal revelation.

In *The Confidential Agent* (1939) – the most straightforward Buchanesque 'shocker' of the three – the protagonist D.'s mission is to buy coal from Britain for his socialist nation (Republican Spain loosely disguised), which is beleaguered by a fascist revolution. The 'infection' of guilt and civil war which D. carries around with him, however, has a quite different effect from the 'hereditary disease' Razumov tries to detect on his face (*Under Western Eyes* 220). D. is the protagonist of an ironic romance centred on the individual, rather than of a political tragedy which sets its characters in a wider social context. Razumov's motive in betraying Haldin is more or less duplicated in *The Confidential Agent* by counter-agent K., who sells out in return for being made a professor; however, the emphasis is almost entirely upon individual conscience. When D. himself rejects the temptation of returning to a quiet academic life of 'long corridors and formal gardens and expensive books' (171), he invokes Razumov's guilty obsession, wondering if it would 'be "getting back" to have a ghost tagged forever at your side as a reminder' (171). There is little suggestion, however, of the intrinsic connection between an individual and his political context which is found in *Under Western Eyes* in the form of 'the dangers menacing the stability of the institutions which give rewards and appointments' (60–1). This is partly due to the novel's setting being almost exclusively in Britain; we never see in any detail the political circumstances in D.'s homeland.

In terms of Peter Brooks's narrative theory, detour or deviation in an individual plot signals a motivation to avoid repressed content.[6] In the same way, Greene's evolving 'mega-narrative' displaces the Conradian political dimension into an interiorised version of Buchan, transforming the political sub-genre into little more than melodramatic background. Nevertheless, Greene does not write a purely formulaic thriller; rather, he uses the Buchan prototype to create a Conradian narrative of ordinary people caught up in unfamiliar and threatening circumstances. This unsettling generic fusion denies us the consolation of formulaic closure, rewriting the solitary protagonist's existential angst in terms of the build-up and release of suspense.

Greene's critical essay on Buchan corroborates his fiction's tendency to press the thriller into the service of an interior narrative. Buchan, he thinks, 'was the first to realise the enormous dramatic value of adventure in familiar surroundings happening to unadventurous men', thereby showing 'how thin is the protection of civilisation' (*Essays* 223–5). However, Greene is talking more of his own methods than Buchan's. In *The Confidential Agent*, he joins adventure with Conradian psychological and existential suspense, defamiliarising what W. H. Auden calls the 'great good place' of the English detective novel (Auden 151)[7] in an almost surrealistic demonstration of the suspicion and danger concealed beneath the surface of a thinly protecting civilisation. As in *Under Western Eyes*, the protagonist's alienation from his surroundings emphasises his isolation. We can see in the English masculine bonhomie of Captain Currie the ignorant complacency of politically secure countries which like Conrad's Switzerland have made 'their bargain with fate' (*Under Western Eyes* 142). Currie is a military type whose chivalrous spirit is manipulated by the counter-agent L. to have D. beaten up for 'walking off' with Rose's bags (*Confidential Agent* 33). Currie tells a couple who stop their car to protest that D. is just 'One of these foreigners.... Glib tongue, you know' (35). At this point it is possible to observe the repressed political narrative appear briefly above the melodramatic surface, suggesting Britain's indifference to the Spanish Republic; however, the emphasis is more upon D. as an isolated individual in an environment which, though apparently familiar, is disturbingly estranged when viewed through his perspective.

Similarly, while Greene retains *The Secret Agent*'s method of dramatising political conflict through individual character, finally he obscures the specific issue. Although, like Verloc, D.'s antagonist L. has no sense of the inherent value of human beings, equating the loss of his art collection with that of D.'s wife, political affiliation remains largely an expression of *individual* personality; we never see exactly what effect L.'s ideology has on Spanish society. Similarly, while Dr Bellows's weak lament at 'all this hate . . . these wars we read about in the newspapers' (43) recalls the empty idealism of the mild-mannered Michaelis, we are never clearly shown the political effects of this muddled thinking. While Dr Bellows also feels Sir Ethelred's repugnance for political details, 'never read[ing] the daily press' because 'in a good weekly paper fact has been sifted from rumour . . . so much less distress' (125), the novel itself seems to share his repugnance too.

The sub-genres of *The Confidential Agent*, then, form a fragmented pattern in which Peter Rabinowitz's 'rules of notice' for determining genre are somewhat confused.[8] Intermittently, we are asked to meditate upon British indifference to the Spanish Civil War by means of a political and psychological narrative which presents D. as a reluctant existential socialist hero combatting the forces of an autocratic or apolitically indifferent bad faith. Ultimately, however, it is the existential drama of the individual which triumphs over both the political and the melodramatic plots. Having made the final lucky escape of the typical adventure story, D. finds his leading lady Rose Cullen aboard the ship which is spiriting him away, a romantic apotheosis which duplicates the end of Conrad's *Chance*. Although Rose herself attempts to qualify this operatic closure with her detumescent reminder that D. 'will be dead very soon' (206), this makes very little difference to the typically affirmative ending of the romantic thriller, in which the role of political reality is largely to provide exotic background.

The Ministry of Fear (1943) develops further this tendency to eclipse the political narrative, creating a novel markedly similar to Buchan's *The Thirty-Nine Steps*. There is an almost exact parallel in the finale when the protagonist Rowe, having officially turned his counter-espionage discoveries over to the authorities as Richard Hannay does, takes over once again and tracks down Hilfe, the principal enemy mole. In this way, the dominant genre of *The Ministry of Fear* is that of a straightforward anti-Nazi spy thriller in which a Buchanesque process of defamiliarisation transforms such quintessentially English stereotypes as Mr Cost the Saville Row tailor or the old man feeding the birds into enemy agents.

In spite of this, *The Ministry of Fear*'s revelation of interior character is more complex than *The Confidential Agent*'s. While Greene sets Arthur Rowe's guilt over the mercy killing of his wife against the formulaic plot, he also creates a metatextual parallel to this through the fiction's speculations upon its own generic origins. In this way, Arthur's quest for renewed selfhood and the merging of interior narrative and thriller plot converge at frequent literary checkpoints. One of these nodal points is to be found in the references to Charlotte M. Yonge's historical romance *The Little Duke* (1854), a Christianised bildungsroman-cum adventure story set in tenth-century Normandy. *The Ministry of Fear* draws its main epigraph and also those of its chapters from this book, which also figures in the story itself through representing one of Arthur Rowe's favourite texts. The references to *The Little Duke* give an alibi, as it were, for *The Ministry of Fear*'s thriller formula, allowing Greene to contrast dream with reality.[9] This is also made clear in Rowe's taste for Dickens's *The Old Curiosity Shop* and *David Copperfield*, which he read 'over and over again till he could have quoted chapter and verse, not so much because he liked them as because he had read them as a child, and they carried no adult memories' (*Ministry of Fear* 20–1).

The Ministry of Fear is written against these narratives similarly to the way in which *Lord Jim* implicitly contrasts itself with the 'light holiday literature' that the protagonist is so fond of. Recalling Greene's essay, 'The Lost Childhood', Arthur Rowe thinks that 'no later books satisfy us like those that were read to us in childhood – for they promised a world of great simplicity of which we knew the rules' (89). Unlike these 'books one had read as a boy', none of which 'had an unhappy ending [nor] was disturbed by a sense of pity for the beaten side' (176), the later books are 'complicated and contradictory with experience' (89). As Rowe gradually remembers his past, 'he [grows] up' in a way which parallels these narratives, 'learn[ing] that adventure did not always follow the literary pattern, that there weren't always happy endings' (180).

This process of working through suggests a paradigm of fictional character and reader maturing together in a process whereby interior revelation merges with thriller plot. As Rowe solves the formulaic 'mystery' of the spy's identity, he reconstructs what Tzvetan Todorov describes as the 'first story' of detective fiction,[10] discovering that Hilfe is the double agent in league with Dr Forester. At the same time, however, he also 'reconstructs' himself, a process which mirrors the reader's own deciphering of the narrative suggestively inscribed when text and detection merge in the first clue Rowe finds in the nursing home. The faint erased pencil marks in the copy of Tolstoy's *What I Believe* keep Digby (alias Rowe) – 'awake and brooding at the end of a day of loneliness and boredom' upon the character of Dr Forester and to conclude that 'You couldn't respect a man who dared not hold his opinions openly' (135). Greene brings the suspect cosmopolitanism of Tolstoy's political thought (which would also have been anathema to Conrad) together with Rowe's gradual growing out of the simplistic narratives of his youth in a way that directly relates them to the development of Rowe's character *and* to the onward impetus of the thriller plot.

In *The Ministry of Fear*, then, the interior narrative is given a weighty role. The effect of this, however, is to relegate the political dimensions of the story to an ideological background which we are encouraged to take for granted. Its publication during World War II perhaps made this inevitable, in contrast with Elizabeth Bowen's novel *The Heat of the Day* (1949), which employs a similar theme and setting. The effect is to deepen the significance of the thriller plot's doubling with a narrative of interior revelation. Rowe's psychological quest, particularly his battle with amnesia, leads to the intricate manipulation of the melodramatic showdown. Marc Silverstein comments that at this point Greene 'denies us the kind of certainty and security we experience at the close of a conventional formulaic thriller where the love of a beautiful woman becomes the hero's reward for saving his country' (Silverstein 42). Rowe's deception of Anna that Hilfe has not reminded him that he killed his wife qualifies the finale more effectively than Rose's token *memento mori* in *The Confidential Agent*. This is due not only to the more consistent portrayal throughout the novel of Rowe's guilty isolation but to the greater depth of the unspoken suspicions and psychological manoeuvres, as when Rowe 'tentatively' tries the stock phrase, 'My dear, my dear, I am so happy', but upon hearing Anna's 'prompt and guarded reply, 'I am too', reflects that 'after all one could exaggerate the value of happiness' (221). In this way, the final scene metatextually sums up the novel's primary generic drive to undermine the conventional love romance with an existential interior narrative.

VI

Written expressly for Sir Carol Reed's film, the short novel *The Third Man* (1947) has a similarly complex interior narrative to *The Ministry of Fear*'s.[11] Relegating the political implications of post-war Vienna to the background, the story again recapitulates the psychological plot of *Under Western Eyes* in Holly Martins's dilemma between keeping faith with his friend Harry Lime and betraying him to Calloway. Although this seems like more of the same, *The Third Man* in fact represents a significant development in Greene's deployment of the Conradian masterplot in its use of *Heart of Darkness*'s narrative structure. Recalling what E. R. Bruffee calls Conrad's 'observer–narrator', the fiction conveys Harry's moral disintegration through the effect of its recognition upon Holly.[12] The consistent processing of the action through Holly's point of view in the film suggests that he becomes a kind of substitute narrator. Like Marlow, he becomes an interior detective who explores himself through attempting to understand his relationship with Harry, resulting in a similar ebb and flow of his sympathies between quizzical admiration and qualified outrage.

Francis Ford Coppola's film, *Apocalypse Now* (1980) suggests a number of cinematic and generic convergences between Greene and Conrad through the mediums of Reed, Marlon Brando and Orson Welles. For example, Coppola uses a similar technique to Reed in order to build gradually up to the representation of Colonel Kurtz. Just as the observer–narrator Captain Willard's investigation proceeds from a taped voice to the dossier containing photos and reports and finally to the climactic emergence of Marlon Brando himself from the shadows, *The Third Man* gradually unveils Orson Welles's Harry by means of a process which metonymically substitutes associated objects for the person sought. Harry's flat, his cat, and a photo which Anna shows Holly in a bar increase in verisimilitude to become the slide photograph which Calloway presents, later the 'ghost' Holly sees in the doorway and finally the 'living' cinematic presence of the man himself beneath the ferris wheel.

There is surely a factor of viewer response involving the delayed and limited appearance of the 'star' actor here, whose importance in the expectations and response of the audience Frank McConnell argues persuasively in his book *The Spoken Seen* (1975). Moreover, the intertextuality between the two films and Conrad's original text acquires an extra *frisson* when we remember that one of Orson Welles'ss uncompleted projects was to play Kurtz in a movie of *Heart of Darkness*. One is tempted to surmise that *Under Western Eyes* may even have been a direct inspiration to Welles's famous improvised gloss on the Conradian contrast between the banality of democracy and the intensity of autocracy: 'In Italy for thirty years under the Borgias they had warfare, terror, murder, bloodshed – they produced Michelangelo, Leonardo da Vinci and the Renaissance. In Switzerland they had brotherly love, five hundred years of democracy and peace, and what did that produce . . . ? The cuckoo clock' (Greene and Reed, *Third Man* 100).

Underpinning the implications of cinematic processing, however, is Greene's generic manipulation of the Conradian masterplot. Like *Heart of Darkness*, *The Third Man* is initially established as a straightforward detective investigation and then gradually transformed first into a psychological investigation of the 'criminal' by the 'detective' and later into one of the detective himself. Like Marlow, Holly conducts a series of interviews with Calloway, Kurtz, Anna, Dr Winkler, Koch and Popescu/Cooler, in an attempt to determine if there has been any 'foul play'. However, after Koch's death this more straightforward sleuthing is complicated by Calloway's decision to reveal the truth about Harry. Cinematic technique streamlines the conventional detective motif which occurs with the 'presentation of the evidence', compressing the minutely detailed 'Sherlock Holmes' denouement into a series of quickly edited shots of slides and other exhibits such as 'finger prints [under a magnifying glass], threads from a coat, files about Lime, still photographs' (79).[13] This telescoping effect emphasises that Harry's guilt can be taken for granted and that the issue at stake is interior psychology. This is confirmed by the camera's continual return to Holly's face to register its gradual progression from scepticism to belief.

With Calloway's presentation, Holly's interior narrative begins a quest for selfhood almost as fraught with ambiguity as Marlow's. 'How could he have done it?' Holly wonders at the end of the sequence (Greene and Read, *Third Man* 79), while in the novel Calloway comments that 'a world for Martins had certainly come to an end, a world of easy friendship, hero-worship' (82). However, Holly still vacillates to and fro in his evaluations of Harry; in fact his temporary rejection is as simplistic as his hitherto unquestioning acceptance. In this respect, his visit to Anna suggests a significant reversal of Marlow's interview with Kurtz's 'Intended' in *Heart of Darkness*. Holly confronts Anna with a truth that she knew all along, and behaves rather as the 'Intended' herself might have done if Marlow had told *her* the truth about Kurtz: 'I feel as though he had never really existed, that we'd dreamed him. Was he laughing at fools like us all the time?' (86). Anna, however, takes a maturer, less worshipful attitude, one more similar perhaps to Marlow's appreciation of Kurtz's complexities at the time of narration: 'For God's sake stop making people in *your* image. Harry was real. He wasn't just your hero and my lover. He was Harry. He was in a racket. He did bad things. What about it? He was the man we knew' (86). In this way, *The Third Man* develops and clarifies the Conradian *Doppelgänger* motif which Greene had employed in a confused and fragmented way in *Rumour at Nightfall*. Holly's existential education consists of learning that he is *not* Harry's double, as he had always in his boyish way wished to be.

The Third Man seems almost consciously to invoke the narrative 'search' of *Heart of Darkness*, a motif often seen in the other major detour of Greene's fiction during these years, in which the examination of interiority is displaced into a Catholic mode. *The Third Man*, in fact, signals the imminent reunion of these two divergent paths through its close merger of the typical 'sanctified sinner' of Greene's Catholic narratives with the villain of a conspiracy plot. Recalling Satan's temptation of Christ in the wilderness, Harry takes Holly up in the ferris wheel and shows him, as it were, the 'riches of the earth'. He asks: 'Would you really feel any pity if one of those dots stopped moving – for ever? If I said you can have twenty thousand pounds for every dot that stops, would you really, old man, tell me to keep my money, without hesitation?' (104). Harry embodies a Catholic sense of evil in a way that recalls Pinkie in *Brighton Rock*, especially when he tells Holly that he 'still *believe[s]* . . . [i]n God and mercy and all that', but that he's 'not hurting anybody's soul. . . . The dead are happier dead' (106). However, Holly's view that Harry has never grown up, that 'evil was like Peter Pan – it carried with it the horrifying and evil gift of eternal youth' (104), gives a clearer, though less satisfactory explanation of Harry's evil than *Heart of Darkness*'s more politically significant portrayal of Kurtz's nihilism.

As in *The Ministry of Fear*, Greene seems self-consciously to be grappling with the various Conradian genres he invokes in *The Third Man*. In this way, generic manipulations of the thriller formula create a formal parallel with Holly's existential education. Recalling Arthur Rowe, Holly grows out of the stereotypical loyalty of the boy's adventure tale into the existential independence of a more probing, psychological narrative. The literary affiliations of Holly and other characters inscribe the analogy between Holly's maturation and the reader's decoding of genre; for example, Holly meets Calloway's accusation that he 'sound[s] like a cheap novelette' with the retort that he '*write*[s] cheap novelettes' (Greene and Read, *Third Man* 25). Similarly, Holly begins his investigation of Harry's death with a doomed attempt to become a hero of one of his own westerns, to be the 'rider who hunted down a sheriff who was victimising his best friend' (32). However, as the plot moves forward we see him figuratively abandon the romance form first for the detective story and then for an intrinsic genre that blends a thriller formula with the interiority of the high literature so beloved by Crabbit and the Cultural Re-Education Society.

These genres clash comically when Holly is mistaken by Crabbit for 'the great English writer Dexter' and must defend Zane Grey against the affiliates of James Joyce.[14] Highly reminiscent of Hitchcock's comically suspenseful portrayal of Richard Hannay posing as the radical candidate in *The Thirty-Nine Steps*, the scene fuses melodramatic comedy with a discussion which is specifically about 'formulaic' versus 'serious' literature; Holly cites Shakespeare in order to defend Zane Grey from Crabbit's charge of being 'just a popular entertainer' (70–1). Later, the argument is further complicated by the self-referential declaration of Holly's – which is also implicitly Greene alluding to his generic intentions – that his next book will be called *The Third Man* (71).

The question of genre definition reflects Greene's larger dilemma at this point in his career between two dissociated strands of the repressed Conradian masterplot in his work. Although *The Third Man* did not inspire him to give up novels and take up screenplays, its excursion into another medium helps to clarify the extent to which the Conradian sub-genres have been displaced into a variety of different textual modes. The film is a kind of homage to his interest in the cinema throughout the thirties, especially to the quality of angst conveyed by Fritz Lang's German expressionist style.[15] What Paul M. Jensen defines in Lang's *Spies* as 'a large web of conspiracy [which] implacably tightens around an individual' (Jensen 78), together with its sense of 'conflict between public and private loyalty and the danger lurking beneath an innocent surface' (78), also applies here. The film's narrative point of view constantly emphasises the dark atmosphere of Vienna and the imagery of the grotesque in nervously edited chiaroscuro shots of threatening faces viewed from skewed and unusual camera angles. The surreal quality is increased by the image of the small child with the ball, recalling the brooding urban threat of Lang's *M*, a film which also provides *The Third Man* with the incongruous carnivalesque note of the balloon seller in the midst of the manhunt. The effect of these disorientating contrasts is uncannily emphasised by the light Viennese music of Anton Karas's zither which is played constantly throughout the film.

In his book *The Cinema of Fritz Lang* (1969), Paul Jensen argues that Lang moved from an imitation of stage expressionism in his films, in which 'directors tended to transfer current styles of decor, acting, and lighting directly to motion pictures' (14), to a 'filmic approach to expressionism [in which] distortions of reality are no longer needed', because 'real settings shown in new ways, by means of close-up and well-chosen angles, will do the trick' (77). Reed also seems to use this approach to develop the atmosphere of existential terror in *The Third Man*. We can observe this especially in the scene where Holly and Anna go to Kurtz's flat to interview him again. As they approach the crowd outside the door, the camera moves back and then hesitates in an unsynchronised rhythm with *their* hesitation. As Holly approaches the crowd to make enquiries, the quick cuts from him to Anna and back to the crowd and the child communicate a general sense of nervousness; this is intensified by the darkness and sense of disorientation as the camera shifts uneasily between Holly's face and the two men he questions. The shrill incongruity of the child's cries, together with the quick, nervous cutting, high-angle shots of the child, the brief glimpses of the old sweeper, an exaggeratedly low angle shot of Anna approaching and one of the child shouting and tugging at Holly's sleeve exacerbate the mounting tension, with high and low camera angles rapidly alternating between Anna, Koch's body and the crowd's suspicious faces.

This visual mode of disorientation is translated into a generic dimension in the chase through the sewers, where melodrama merges visually with the existential uncertainty of the divided Conrad–Greene protagonist. Like Harry, we have no idea where we are in the maze of tunnels, which is cinematically simulated by a labyrinthine succession of shots of Harry, the police, Holly, the tunnel-openings, doors behind waterfalls and ladders. This sequence culminates in Harry standing at the entrances to a group of tunnels unable to tell from the sound of the echoes where his pursuers are, while the final appearance of his hands through the grating constitutes an enigmatic return to the metonymic mode with which he was introduced. In this way, cinematic form rejects a consolatory ending in which good vanquishes evil. The final shot of Holly after he has killed Harry provides a conclusion that parodies one of his own western heroes, for instead of riding *into* the sunset to disappear into some impossible form of narrative quiescence, Holly emerges *out* of the searchlight, as though to signal his initiation into the complex 'mixed genres' of adult life.

VII

It has long been a critical truism that Greene's contact with the cinema influenced his narrative style. However, it would seem that his collaboration on the film of *The Third Man* marks the end of a process in his fiction rather than a beginning, the point at which he almost reaches the full extent of his detour towards realistic melodrama. I say 'almost', because his writing can be seen in hindsight at this point to suffer a temporary relapse into the quiescent acceptance of Conrad's influence. In 1948, Greene wrote *The Tenth Man*, which later he astonishingly claimed to have forgotten about till 1985,[16] an almost literal repression of Conrad, for this short novel is about the closest he ever comes to repeating *Under Western Eyes* wholesale. Fortunately, however, *The Tenth Man* is a temporary aberration, a drawing back perhaps in order to prepare for the eventual return of the reluctantly involved protagonist within a political narrative.

Imprisoned as a hostage in wartime Paris, the lawyer Louis Chavel buys his life in exchange for his fellow prisoner Janvier's, when he is chosen in a lottery as one of ten prisoners to be shot in a Nazi reprisal. Closely recalling Conrad's structure, the narrative subsequently shows Chavel – now known as Charlot – as he looks for work at his former residence, now the home of Janvier's mother and sister Thérèse. Like Razumov he has 'no – one – to – go – to' (*Under Western Eyes* 327); he finds Thérèse Janvier distraught over her brother's death and anxious to revenge herself while the mother, old and ailing like Mrs Haldin, has not been told the circumstances of her son's execution.

Chavel's belief, in prison, that he should be exempt from the political persecution suffered by his fellows results in a similar alienation to Razumov's from the community of mankind. A middle-class lawyer, he attempts desperately to deny that he is involved in the same circumstances as the other hostages. Because he 'never consented' to take part in the lottery, he protests: 'You can't *make* me die like the rest of you' (*The Tenth Man* 50). His process of denial continues later when he is free. Unpicking, with 'his lawyer's mind . . . the threads of the case' (98), he also tries to project his own guilt onto Janvier as Razumov does Haldin: 'After all,' he tells himself, 'only Janvier is responsible for Janvier's death: no guilt attaches to me whatever I may feel' (98). However, guilt is forced upon him through his involvement with the very people his act has most affected, Janvier's mother and sister. As in *Under Western Eyes*, this process also blends the psychological portrayal of the protagonist with the promise of a romantic narrative when Chavel begins to fall in love with Thérèse, lending a further dimension to the melodramatic suspense as to whether his secret will be discovered. As Charlot falls in love with Thérèse, he begins to perceive her grief and his own guilt, finding now 'a different quality in his despair' whereby 'he no longer despairs of a livelihood' but 'of life' (97).

This specifically Conradian configuration of betrayal is also shown by the marked presence of another Conrad novel – *Lord Jim*. In her discussion with 'Charlot' of 'Chavel's' betrayal, Thérèse momentarily takes on the role of Conrad's French Lieutenant. She disagrees that Chavel was merely 'unlucky' in the fact of his act of cowardice proving 'so spectacular' (95), asserting: 'That thing happens to everyone once. All one's life one has to think: Today it may happen. . . . When it happens you know what you've been all your life' (95). With these transparent references to Conrad, it is only towards the end, with the arrival of Carosse, that the plot of *The Tenth Man* falls back into the more typical melodrama of the entertainments. Carosse, a con-man pretending to be Chavel, is a stock figure of nemesis in contrast to the more subtle psychic processes which cause Razumov to confess. Carosse's figure 'stretched on [Chavel's] bed' is a similar but more formulaic manifestation of the *Doppelgänger* motif in *Under Western Eyes* (*The Tenth Man* 122). Carosse's cynical knowledge caricatures Chavel's not unworthy motivations: 'Here you are,' he tells him, 'living alone in the house with a quite attractive young girl. . . . Add to that you have been a long time in prison – and knew her brother. It's just a chemical formula, my dear fellow' (124). Just as Razumov's last temptation leads to his confession and redemption, Carosse's cynicism finally inspires Chavel to reveal the truth when, confronting Carosse embracing Thérèse, he 'no longer felt the desire at all: only an immeasurable tenderness' (152).

With *The Tenth Man,* Greene reaches a point of stasis, a momentary return to the compliance with the Conradian influence seen in his early novels; it is perhaps no wonder that he repressed the memory of writing it for so many years. Within a larger perspective, however, this close recapitulation of *Under Western Eyes* may have helped clarify for Greene the essential point of interest in his Conradian subject, the divided protagonist within a political situation. The decades of the thirties and forties represent a period during which it is possible to observe Greene's fiction laying the groundwork in preparation for a renewed engagement with Conrad which synthesises these dispersed genres of the repressed masterplot. Before arriving at that point, however, we must first enquire into Greene's engagement with interiority in its Catholic form during these years, an engagement which will reveal an even greater concentration on the isolated individual, now pursued, not by enemy agents, but by God.

3

'A Distant Memory of the Sanctus Bell': Greene's Catholic 'Heart of Darkness'

I

While Catholicism in Greene's entertainments is generally subordinated to psychological melodrama, the reverse is the case in his other novels of this period. Here, theology reveals interior consciousness, while still repressing the political narrative. In *Ways of Escape* (1980), Greene writes that at first his 'professional life . . . and religion were contained in quite separate compartments' (*Ways of Escape* 75); only 'the socialist persecution of religion in Mexico, and . . . General Franco's attack on Republican Spain' overcame his reluctance 'to bring them together' (75). I would argue, however, that even though the main focus of Greene's fiction is on Catholicism in the late thirties, it is much later before it becomes 'inextricably involved . . . in contemporary life' (75). During the thirties and forties, Greene experiments with the interior narrative both in his Catholic novels and in his melodramatic entertainments, leaving the political narrative largely in abeyance.

Although Conrad hardly ever refers explicitly to religion in his work, his protagonists' struggle to be redeemed after an early betrayal – especially in *Lord Jim* and *Under Western Eyes* – often has strong religious overtones. Greene, however, thinks that 'little more' was left of Conrad's religious sense 'than a distant memory of the Sanctus bell and the incense', and that all he 'retained of Catholicism' was 'the ironic sense of an omniscience and of the final unimportance of human life under the watching eyes' (*Essays* 184). Greene's depreciation of Conrad, however, gives him an alibi, as it were, for his own creative aspiration to translate Conrad's more political mode of betrayal into one in which issues of religious conscience are at stake.

As we have seen in works such as *It's a Battlefield*, Greene shares Conrad's wider, more social form of compassion for human suffering, especially at the hands of a corrupt political establishment. As if to signal the enduring quality of these sentiments, a more political narrative intermittently surfaces in his novels during these years, most strikingly in the middle of the Catholic cycle in *The Power and the Glory* (1940) and at the end in *A Burnt-Out Case* (1960). Like Conrad, Greene is less interested in elections and parliamentary business than in political processes in developing societies. Neither does he forget the individual's interiority when constructing a political plot, stressing the need for both a spiritual and a political dimension in human life.

Biographical parallels between Greene and Conrad are also important here. Like Conrad, Greene's visits to Africa make an essential contribution to the eventual reunion of the political and religious narratives within his work. In 1935, he made the well-known Liberian journey which he recounts in *Journey without Maps* (1936). As if to circumvent his self-imposed ban on reading Conrad, this travel narrative displaces *Heart of Darkness*'s interrogation of primitive human motivations into a documentary mode based on Greene's own life experience. In spite of this, the first novel dealing with Africa, *The Heart of the Matter* (1948), fails to deliver on its initial promise to become a critique of African colonialism; like *Brighton Rock* (1939) and *The End of the Affair* (1951), it concentrates exclusively upon a romanticised sinner, creating a largely abstract portrayal of theological issues such as sin and damnation. In contrast with these earlier novels, *A Burnt-Out Case* (1960) takes up where *Journey without Maps* (1935) leaves off. Returning to the political and social dimensions of the interior novel set in Africa, it transforms Greene's entire relation to Conrad through representing faith in terms of a secular as well as religious view of social obligations, even going so far as to parody *Heart of Darkness* itself in the process.

II

Brighton Rock (1939) and *The End of the Affair* (1951) represent the purest examples of Greene's narratives of Catholic interiority. While

Brighton Rock begins as a detective story which quickly becomes a theological drama, *The End of the Affair*'s narrative of adultery is transmogrified into hagiography. These two novels are confined within individual problems of faith and estranged from a larger Conradian vision of society, confirming Bruce Harkness's view that Greene 'rejects the outer society which, for all his pessimism . . . Conrad ultimately accepted' (Harkness 71).

In its earlier stages, *Brighton Rock* attempts to create a bridge between Greene's Catholic and melodramatic displacements of Conrad. Greene recalls that he 'began [the novel] as a detective story and continued, [he is] sometimes tempted to think, as an error in judgement' (*Ways of Escape* 73), Although Greene makes fun of his gaining the reputation of being 'detestable term! – a Catholic writer' (74), *Brighton Rock*'s bifurcated genre does arguably represent an 'error', in aesthetic judgement at least. The theological narrative of mortal sin and redemption which takes over the pursuit motif of the thriller plot transforms melodrama into a kind of sugar coating to sweeten the Catholic medicine; Greene may have employed this method quite consciously, even calculatingly, judging from his remark that 'if you excite your audience first, you can put over whatever you will of horror, suffering, truth' (Phillips 172).

Greene translates into theological terms, then, the prototypical Conradian narrative of the haunted man. Pinkie experiences a similar isolation to Razumov's, 'a sense of loneliness, a lack of understanding' (*Brighton Rock* 51), which causes him to feel rage and bitterness against the world. Both Pinkie and Razumov also decry the world's materialistic values and call for a passionately intense engagement with the reality, in contrast to the utilitarianism of their surroundings. *Brighton Rock* celebrates Sophie Antonovna's pronouncement that 'You have either to rot or burn' (*Under Western Eyes* 246), while Rose's more infernal preference to 'burn with [Pinkie] than be like [Ida]' (*Brighton Rock* 114) contrasts with the confession of Prewitt, Pinkie's crooked lawyer, that he can only 'rot' (209). The difference is that *Under Western Eyes* is not specifically theological; Razumov refers more circumspectly to his own games with 'the devil' and his thoughts of stealing Natalia's soul than Pinkie, who wholeheartedly embraces mortal sin both in word and deed when carrying out his similar plan to gain immunity by marrying the key witness to his crime.

Pinkie's interior processes remain confined within his tormented consciousness rather than being integrated with a political vision of society. Although some critics emphasise Pinkie's deprived childhood – Neil Nehrung even sees him as a figure of proto-punk protest[1] – the theological insistence almost completely obscures social and political motivation. This is clear from a brief comparison of *Brighton Rock*'s protagonists with *The Secret Agent*'s. While both novels portray marriages which are based on deception, Verloc's and Winnie's relationship has more far-reaching social implications, for Verloc's treatment of her directly reflects his attitude to society. Pinkie's and Rose's predicament seems isolated by contrast; the crimes in which Pinkie attempts to gain Rose's complicity seem isolated from ordinary life beside Verloc's bungled terrorism in *The Secret Agent*. Indeed, the crimes themselves are not the issue but rather Pinkie's 'sins', which, it is implied, may even make him a better person than people who don't happen to commit murders.

This fundamental difference between the two novels is reflected in their treatments of the detective story. *Brighton Rock* adapts the genre to the pursuit of a spiritually intense criminal, Pinkie, by a banal, sensual detective, Ida Arnold; while *The Secret Agent*, through depicting a society with many intricately interwoven networks of obligation, presents a far less schematic picture. The Assistant Commissioner and Inspector Heat are portrayed as fallible human beings, worried as much about the harmony of their domestic lives or reputations as the pursuit of justice. In contrast to *Brighton Rock*, their mixed motives show *The Secret Agent*'s capacity to cross thematic and generic boundaries.

The aim of Greene's novel is romantically to exonerate Pinkie in order to vilify Ida, who has substituted the spiritualist movement for Catholicism, choosing not to 'believe in heaven or hell, only in ghosts, ouija boards, tables which rapped and little inept voices speaking plaintively of flowers' (*Brighton Rock* 36). Greene seems to have created her almost to indulge a personal grudge; such comments as his insistence on her maternal style of sexuality – 'You thought of sucking babies when you looked at her' (77) – represent an unusual obsession in the mind of a narrator. Particularly disingenuous is the lip-service paid to indeterminism when, having told us that 'You could only guess at the goods behind' her eyes, the narrative immediately defines them as follows: 'justice, an eye for an eye, law and order, capital punishment, a bit of fun now and then' (77). Altogether, the portrayal of Ida as a secular moralist is a caricature. Although she's 'not a Puritan', she says, and she's 'done a thing or two in [her] time', she's 'always been on the side of

Right' (122); when 'the stout [comes] back up her throat again' (122), at this point, however, to betray the blowsy nature of her morality, Greene seems to stack the cards too outrageously against her.

Similarly, the employment of a Blakean Satanic archetype to romanticise Pinkie at the expense of Ida's ordinary morality is too heavy-handed a treatment for the slightness of his character depiction. The result is an unfortunate caricature of Catholic interiority that occasionally borders on the Monty Pythonesque:

> 'These atheists, they don't know nothing. Of course there's Hell. Flames and damnation,' [Pinkie] said with his eyes on the dark shifting water and the lightning and the lamps going out above the black struts of the Palace Pier, 'torments.' (52)

The slight rhythmic pause just before Pinkie's last word lends a quality of farcical exaggeration to the passage which Greene surely did not intend. Nor is this an isolated case, for a similar instance with an almost identical final hesitation occurs in Pinkie's description of life as 'Worms and cataract, cancer. You hear 'em shrieking from the upper windows – children being born' (226).

Greene's apparent intention is to portray Pinkie as an incarnation of pure evil, a hair's breadth from goodness. However, the first of Greene's long series of 'prêtres manqués' seems more like an abstract principle, compared for example with the conflicting attributes of the lieutenant's character in *The Power and the Glory*. Regarding Conradian prototypes, Cedric Watts compares Pinkie with Conrad's Kurtz in terms of their common 'dependence on the ancient theological paradox that in the eyes of God, those who are evil may have greater moral worth than those who are morally nondescript' (Watts, *Deceptive* 25). While this certainly seems to be Greene's intention, the theological ramifications tend to obscure rather than clarify Pinkie's interiority; Kurtz, on the other hand, remains a shadowy, mysterious figure who serves more as a catalyst for Marlow's ambiguous ruminations upon empire. In so far as Kurtz's romantic Satanism emerges into the foreground, it is implicitly condemned as a paradigm of the European impulse to empire. Pinkie, however, lacks a significant political narrative; he is at once too prominent in the fiction and too sketchily drawn a character to bear such an allegorical burden.

This tendency to formulate interiority by means of a set of theological abstractions is most clear at the end of the novel in the first of a series of priestly epitaphs, a motif which later becomes a defining characteristic of Greene's Catholic works. The narrative of *Brighton Rock,* while paying lip service to such values as ambivalence and indeterminism, strongly suggests that Pinkie *is* saved 'between the stirrup and the ground'.[2] Pinkie is the first example of what George Orwell calls Greene's 'sanctified sinner', a figure drawn from the writings of the Catholic mystic Charles Péguy, who emphasises the central role of sin in the processes of salvation. Péguy himself in fact seems to be the Frenchman who, the priest tells Rose, 'lived in sin all through his life because he couldn't bear the idea that any soul could suffer damnation' (246). The priest implicitly links Pinkie with Péguy in his remark that neither he (the priest) nor Rose can conceive 'the appalling strangeness of the mercy of God' (246). In these ways, *Brighton Rock* gathers pretensions to more theological weight than it has ballast to support.

In *Brighton Rock* and other Catholic novels, Greene displaces Conradian interiority by a narrative of the kind written by François Mauriac, in which there is a marked dissociation between the realistic depiction of character and the Catholic world vision that contextualises it.[3] In his 1945 essay on Mauriac, Greene uses the French novelist as a stick with which to beat the English modernists, dismissing the characters of Woolf and Forster as wandering 'like cardboard symbols through a world that was paper thin' (*Essays* 115). Greene argues that 'with the death of James the religious sense was lost to the English novel, and with the religious sense went the sense of the importance of the human act' (115). Mauriac, on the other hand, belongs to 'the company of great traditional novelists'; he is 'a writer for whom the visible world has not ceased to exist, whose characters have the solidity and importance of men with souls to save or lose . . . who claims the traditional and essential right of a novelist, to comment, to express his views' (116).

Significantly, Greene does not mention Conrad in the context of this loss of the 'religious sense'. This avoidance may be due to Conrad's being both a nineteenth-century novelist and a modernist, who while presenting characters within the framework of a moral code also allows for multiple interpretations of them. Greene cannot criticise Conrad for a lack of religious sense manifested either by a diminished visible world or by unimportant human acts, for Conrad's fictional worlds are all too visible and the acts of his characters too similar to Greene's. Greene suggests that 'a book such as *Lord Jim*' is 'romantic and false in comparison' with 'events in

Mauriac's novels [which] are to reveal rather than change characters' (120). However, both Greene's and Conrad's characters do change and develop within the larger moral structure of their fictions. Greene protests too much, betraying how much during these years he was attempting to differentiate himself from Conrad by over-identifying with a Catholic world view.

This over-identification also characterises *The End of the Affair* (1951), in which Greene reaches the furthest point of his theological detour. Blending a tale of adultery with hagiography, the narrative places any hint of a thriller plot entirely at the service of the Catholic narrative, as for example in Bendrix's feeling, when he discovers that Sarah had been baptised a Catholic, like 'a man who has committed the all-but-perfect crime and watches the first unexpected crack in the wall of his deception' (*End of the Affair* 203). Like Razumov (and also like Lord Jim), Sarah and Bendrix are 'pursued' by their consciences, rather than by villains or detectives. Bendrix plays the role of an 'average sensual man' who confronts and attempts to resist 'an infinite tide' (78). Forced to believe in God by the pattern of events throughout the novel, he tells Him finally that he's 'too tired and old to learn how to love', and to '[l]eave [him] alone forever' (240). Implicitly, however, we are invited to understand that in the end Bendrix the sinner will be saved. Although Greene attempts to dramatise the perspective of the non-believer, this apparent openness seems a subterfuge for dice which are palpably loaded. As in *Brighton Rock*, where our only alternative lies between the vapid sensuality of Ida or the vicious spirituality of Pinkie, the only viable choice here is between the saintliness of Sarah and the jealous bitterness of Bendrix.

Conrad does not need to manipulate the reader or the protagonist in this way, because he constantly refers to publicly recognisable criteria. Sarah's compulsion to carry through her promise shows a great contrast, for example, with Jim's determination to keep faith with the seaman's code of conduct, even though it seems to be centred upon a 'bit of ass's skin (*Lord Jim* 161). Jim's crime is very clearly a breach with the solidarity of mankind, while Sarah's and Bendrix's struggles seem claustrophobically confined to their own personal spheres.

Marlow's distance and ambivalence suspends final judgement on Jim. Although Marlow seems at the end to validate Jim's adherence to the code, asking if he 'was so very wrong after all' in '[standing] up to answer for his eternal constancy' (416), he questions whether a final verdict on Jim is, in fact, possible: 'Who knows? He is gone, inscrutable at heart . . .' (416). One thing we do know, however, is that Jim's code involves a felt sense of society; he offers himself up to execution, taking responsibility for the disaster which befalls the Bugis, who perhaps retain their faith in the white race because Jim lives up to his reputation. In this way, *Lord Jim* plays an interior narrative of betrayal against a public dramatisation of colonialism, creating a dialogical interplay of genres which contrasts with the monological insistence on the Catholic processes of faith and doubt in *The End of the Affair*.

The End of the Affair finally resembles more a medieval allegory than a realistic novel. While later 'magic realists' such as Gabriel García Márquez and Salman Rushdie have yoked such genres together with less violence, Greene's Catholic displacement of the interior narrative has become incompatible with the fiction's realistic premise. It is this sense of incongruity with which many critics of the novel struggle to come to terms. Ian Gregor and Ray Snape condemn its tendency to religious propaganda, while Robert Murray Davis amongst others investigates more closely the connections between its complex narrative structure and its theological vision. Davis argues that, like Evelyn Waugh, Greene chose a first-person mode of narration 'for the way in which it allowed [him] to break through the social veil, to allow for uncertainty, mystery and the breaking of "the chain of cause and effect"' (409). However, Davis thinks that both novelists also 'refused to abandon the texture and many of the techniques of the novel', thus creating a 'fusion of genres' which 'ultimately proved unstable' (409). The inherent realism of the novel as a genre is historically bound up with an ontology of 'becoming' rather than of 'being', together with a sense of larger social and political circumstances which contextualises individual characters. Greene's continued interest in this larger social dimension almost in spite of himself creates a dissociated insistence on the specifically Catholic formulation of personal inner experience.

III

The Power and the Glory (1940) is a different story altogether. One of the few novels of Greene's early career which unites the interior narrative and the political thriller of the repressed Conradian masterplot, it combines a Catholic struggle for faith with a plot of pursuit and escape. Dramatising the direct effect of religious persecution on Mexican society, the conflict of church and state makes the Catholic theme a more vital and central part of the social, political and personal plots. Moreover, the combination of the lieutenant's pursuit of the priest with the priest's 'hunt' for himself creates a doubling of the adventure narrative; this eventually subverts the protagonist's successful 'escape' when he chooses to return and die, thereby keeping faith with his 'code' in the same way as Conrad's Lord Jim.

It is Greene's personal experience of Mexico which draws him temporarily back to this more political drama. However, *The Power and the Glory* is not political in a democratic or parliamentary sense; as Coral tells her father, the pursuit of the priest 'isn't politics' in the way that the Reform Bill is (37). Rather, the removed setting of Tabasco – a 'small state' as self-contained as Conrad's Costaguana in *Nostromo* with its 'mountains on the north, the sea on the south' (*Power and the Glory* 23) – makes possible a realistic conflict between the private narrative of faith and the exterior political one of religious persecution. This duality is seen constantly throughout the novel, as in the opening paragraph, where 'the bust of an ex-president, ex-general, ex-human being' (7) ironically contrasts the transience of political status with the more fundamental temporariness of human life.

Unlike many of the novels of this period, *The Power and the Glory* represents religion in terms of more general human needs. 'The Bystanders', a variety of Catholic and non-Catholic characters, provide a range of responses to the pursuit of the priest, emphasising that he has a social as well as a religious function. Mr Tench, whom we first encounter wandering down to the port with the polysemous question running through his head, 'what am I here for?' (8), regains enough sense of purpose from his 'interesting afternoon' (47) with the protagonist to attempt to resolve his pathetically disordered private life. The priest may also have a salubrious effect on the spiritually abandoned Coral Fellows, who 'went on afterwards', her father says, 'as if he had told her things' (214). Characters such as Coral's neurotic mother, with her taboo on even the remotest allusion to death, emphasise the need for *some* religious view of life, if not a specifically Catholic one.

Representing the religious and the political spheres, the priest and the lieutenant contend for the allegiance of these 'bystanders'. Although apparently antagonists, they are also 'secret sharers'; there is 'something of a priest in [the lieutenant's] intent observant walk – a theologian going back over the errors of the past to destroy them again' (24), while the priest emphasises what J. F. Desmond calls 'the immediate presence in the concrete world' of 'a transcendent vision of reality and history' (62). In this way, the lieutenant is more like a stereotypical version of a priest, while the priest resembles a conventional *homme moyen sensuel*.[4]

Their 'search' for each other – the lieutenant's physical pursuit of the priest and the priest's more transcendental interrogation of the lieutenant – suggests a complex variation on Marlow's quest in *Heart of Darkness*. These two modes of pursuit are doubled at a generic level by the fusion between the pursuit narrative of the thriller and the interior narrative of conscience. In this way, the plot is contingent upon two types of *anagnorisis*, with the priest recognising that the lieutenant is 'a good man' (140) much earlier than the lieutenant more literally identifies him. Again, the dramatic details of the chase realistically project the priest's divine immunity implicit in his apparent inability to be captured. The lieutenant's attempts to decode his quarry from an old photograph, as in *Heart of Darkness* and *The Third Man*, are more effective than *The End of the Affair*'s hagiography in relaying metaphysical implications. Even when the lieutenant catches the priest, the 'chase' continues in their debate, which reverses the melodramatic roles of pursuer and pursued. This discussion differs from the 'rigged' contests of *Brighton Rock* and *The End of the Affair*, for an authentic dialogue occurs between the priest and the lieutenant – mirroring the interplay of the interior and political genres at a metatextual level. Each concedes some ground to the other. The priest admits the partial truth of the lieutenant's criticism of the church, together with his own faults and those of other corrupt clergy, though he still insists on the central mystery of his religion. In his turn, the lieutenant acknowledges that the priest isn't 'a bad fellow' (201) and attempts unsuccessfully to get Padre José to hear his prisoner's confession.

Finally, it is as though the priest's narrative of a struggle for faith triumphs over the lieutenant's melodramatic one. The almost postcoital sadness the lieutenant feels after the execution, in the flatness and deadness of 'the dynamic love which used to move his triggerfinger' (220), suggests that he is left stranded and alienated within the sequential mode of the thriller formula; the priest, on the other hand, reaches the narrative closure of death with a relatively clear conscience. Finally, the larger pursuit of man by God subsumes the lieutenant's hunt for the priest. While the lieutenant feels the need for another quarry in spite of his belief that he has hunted down the last priest, the priest may have arrived at sainthood through the paradoxical virtue of believing he hasn't; he realises, on the threshold of his execution, that 'to be a saint' was 'the only . . . thing that counted' but simultaneously concludes that he has failed in this regard (210). Through setting an interior, religious narrative against a realistic political thriller, the novel's multi-generic levels suggest a more dynamic, ongoing Christian spirituality than has been the case in Greene's novels so far.

This fusion of interior quest and adventure story in *The Power and the Glory* has significant resonances with Conrad's *Lord Jim*. Jim's struggle to keep faith with a code of conduct conflicts with reader expectations derived from more typical adventure stories that Jim will attempt to escape the wrath of the Bugis and take Jewel back to civilisation. However, this kind of escape represents Jim's greatest danger, for he would be left with the record of a second 'Patna'. *The Power and the Glory* confronts its reader with a similar dilemma. On the one hand, we wish that the whisky priest will ignore the half-caste's message regarding the dying bank robber and continue to the capital while, on the other hand, the narrative of religious interiority prompts us (as well as the priest) with the knowledge that such a response is inadequate, in terms both of religious faith and of secular psychology. As the priest himself realises, 'It wouldn't really have been a good dream – that confession in Las Casas when he would have had to admit, as well as everything else, that he had denied confession to a dying man' (180–1).

A formulaic sub-text adds a further dimension to this conflict of interior and melodramatic genres in *Lord Jim* and *The Power and the Glory*. Jim reads 'light holiday literature' (6) but becomes the hero of a 'real' adventure story, while the priest becomes a fully realised version with his illegitimate child and alcoholism of the cardboard figure, Father Juan, in the pious tale the mother subjects her children to in *The Power and the Glory*. At the end of the novel, this homily and the main plot unite to produce a reborn priest to carry on the fight. The boy Luis is largely responsible for joining together these narrative modes. Luis himself struggles throughout the novel to come to terms with the disjunction of formula from realism. The predictable, pious tale his mother reads aloud bores him; it must be accepted at face value, for his mother allows no discussion, protest or even interaction. Luis, however, prefers the equally unidimensional genre of the unadulterated thriller, in the form of the exploits of Villa, Obregon and Madero which he acts out with his friends. Nevertheless, at the end of the novel, both these sub-genres merge for him in the 'real' narrative of the whisky priest, whose execution occurs the same day that the mother reaches the account of Father Juan's in her reading. Within this concatenated merging of narrative levels, Luis and the lieutenant also briefly become surrogate 'readers' of the novel. For the lieutenant, the monotonous pursuit of a simplified political conflict will probably resume: 'Of course,' he tells himself, 'the dynamic love which used to move his trigger finger . . . will come back' (220). Luis, however, rejects the lieutenant's narrative desire for another formulaic plot by welcoming the new priest into the house, thereby we suppose initiating another 'religious thriller' of a similar mixed genre to *The Power and the Glory*.

The interlocking of the Conradian genres in this early novel represents a promissory note for Greene's later work, where religion is set within a broader social and political context. The priest expresses this necessary connection between God and man in his belief that 'at the centre of his own faith there always stood the convincing mystery – that we were made in God's image' (101). However, the generic integration of the interior and political narratives here is only a serendipitous instance in the Catholic cycle. The full political narrative does not return into Greene's narrative *opus* until *The Quiet American* (1955) and although implicitly visible in *A Burnt-Out Case* (1960) does not engage in so complex a dialogue with religious interiority until *The Honorary Consul* (1972). Until then, like the whisky priest himself, Greene is unable to survive 'across the border' where religion and politics meet.

IV

It is possible to connect Greene's own Mexican journey, which he recounts in *The Lawless Roads* (1939), with the temporary return of the 'repressed' political narrative in *The Power and the Glory*. Like Conrad, Greene often uses his travel experience of Africa, South America and South-East Asia as subject matter for his fiction. Before the Mexican trip, however, it is in *Journey without Maps* (1935), the account of his journey on foot through the Liberian interior, that Greene first clearly merges a narrative of Catholic interiority with a meditation upon social and political reality. Indeed, Africa inspires a number of books in which it is possible to trace a kind of blueprint of the Catholic novel's development in relation to the Conradian masterplot.

In June 1932, Greene re-read *Heart of Darkness*, later noting that it was 'odd how central Africa has become symbolically important to the imagination', a process which he thinks 'Conrad's [novel] perhaps began' ('Diaries' 19 November 1932). His own journey results in an autobiographical displacement of *Heart of Darkness* into the mode of the travel narrative. However, Greene discovers a different Africa from Conrad's Marlow's through coming closer to the land and its people. More *about* Africa than is *Heart of Darkness*, *Journey without Maps* leads the narrator to an entirely different confrontation with the interior self. Despite the intolerable conditions and forced marches, which cause him to fall seriously ill, he finally discovers in his own 'wrestle with death' not Marlow's 'impalpable greyness with nothing underfoot . . . without glory, without the great desire for victory' (*Heart of Darkness* 69), but 'a passionate interest in living' (*Journey* 213). Like Conrad, Greene describes his journey into the 'primitive' within the typical framework of the quest romance, in which the hero confronts danger and brings back an important truth. He observes that 'there are times . . . when one is willing to suffer some discomfort for the chance of finding – there are a thousand names for it, King Solomon's Mines, the 'heart of darkness' (19). Like Conrad, however, Greene wanted to go beyond Rider Haggard by also presenting his journey as a heuristic quest which engages with a psychological mystery.

As well as undertaking a search for the self, *Journey without Maps* and *Heart of Darkness* are also political narratives which represent Africa and Europe as distorting mirrors of each other. Just as European culture and history provide more familiar manifestations of the 'heart of darkness' in Conrad's novel, Greene also continually resets his 'smash-and-grab raid into the primitive' (119) in the context of his own civilisation. Comparing their qualities of 'seediness', he asserts that 'you couldn't talk of darkest Africa with any conviction if you had known Nottingham well' (100–1) and finds 'a reminder of darkness' in the weeping girl in the Queen's Bar' (35) as well as in a series of European vignettes such as the philandering Major Grant, the prophetess Miss Kilvae and the mad Charles Seitz. In a more specifically mythological mode, he speculates that '[h]ere in Liberia again and again one caught hints of what we had developed from' (93), recalling the Jack-in-the-Green he saw when he was four, whose dance 'as late as the ninth century in England had religious significance [as] part of the rites celebrating the death of winter and the return of spring' (92–3).

Both narrators, then, wish to find out something about their own civilisation. Like Marlow, Greene meets the wrecks of Europe in Africa, figures which reflect back on the woeful state of contemporary Western culture such as the German 'stranger' who, recalling Conrad's Russian harlequin, gave no indication of why he had come or where he was going or what he doing in Africa at all' (58). There is even a Kurtz figure, a diamond prospector in conflict with big business (55); meeting him, Greene echoes Marlow in his comment that the event 'cast a light in so many directions, the satiric, the social, the psychological' (55).[5] As in *Heart of Darkness*, Africa reflects contemporary Europe in more specifically political ways too. Just as Kurtz himself is a proto-fascist beginning to practise his skills at rousing the masses with his rhetoric, Nazism hovers in the background of *Journey without Maps*, in the suicide of the German 'Dr D' about to be called back to Hitler's Germany (67).

Like Conrad, Greene also uses this analytical adventure story to reflect upon white and black racial issues, concluding that the true primitive wins out over 'seedy' levels of civilisation. In *Heart of Darkness*, Marlow sees the 'bone, muscle, a wild vitality, an intense energy of movement that was as natural and true as the surf along [the natives'] coast' (17), but is disillusioned when he sees the effects of European colonisation upon the culture, as in the sick slaves dying in the grove. Similarly, Greene reports: 'Everything ugly in Freetown was European . . . if there was anything beautiful in the place it was native' (*Journey* 38). At Kailahun in Sierra Leone, Greene even encounters 'irons' used as currency in the same way as the natives on Marlow's riverboat were paid in brass rings. In the interior of Liberia, however, the situation is different: 'The Englishmen here didn't talk about the "bloody blacks" . . . the real native was someone to love and admire' (54).

Journey without Maps represents another of the intermittent points during the thirties and forties where Greene writes a fully political narrative. While in *Heart of Darkness*, Marlow is a well-meaning white man reluctantly involved in the imperial situation of Africa, it is as impossible for him to break through European repression of the realities of imperialism as it is for him to tell the truth to Kurtz's 'Intended'. In this way, Conrad's novel tells of the impossibility of remaining uninvolved with the colonial situation, no matter how good one's intentions are. Although this is not Greene's problem in the anti-imperialist climate of the thirties, he admits that the need for survival often forces him into traditional role patterns which govern the interaction between the two cultures. Throughout *Journey without Maps,* Greene describes a conscious dilemma between his inherent liberalism and an imperialism he feels the need to simulate if he is to survive the journey, such as refusing the carriers more than one meal each evening as they become sick and tired or treating them 'like schoolboys who are testing a new master's discipline' (122). The reference to the public school ethos is not without significance.

In spite of this, Greene comes much closer to the African countryside and its people than Marlow does. Travelling entirely by land, he attempts to observe the culture from within rather than as the captain of a riverboat who only sees the natives at some distance. Although he also notes 'the deadness of nature' (154) and acknowledges that 'the quality of darkness . . . the inexplicable' in Africa 'may take the form of [the] unexplained brutality [which] Conrad noted in his Congo diary' (20), he manages to see charm as well as squalor. He observes more instances of primitive harmony than Marlow's brief glimpse, as in the natives' 'sense of warm and sleepy beauty, of enjoyment divorced from activity and the weariness of willing' (33). He notes 'the sense of a small courageous community' (79) and reports several times an inexplicable happiness that descends on him (55, 126, 134), even though he himself cannot reach the carriers' 'unthinking tidal urge to joy' on the night of the full moon (183).

Greene's quest for 'one's place in time' (19) through his Africa journey represents an attempt to vivify and renew his religious faith. He states near the beginning of *Journey without Maps* that he is a 'Catholic with an intellectual if not an emotional belief in Catholic dogma' (17); however, the narrative itself steers away from this intellectual form of belief to suggest that primitive Christianity and primitive Africa have much in common. Recalling his baptism in Nottingham, he remembers that he 'couldn't help feeling' that he 'had got somewhere new by way of memories [he] hadn't known [he'd] possessed' (101–2). Implicitly, he equates this feeling with his Liberian journey in the thought that he had taken up the thread of life from very far back, from as far back as innocence' (102). Encountering an American Episcopal mission, he comments: 'the sound of the Latin represented a better civilisation than the tin shacks of the English port . . . the little group of priests and nuns had a standard of gentleness and honesty equal to the native standard' (82). In this way, he holds up Christianity, together with the best elements of native culture, as a criterion against which to set civilisation, a moral foil which is developed in his later novels.

V

Journey without Maps shows how intimately involved with Conrad Greene remains during this period – especially the Conrad of *Heart of Darkness* – even though only two or three years have elapsed since he determined to give up reading him. This connection is also shown in the short story 'A Chance for Mr Lever' (1936), where there is a vein of absurdity, almost farce, about the disintegration and corruption of the white anti-hero in Africa which recalls Conrad's short story 'An Outpost of Progress'.[6] However, this is not the case in Greene's first African novel, *The Heart of the Matter* (1948), where a more abstractly theological Catholicism takes over, as in *Brighton Rock* and *The End of the Affair*. Despite Greene's lengthy sojourn in West Africa during the war, *The Heart of the Matter* engages only fleetingly and tantalisingly with its full political implications, dissociating the political adventure story of a white colonist from the interior narrative of private guilt which increasingly takes it over.

In its early stages, the narrative seems to suggest many potential directions. At the opening, the undercover detective Wilson sits on the 'balcony of the Bedford Hotel with his bald pink knees thrust against the ironwork' (*Heart of the Matter* 11). This lonely young white man in a British African colony with his vulnerable flesh protected by the products of European industry engenders expectations that *The Heart of the Matter* may be a political narrative of imperialism. This seems to be confirmed by Wilson's discussion of 'niggers' with Harris and, shortly afterwards, by the difficulties Scobie experiences in dispensing justice to the natives. The novel then moves to Scobie's domestic circumstances, briefly to introduce the issue of Catholicism in Mrs Scobie's accusation that he converted for the sole purpose of marrying her (25). The reader is unsure whether to expect a political narrative of imperialism, a domestic novel or a blend of both. Soon also, a thriller motif is introduced in the Syrian trader Yusef, a more or less conventional villain who recalls Abdulla's ruthless economic success in *Almayer's Folly* and *The Outcast of the Islands*. The second chapter of *The Heart of the Matter*, however, clarifies that the focus will be more upon a depiction of Scobie's conscience and the processes of his corruption due to pity rather than the creation of a colonial narrative. When he covers up for a Portuguese sea-captain by burning an incriminating letter, it is interesting that 'Only his own heart beats told him he was guilty – that he had joined the ranks of corrupt police officers' (55), and not the thought of how many people his act might actually harm.

This emphasis upon private rather than public guilt anticipates a passage in which there is a stronger intimation that Scobie's interiority will be conveyed largely in the term of the Catholic theme. Reflecting upon 'his terrible private vow that [Louise] should be happy', he thinks to himself:

> Despair is the price one pays for setting oneself an impossible aim. It is, one is told, the unforgivable sin, but it is a sin the corrupt or evil man never practises. He always has hope. He never reaches the freezing-point of absolute failure. Only the man of goodwill carries within him this capacity for damnation. (60)

If we compare this with a slightly earlier depiction of Scobie's thoughts, we can see that the first is characteristic of a policeman, while the second is not. A few pages before, Scobie thinks that 'People talk about the courage of condemned men walking to the place of execution', while 'sometimes it needs as much courage to walk with any kind of bearing towards another person's habitual misery' (56). This is a realistic and secular response to a domestic situation – genuinely free indirect discourse – in contrast to the later extract, which is authorially constrained and pseudo-indirect. Scobie's interest in the knotty problems of Catholic theology seems to come out of the blue, with little if any explanation. In this way, the narrative modulates into the voice of the implied author, who, we can infer, *is* interested in religious theory from his choice of the Péguy epigraph: 'Le pécheur est au cœur même de chrétienté. . . . Nul n'est aussi compétent que le pécheur en matière de chrétienté. Nul, si ce n'est le saint.' The first passage illustrates the inherently monological tendency of Greene's earlier Catholic fiction, while the second points towards the possibility of a narrative of conscience brought effectively into conjunction with other, more public human stories.

Although Greene denies that he intended Scobie to be interpreted as a saint (Devereux 112), this is not clear from the novel itself. George Orwell aptly calls him a 'sanctified sinner', arguing that Greene's preoccupation with fashionable theological issues obscures *The Heart of the Matter*'s potential investigation of British colonialism: 'Except that one of the characters is a Syrian trader, the whole thing might as well have been happening in a London suburb' (Orwell 106). Orwell notes that 'although we are shown [Scobie's] thought in considerable detail, he seldom appears to think about his work . . . never about the war', and that 'All he is interested in is his own progress towards damnation' (106).

In this way, the repressed political narrative tantalises us by surfacing at intermittent intervals briefly to reveal its secret sharing with *Heart of Darkness* and then to disappear once more. We get a hint of a structural parallel with Conrad's search motif for an alter ego when Scobie travels into the bush to investigate Pemberton's suicide. At this point, there is also an intimation of a more politically orientated analysis in the form of Scobie's happiness driving through the forest with Ali, his servant, towards whom he feels more affection than for his wife. This hint that he can only relate to others on the basis of paternalistic superiority suggests a relevance to his political role which is never followed up, however. Instead the purpose of the Pemberton episode appears to be to introduce Scobie's ruminations on the issue of suicide in a Catholic context. Echoing *Brighton Rock*, it seems to Scobie 'that unquestionably there must be mercy for someone so unformed' (88).

When Scobie makes his momentous decision to borrow money from Yusef so that Louise can go to South Africa, the narrative's political implications begin to be increasingly phased out in favour of a thriller given over to the service of the Catholic interior narrative. As in the ambiguous narrative structure of *The End of the Affair*, Greene slips into a mode of plotting whereby realistic action mirrors theological necessity. As a consequence of his adultery with Helen Rolt, Scobie gradually falls more and more into the clutches of Yusef, with something of the forced irony of a Hardy novel. In this way, Scobie begins a love affair which he doesn't particularly enjoy and then hears that his wife Louise is on her way home. Recalling the straying letters of *Tess of the D'Urbervilles* and *The Return of the Native*, Scobie's indiscreet note to Helen falls into Yusef's hands and becomes an invaluable tool for blackmail.

The action increasingly focuses on Scobie's soul and upon his leap into damnation, while continuing to tease us with repressed hints of a political narrative. Scobie's betrayal of Ali, with its implicit allusion to a larger relationship between whites and blacks, is never developed in the way that Almayer's servant – also named Ali – provides many occasions for reflection upon cultural identity. The scene in which Scobie realises what has happened to Ali demonstrates this. Concrete detail surrealistically heightens the action, conveying the intense emotion behind Scobie's realisation that his own corruption is responsible for Ali's death: 'pain and fear . . . swam up like a drowning animal for air, and fell again into the darkness of the room, into the whisky, under the desk, into the basket of wastepaper, a discarded, finished cry' (246). The theological issues of confession and damnation expressed in Scobie's interior dialogue with God finally obscure the political implications of white master's betrayal of black servant to Arab trader (258).

While Scobie's pronouncement that 'No human being can fully understand another' (85) echoes Marlow's suggestion that 'We live, as we dream – alone' (*Heart of Darkness* 30), Marlow's despair arises from the political problem of imperialist abuses in Africa. *The Heart of the Matter* is mainly concerned to portray, if not romanticise, the sick state of Scobie's soul. In the final spiritual 'post-mortem' often depicted in Greene's Catholic novels, Father Rank paraphrases Marlow in his pronouncement to Louise that 'The Church . . . doesn't know what goes on in a single human heart' (*Heart of Darkness* 272); at the same time, however, Rank thinks that from what he 'saw of him', Scobie 'really loved God' (272). However, he dodges Louise's pointed comment that Scobie 'certainly loved no one else' with his lukewarm agreement that she 'may be in the right of it there too' (272). In this way, the social dimensions of the narrative remain suspended.

Nevertheless, there is one significant point in *The Heart of the Matter* where Greene metatextually alludes to the inherent dissociation of genres. To entertain a young boy recovering from a shipwreck, Scobie demonstrates an uncharacteristic sense of mischievous humour in converting the pious novel *Bishop Among the Bantus* into a Buchanesque thriller. One is tempted to see Greene mocking his own religious pretensions, especially in Mrs Bowles's stern reminder that 'we are not teaching the children here . . . in order that they shall read – well, novels' (127). Scobie also seems to caricature the plot of *The Heart of the Matter* when he describes his fake narrative as 'a kind of detective story . . . because [Arthur Bishop] is a secret agent of the British government [who] falls in love with the daughter of the captain of the Bantus and that's when it turns soppy' (129).

This episode serves to emphasise the abstractness of the rest of the novel. Paradoxically, however, Catholicism tends to reify the metaphysical issues more than in Conrad's fiction. Conrad's title *Heart of Darkness* embodies the utter mystery of human motives and the relativity of human cultures, a mystery which the fiction explores but refuses to solve: 'to Marlow, the meaning of an episode was not inside like a kernel, but outside, enveloping the tale which brought it out only as a glow brings forth a haze' (9). By contrast, Scobie's speculation as to whether one would 'have to feel pity even for the planets . . . if one reached what they called the heart of the matter' and 'knew . . . the facts' (122–3) proposes that there actually *is* a teleological scheme that it is possible to know. For Conrad, however, 'facts' are more often 'confounded' ones that 'we men have been living contentedly with ever since the dawn of creation', such as the propensity of white men to scramble for loot (*Heart* 16). The narrative of the 'sanctified sinner' denies a social and political context. Despite the interspersed vignettes of colonial life, public roles are in abeyance, and all we are left with is Scobie's relation with God. The religious themes of guilt, confession and redemption do not seem to apply to the lives of human beings as they do in *The Power and the Glory* and later in *A Burnt-Out Case* (1960). Scobie has little personality, little real interiority in fact, beyond his fear of hurting anybody's feelings and the final verdict that 'he really loved God' but 'no one else' (272). The self-cancelling nature of this pronouncement alludes to the difficulty of constructing a narrative of religious interiority within the traditionally secular form of the novel, which demands, as Christianity itself does, a concern for others and 'other' experience.

VI

In 1953, Greene told Martin Shuttleworth and Simon Raven that the group of his novels comprised of *Brighton Rock, The Power and the Glory, The Heart of the Matter* and *The End of the Affair* was 'now finished', and that his next (which would be *The Quiet American*) would 'not deal primarily with Catholic themes at all' (Shuttleworth 159). Although *The Quiet American* (1955) is a more secular narrative dealing with a crisis of conscience in the political world, Greene by no means abandons Catholicism. *A Burnt-Out Case* (1960) comes full circle to meet *Journey without Maps* (1936), uniting Greene's religious sense with his passion for Africa and making explicit his long-standing connection with Conrad's *Heart of Darkness*.[7] In spite of Greene's assertion in the preface that the novel is 'removed from world politics', it remains political in the primary sense of relating the individual and society through a Catholicism which encourages practical action in the world and service to others.

Bringing this sense of society together with the last narrative of the 'sanctified sinner', the novel is a self-conscious rewriting of *Heart of Darkness* in which Greene tackles Conrad – literally on his own ground of the Congo – by means of a parallel theme and structure, as well as direct parody. The African 'search' is as much for the Conradian political narrative as for the interior self; indeed *A Burnt-Out Case* explicitly affirms their intrinsic and necessary connection. In his travel narrative *In Search of a Character* (1960),[8] Greene recounts his own journey up the Congo, during which he reads Conrad for 'the first time since [he] abandoned him about 1932 because his influence . . . was too great and too disastrous' (31). Greene continues:

> The heavy hypnotic style [of *Heart of Darkness*] falls around me again, and I am aware of the poverty of my own. Perhaps now I have lived long enough with my poverty to be safe from corruption. One day I will again read *Victory*. And *The Nigger*. (31)

Manifesting some Bloomean anxiety, however, Greene still wonders if he has fully differentiated himself:

> Conrad's *Heart of Darkness* still a fine story, but its faults show now. The language too inflated for the situation. Kurtz never really comes alive. It is as if Conrad had taken an episode in his own life and tried to lend it, for the sake of 'literature,' a greater significance than it will hold. And how often he compares something concrete to something abstract. Is this a trick that I have caught? (33)

Karen Marguerite Radell, in her comparative study of Greene and Ford Madox Ford, argues that 'the language and tone of *A Burnt-Out Case* are so different from that of *Heart of Darkness* (the former is sparing and light, the latter is heavy and dense) that we must wonder at the profusion of comparisons between the two books' (Radell 131). While this remark applies generally to Greene's and Conrad's styles, the numerous, apparently superficial parallels between the two novels accumulate, with the effect of foregrounding an explicit intertextuality, a conscious reply to *Heart of Darkness* in the form of a number of metatextual signals which call attention to Greene's Catholic adaptation of Conrad's socio-political narrative. The protagonist Querry, like Greene himself in *Journey without Maps*, comes closer to the continent's people than Marlow does in *Heart of Darkness*. The natives are no longer alien savages hidden along the bank, but more familiar human beings who come to Mass on the riverboat and disappear into the bush, swinging lanterns like New England carol singers (10). Moreover, their own point of view is directly communicated rather than merely surmised, as by Conrad's narrator; in fact the first independent narrative viewpoint of Querry is when the captain translates their 'not altogether complimentary' song about 'a white who is neither a father nor a doctor', who 'has no beard' and 'tells no one to what place he is going or why' (11). Like Doramin's mother in *Lord Jim*, they identify the central symptom of Querry's spiritual malaise in his lack of immediate community.

However, Greene reverses Conrad's denouement in *Heart of Darkness*, for the Congo in a sense 'cures' Querry. Greene's Africa is not an alien 'dark' continent where hitherto repressed European barbarism can be released. Indeed, in the manuscript Greene appears to have adapted Marlow's denigratory reference to natives howling and dancing (*Heart of Darkness* 38) in Dr Colin's more Arcadian suggestion that perhaps Querry feels 'a need to run and dance and sing . . . in a clearing in a forest by a stream' ('Composite T' 46). The Congo may be familiar and friendly. Dr Colin also speculates 'whether the Apostles would find [the strange Christianity of Africa] as difficult to understand as the collected works of Thomas Aquinas' (*Burnt-Out Case* 58), while Querry wonders if it isn't 'just as possible for a god to exist in this empty region as in the empty spaces of the sky where men had once located him' (55). In this way, Greene builds upon the association forged in *Journey without Maps* between primitive Africa and primitive Christianity, going beyond 'intellectual faith' and returning to one of the basic teachings of the New Testament: 'love thy neighbour as thyself'.

A Burnt-Out Case suggests that religious faith may regenerate both society and the individual in a way that the agnostic vision of

Heart of Darkness cannot. Querry's deathbed statement in the form of a 'distorted laugh' and a cryptic hint of an existential leap of faith – 'Absurd . . . this is absurd or else . . .' (196) – clearly contrasts with Kurtz's famous last words. Querry himself is initially an intellectual Catholic who has declined into cynicism and despair. Irritated at first during his stay at the seminary by the priests' laughter, he thinks scornfully of their domestication of God in terms of a 'marriage like the world's marriages [which] was held together by habits and tastes shared in common between God and themselves' (14). Finally, however, Querry learns, unlike Major Scobie in *The Heart of the Matter*, to love other people as well as God. As Dr Colin observes after his death, 'He'd learned to serve other people . . . and to laugh' (198). The ability to appreciate comedy is one which becomes increasingly important in Greene's later religious vision.

Querry's last laugh reflects the novel's wider quest to renew the connection between Christianity and everyday social life. The Superior builds such bridges in his sermons: 'It is much easier to show mercy because a child weeps or to love because a girl or young man pleases your eye. That's not wrong, that's good. Only remember that the love you feel and the mercy you show were made in you by God' (82). With this reunion of the transcendent and the mundane, we can see Greene moving towards his later 'Catholic agnosticism',[9] a state of mind he had previously implied was Conrad's rather than his own. Together, the atheist Dr Colin and the Superior embody this paradoxical philosophy. 'Close friends' through their 'struggle with the common enemy [leprosy]' (20) rather than adversaries like the priest and the lieutenant in *The Power and the Glory*, both men play down dogma against virtues lived out in the world which Christianity cannot lay exclusive claim to. Dr Colin tells the Superior: 'Gentleness isn't Christian, self-sacrifice isn't Christian, charity isn't, remorse isn't' (76–7); he concedes, however, that 'the Christian myth is part' of the great 'evolutionary wave', going on to speculate that 'it may be the most valuable part' (124). The Superior, in his turn, is sceptical of intellectual Catholics like Rycker with their narcissistic spiritual problems; interestingly, his analysis appears to validate Winnie Verloc's depreciation of interiority in favour of a less reflective solidarity with one's immediate community: 'There's no real harm in a superficial judgement but if I begin to probe . . . I might find some terrible things' (*Burnt-Out Case* 23).

Querry's journey results in a renewed and simplified sense of spiritual purpose, in contrast to the moral perplexity which overtakes

Marlow. *A Burnt-Out Case* is written quite explicitly against *Heart of Darkness*, as the number of parodic inversions of Conrad's novel demonstrates. For instance, Querry reverses the reflection that 'meaning ... was not inside the kernel but outside' (*Heart of Darkness* 9), finding peace 'like a nut at the centre of the hard shell of [his] discomfort' (*Burnt-Out Case* 9). His journey is not into the 'heart of darkness', but away from the moral and spiritual bankruptcy of his Western self in the direction of an interior version of Pendélé, the mythical place where his black servant Deo Gratias tells him with a grand and moving simplicity: '*Nous étions heureux*' (78). The less specific rendering distinguishes this from Scobie's teleological meditation on 'facts' in *The Heart of the Matter*. Similarly, Greene transforms Marlowe's horrified discovery of the 'black, dried, sunken' heads (*Heart of Darkness* 57) stuck up around Kurtz's house into a mere comparison of the 'nuts for the presses and the ovens' being loaded in Marie's yard to 'dried and withered heads, the product of a savage massacre' (*Burnt-Out Case* 138).

If the terms of Marlow's spiritual quest are altered, the spatial dimensions of *A Burnt-Out Case* are also reversed to mirror this. Querry arrives at the 'furthest point of navigation' as early as the second chapter and apart from occasional excursions into civilisation, his journey now takes place within himself. In this way, the focus of the novel is backward-looking, for there are no new physical frontiers to be breached; in contrast to Marlow's journey from Europe to the coastal colony and thence into the centre of the 'dark continent', Querry watches 'the steady khaki flow of the stream ... *out* of the heart of Africa, towards the far-off sea' (my emphasis; 26). When Querry arrives at the leper colony, he has already 'come to ... the end of everything' (16). In this way, *A Burnt-Out Case* begins where *Heart of Darkness* leaves off; Querry rediscovers his vocation, in contrast to Marlow's stoic adherence to the values of unthinking toil. While Marlow merely vacillates between the banal, commercial aspects of imperialism and its romantic, Satanic nightmares, Querry progresses, always wishing to 'go a little further' in his voyage of self-discovery. This is even reflected at the level of narration; where Marlow is trapped, as it were, within his compulsion to deliver what Peter Brooks calls 'an unreadable report' (Brooks 238–63), the free indirect discourse of *A Burnt-Out Case* mediates more flexibly between an interior and a public ontology.

Paradoxically, this places Querry more at the centre of his novel than Marlow in his, for he learns the way of simplicity from a desperate awareness that he has arrived at a point of Conradian perdition. When he dreams that he is unable to 'make his confession and obtain wine with which to celebrate Mass' (51), it seems to him 'as though he had had an appointment with hope at this turn of the road and had arrived just too late' (*Burnt-Out Case* 52). This motivates his discovery that he can still be an architect with a social as well as an aesthetic purpose, with the result that he finally agrees to design the hospital and re-enter the 'community of mankind'. His rescue of Deo Gratias from the jungle contrasts strikingly with Marlow's inefficacious sympathy with the sick negroes dying in the grove, for Marlow can present only ironic vignettes which embody the absurdity of European colonialism. Querry, on the other hand, stays with Deo Gratias through the night, becoming more like the saviour figure Lord Jim. His similar status as a sacrificial 'god-king' figure is especially apparent when Deo Gratias, recalling Jewel's anxiety, worries about his eventual departure (*Burnt-Out Case* 177).

Querry, however, like Marlow in *Heart of Darkness* and *Lord Jim*, undertakes a 'hermeneutic' quest, in which he 'does battle', so to speak, with a series of 'monstrous' interlocutors. Querry encounters versions of Kurtz in Rycker, who likewise is 'tall, stooping, and overgrown', with a 'narrow and flat and endless [face], like an illustration of the law that two parallel lines never meet' (33). Rycker tells Querry his 'inmost thoughts' (191), as Kurtz does Marlow; he too has a complex inner life that has gone rancid. Dramatising himself as passing through the 'Dark Night of the Soul' (142), he is the intellectual Catholic *par excellence*, an indication of where Scobie's exclusive love for God might lead. Recalling another of Marlow's antagonists, the 'papier-mâché Mephistopheles' (*Heart of Darkness* 29), Rycker's lack of substance is described in his comparison to 'a wall so plastered over with church announcements that you couldn't even see the brickwork behind' (*Burnt-Out Case* 144).

Rycker's young wife, Marie, completes a triangle that parallels the one made up of Kurtz, Marlow and the Intended. However, while Marie initially seems to take on the identity of the Intended transplanted to Africa and subjected to the 'abominable rites' of Rycker's unwelcome pseudo-religious, sexual and emotional bullying, *A Burnt-Out Case* again reverses the outcome of *Heart of Darkness*. Conrad portrays the subjugation and deceptive sheltering of women as largely responsible for the continuation of imperialistic abuses; in *A Burnt-Out Case*, however, it is Marie herself who lies (about Querry's responsibility for her pregnancy) in order to protect and separate herself from Rycker. For the first time, Querry finds 'an egoism as absolute as his own' (184), which leads to his symbolic 'execution'.

As well as these larger parallels, Greene's references to Conrad often take on an explicit form not seen since Conrad Drover's death in *It's a Battlefield*. In this way, Querry himself briefly becomes a Kurtz figure, who is in turn approached by the fat journalist Parkinson parodying Marlow. Parkinson journeys up the river to find Querry, whose myth Rycker has tried to inflate to Kurtzean proportions, calling him 'the greatest thing to happen in Africa since Schweitzer' (*Burnt-Out Case* 63). However, when Parkinson echoes Marlow's taste for conversation with Kurtz in his intimation that Querry and he have 'got to have a talk' (109), it is Querry who like Kurtz dominates the conversation. Consciously seeing Parkinson as a 'looking glass' to whom he can confess, he admits that he has been 'waiting for someone like [him]' (116).

Nevertheless, unable to face the truth counter-reflected by Querry, Parkinson goes beyond Marlow's 'cover-up' job, intentionally and spitefully building up Querry as a saint: 'How do you know Rycker's not right about you?' he asks him, commenting with another Conradian echo, 'We none of us really know ourselves' (111). Parkinson's newspaper article does what it can to cheapen Querry's interior quest by translating *Heart of Darkness* into tabloidese, telling how 'Unconscious and burning with fever, [Parkinson] was carried on shore from [his] pirogue, the frail bark in which [he] had penetrated what Joseph Conrad called the Heart of Darkness . . .' (133). It is as though Greene was mocking the critical view current in Albert Guérard's work, amongst others, of *Heart of Darkness* as representing primarily a quest into the interior psyche, rather than one which also reintegrates an important political narrative.

Querry's feeling, after Parkinson's departure, that 'some persistent poison had been drained from his system' (123) suggests a parallel with Greene's transformed relationship with Conrad in *A Burnt-Out Case*. Although 'Greene' is not 'Querry' in the simplistic sense he so often denies regarding the links between his life and his characters,[10] the narrative of *A Burnt-Out Case* rediscovers the Conradian political theme in a fundamental concern with other human beings. Frank Kermode misses the point when he sees Greene posing as the 'tortured artist' who is suspended between the material and the transcendental in the parable of the eggs and crosses

Querry tells Marie.[11] Rather, this parable represents a metatextual confession of Greene's boredom with his reputation as a Catholic novelist, 'especially [among] those who claimed to know and love the King [God]' (157). In Querry's fable, these critics' 'books all said much the same thing, and when our hero had read one he had read them all. There was nearly always a chapter called "The Toad in the Hole: the Art of Fallen Man" . . .' (157).

Greene's urge to redefine his intrinsic genre, then, is embodied throughout *A Burnt-Out Case* in a new dialogue between Catholic interiority and a vision of human beings as they relate to their social and political setting. Although Greene believed at the time that the novel would be his last (*Ways* 300), this Catholic 'heart of darkness' leads directly forward to a point at which he can unite the hitherto discrete versions he has created of the Conradian masterplot's sub-genres in new, varying combinations. In this way, Greene writes his late fictions in the spirit, rather than the letter, of Conrad's work, setting the political and religious narratives 'in pursuit of each other', to discover fresh representations of his developing philosophy of Catholic agnosticism.

4

'He Who Forms a Tie': The Conradian Protagonist in Greene's Later Novels

I

In his book *Reading for the Plot* (1984), Peter Brooks discusses narrative repetition as 'a *return* in the text, a doubling back . . . a return to origins or a return of the repressed' which 'works as a process of *binding* towards the creation of an energetic constant-state situation' (Brooks 100–1). What Brooks means by this is that narratives moving towards their conclusions seem to 'come together', integrating hitherto fragmented material in new and significant ways. Applying this to the Conradian masterplot in Greene's later fiction, we can see a return *to* and a return *of* the repressed political narrative, 'both the recall of an earlier moment and a variation of it' (Brooks 99–100). In *The Quiet American* (1955), *The Comedians* (1966), *The Honorary Consul* (1973) and *The Human Factor* (1978), the political narrative returns with full force to become more integrated with the Catholic interior narrative and thriller plot.

As in Brooks's suggestion that a single narrative represses its secret or solution until the denouement, allowing an occasional glimpse of its repressed contents during the earlier stages, Greene's literary career also assumes the form of a plot, with conflict, development and denouement, which is governed by a 'principle of interconnectedness' (Brooks 5). As we have seen in Greene's Catholic and melodramatic displacements of the divided protagonist's narrative, a repressed story which is more concretely political intermittently reveals itself, often raising false expectations by the reader. By contrast, Greene's later career represents what Brooks calls 'a narrative that somehow mediates and forcefully connects its discrete elements' (10); it does this through 'a "binding" . . . of textual energies that allows them to be mastered by putting them into serviceable [i.e. perceptible] form' (101). In this way, Greene's later fiction unites the interior narrative of conscience, with both the thriller and the political narrative, to create a dialogue between these genres, as opposed to their isolation in the earlier fiction.

Drawing together the narrative of interior conscience with a conspiracy plot centred upon global politics, *The Quiet American* (1955) represents the watershed of Greene's career.[1] The novel creates a new synthesis of the three principal components of the Conradian masterplot; never again will Greene write so exclusively in the genre of either the Catholic novel or the thriller. This marks the beginning of a mature phase in which his fiction becomes fully political once more in a way it has not been since *Stamboul Train* (1932) and *It's a Battlefield* (1933). *The Comedians* (1966), *The Honorary Consul* (1973) and *The Human Factor* (1978) also take as their point of departure the crisis of faith experienced by a more or less detached individual within a political situation. However, because Greene has worked through two major Conradian displacements in the form of the thriller and the Catholic narrative, these novels are more individual, original works, which intricately synthesise the Conradian masterplot with other major influences on Greene during these years, such as James, Ford, Buchan and Mauriac. Just as Peter Brooks describes the detours of plot as 'arabesques', intricately curved lines designed around a basically symmetrical pattern, Greene's reworkings of the Conradian masterplot become a series of 'arabesques of influence' in his later fiction. In this way, a solid generic infrastructure of interior narrative and political thriller underpins multiple variations on Conrad's fiction.

Greene's intention to lift his self-imposed ban on reading Conrad, which he announced in the 'Congo Journal' (1960), corroborates this new sense of an ability to control the formerly 'disastrous influence'. However, although Greene re-read *Heart of Darkness* at this time, initially he concentrated less on the fiction than on critical biographies. The monthly lists of books he kept during these years note that he read Jocelyn Baines's *Joseph Conrad: A Critical Biography* in July 1960 and Norman Sherry's *Conrad's Eastern World* a few years later in 1966, when he also re-read *Victory*. Whenever he read Conrad criticism after this, he seems to have chosen an almost unmitigated diet of Sherry, later choosing him as his official biographer. In 1971 he read *Conrad's Western World*, followed in 1974 by *Joseph Conrad: The Critical Heritage* and *Conrad and his World* in 1975. These studies would have recalled to Greene the geographical and cultural settings Conrad and he shared. During 1976 and 1977 he returned to Conrad's fiction, re-reading *Victory*, *Heart of Darkness*,

The Rescue and *A Set of Six* ('Appointment Books' 1960–77).[2] It is possible that his inclination to revisit Conrad first in overview and later through primary texts is indicative of a gradual rather than sudden feeling of independence. Defensively parodic in *A Burnt-Out Case* (1960), he is able by the end of the cycle to range freely across Conrad's territory, conforming to the spirit rather than the letter of his work.

II

Like the earlier entertainments, *The Quiet American*'s dramatisation of an individual's crisis of commitment within the structure of the political thriller clearly has many resonances with *Under Western Eyes*. The relation, however, is more than thematic, for the narrative structure also recalls that of *Heart of Darkness* in Fowler's search for his elusive antagonist, Pyle, within an imperial setting. With its combination of the interior narrative of faith and betrayal and a political and psychological detective story, *The Quiet American* creates a new synthesis of Conradian elements which during Greene's earlier career had been dispersed in different and unequal emphases throughout his fiction.[3]

Like Razumov, Fowler is an individual with a highly specified inner life who is caught up in a crisis of faith and betrayal within a political context. His creed of non-involvement, together with his final betrayal of Pyle to the Vietnamese Communists, closely follows Razumov's rationalisations of his own treachery towards Haldin. Both Razumov and Fowler confuse personal and public motives, only to find that they cannot help becoming involved in their political surroundings. They attempt to convince themselves that they are aiding in the suppression of misguided and dangerous idealists and that their actions of betrayal are ratified by a commitment to the Russian or Vietnamese people. Razumov's and Fowler's motives, however, are at best partly personal, for Haldin and Pyle have disturbed their lives – Haldin by threatening Razumov's civil service career and Pyle by absconding with Fowler's mistress, Phuong. In both cases, the situation is complicated by the fact that the rationale for betrayal – the desire for legality and political stability – is apparently such a good one.

Because Greene has undergone the process of exploring separately the individual components of Conrad's fiction during the early part of his career, he is able to create a new synthesis of them at this point. The result is that, although *The Quiet American* follows *Under Western Eyes* even in quite specific details, it is not an imitation of Conrad in the same way that *It's a Battlefield* follows *The Secret Agent*. By the time of *The Quiet American*, Greene is writing in the *tradition* of Conrad and other major forebears such as Dickens, Dostoevsky, James, and Turgenev. For this reason, it is possible to detect close affinities between *The Quiet American* and a number of Conrad novels yet simultaneously to perceive *The Quiet American* as a renewed fictional struggle with the interior political thriller.

Both *The Quiet American* and *Under Western Eyes* are obsessed with the themes of guilt and betrayal. The impulsiveness with which Razumov and Fowler decide to deliver up their victims shows their lack of insight into the complex and contradictory reasons behind their acts. After Pyle's terrorist attack on innocent Saigon civilians, Fowler bursts into the communist agent Mr Heng's house, causing a domestic upset similar to the one Razumov instigates at Prince K.'s with his desire to betray Haldin. Fowler and Razumov work through similar processes of guilt over these betrayals. Razumov's feelings develop after the event, as he becomes obsessed with the image of Haldin lying in the snow or on Razumov's bed. Similarly, Fowler begins to feel affection – even a sense of identity – with Pyle, and despite his exasperation with the quiet American's political naivety finds himself giving the same advice regarding Phuong (now Pyle's girlfriend) as Pyle might have given him a month previously (*Quiet American* 156).

Both *The Quiet American* and *Under Western Eyes* use the motif of the police interrogation to reveal their protagonists' inner feelings of guilt. 'Not guilty', Fowler tells Vigot, the detective investigating Pyle's murder; nevertheless, he has to deceive himself 'that it was true' and that 'no one but Pyle was responsible' (18). Similarly, Razumov's inner torment is exacerbated by Councillor Mikulin's quiet insinuation that Razumov is bound to him and has nowhere to 'retire' (*Under Western Eyes* 130). In this situation, both protagonists become angry, defensive and sarcastic. Razumov protests, 'by what bond of common faith, of common conviction, am I obliged to let that fanatical idiot [Haldin] drag me down with him?' (82); Fowler, on hearing Pyle suggest that the victims of his bomb attack 'died for democracy', suddenly feels 'very tired' and declares that he 'wanted him to go away quickly and die' so that he (Fowler) 'could start life again – at the point before [Pyle] came in' (179).

Fowler also experiences a kind of inversion of Razumov's violent, guilty and frustrated urge to pummel the drunken peasant Ziemianitch, reporting, on the brink of a quarrel with the American journalist Granger, that he 'would not have minded if [Granger] had beaten [him] unconscious', explaining that 'We have so few ways in which to assuage our guilt' (184).

These themes of guilt and betrayal are triangulated by means of a female protagonist both in *Under Western Eyes* and in *The Quiet American*, although characteristically the theme of sexual infidelity is more central in Greene. In this way, Natalia and Phuong (Haldin's sister and Pyle's fiancée) mediate the sense of uneasy communion between betrayer and betrayed. Each of these women also has a close connection with the betrayer himself, whose actions she is ignorant of. Natalia is attracted to Razumov, while Phuong returns to Fowler quite unquestioningly on the night of Pyle's death. Razumov finally confesses to Natalia, however, whereas Fowler is left tormented by his inability to tell the truth. The guilt he feels over his secret, together with his success at getting Phuong back, acts out the macabre, self-tormenting temptation Razumov resists in *Under Western Eyes* to marry Natalia and 'steal [her] soul', as he puts it to himself (331). Fowler, by contrast, remains isolated with his secret. Like Razumov with his mournful cry, 'no one – to – go - to' (327), he declares at the end of the novel: 'Everything had gone right with me since [Pyle] had died, but how I wished there existed someone to whom I could say that I was sorry' (189).

While Natalia (and possibly Mrs Haldin) are the only people to whom Razumov can apologise, Greene introduces a series of moral foils who throw into relief Fowler's muddled and self-deceiving attitude of compromise. The contemplative mode of detachment Fowler's assistant Dominguez achieves from the discomfort of his illness administers a silent rebuke to Fowler's egotism (123); Trouin, the French pilot, recalls a phrase from *Lord Jim* in his view that Fowler 'would not understand the nonsense', because he is 'not one of us' (152). In a similar spirit, the communist Heng declares to Fowler at their final meeting: 'Sooner or later, one has to take sides. If one is to remain human' (174).

The thriller formula which structures *The Quiet American* also serves to develop these hints of a Catholic dimension to the interior narrative. The police officer, Vigot, is both 'priest' and detective, investigating Fowler's soul as well as his alibi; seeing the inherent contradiction between Fowler's betrayal of Pyle and his professed non-involvement, he tells him that he doesn't follow his own principles, that he is '*Engagé*, like the rest of us' (138). Vigot's psychological insight into Fowler's dilemma is reminiscent of Councillor Mikulin's insidious comment on Razumov's retirement: 'Where to?' (*Under Western Eyes* 130); however, his role of father-confessor bypasses *Under Western Eyes*, more to resemble Porphyry's in Conrad's own despised original, *Crime and Punishment*. Fowler thinks that Vigot looks at him 'with compassion, as he might have looked at some prisoner, for whose capture he was responsible, undergoing his sentence for life' (*Quiet American* 139). Although Fowler tells Vigot that he 'would make a good priest' (168) and is disturbed by his visit in a manner which goes beyond the fear of discovery, he nevertheless refuses the detective's invitation to confess and 'see himself clearly as he is' (168).

Daphna Erdinast-Vulcan suggests that 'Vigot assumes the role of the chorus.' Observing the drama and commenting on it, 'he does not actively interfere', although his 'intimacy with Fowler gives him the authority to correct Fowler's narration, to present the reader with a description of Fowler that is closer to the omniscient viewpoint' (Erdinast-Vulcan 59). In this way, Greene merges Fowler's immediate, first-person narrative with Vigot's more transcendental perspective, solving the problem of generic ambiguity in *The Heart of the Matter* and *The End of the Affair*. While there is a disjunction in these novels between a first-person narration bearing witness to religious mystery and a realistic texture more germane to the traditional novel, *The Quiet American* introduces a more varied perspective which moves between a realistic narrative of international intrigue and the interior revelation of individual conscience.

The Quiet American, then, is not exclusively about Fowler and Pyle but, like *Under Western Eyes*, dramatises a larger political crisis, sceptically appraising both secular optimism and the autocratic tendencies of imperialism. The democratic Geneva of *Under Western Eyes*, which has 'made its bargain with fate' (142), finds a counterpart in the biting satire of the American presence in Vietnam. Walking in the Bastions discussing Razumov, the professor–narrator and Natalia encounter a Swiss couple, 'whose fate was made secure from the cradle to the grave by the perfected mechanism of democratic institutions' (*Under* 189). Their colourless placidity embodies the joylessness of the Swiss democratic state just as Fowler's comments on the asexuality of two American girls whom he finds it 'impossible to conceive . . . as a prey to untidy passion' (159–60) create a metaphor – coming just before Pyle's bomb attack – for the sanitised rationalism of American involvement in Vietnam. Greene complicates the Conradian metaphor of democracy by emphasising the paradox of its sublimated ruthlessness, oxymoronically embodying in Pyle's own 'innocent' fanaticism the contrast of the girls' self-containment with the explosion which follows.

In spite of these numerous intertextual resonances, however, the Conradian masterplot in *The Quiet American* is fundamentally a question of generic affinity rather than of thematic correspondence and as such cannot be paired exclusively with one single novel. Besides *Under Western Eyes*, *Heart of Darkness* provides another major Conradian intertext in which a first-person narrator studies an inscrutable protagonist to discover their secret sharing in the guilt of empire.[4] The observer-narrator's investigation of this antagonist is doubled with an enquiry into the political problem the antagonist embodies – savagery masquerading as an idealistic enterprise. Pyle is linked with Kurtz through the combination of political ruthlessness with a veneer of civilised enlightenment. In their turn, Fowler and Marlow feel some affinity for these antagonists, but finally remain ambivalent. Fowler's reluctant admiration and simultaneous disapproval for the idealistic Pyle echoes Marlow's for Kurtz; in fact, he throws Kurtz's comment about the necessity of '[taking] care of the motives – right motives always' (*Heart of Darkness* 67) back to Pyle, telling him sarcastically: 'I know your motives are good, they always are' (*Quiet American* 133).

In both novels, the difficulty in communication between the narrator and his antagonist dramatises the search for a solution to a complex political problem. Marlow tells us he 'had to deal with a being to whom [he] could not appeal in the name of anything high or low' (65), while Fowler is similarly frustrated in his attempt to make Pyle see the horror of his acts of terrorist provocation. He observes that Pyle 'was as incapable of imagining pain or danger to himself as he was incapable of conceiving the pain he might cause others' (62). Both antagonists embody an implacable imperialism, as is demonstrated when Greene adapts the incident of the helmsman's death, in which Marlow's shoe is covered in blood, to dramatise Pyle's innocent callousness at the bomb attack. While the horrified Marlow's divesting himself of his shoes and throwing them overboard seems to hover ambiguously between trauma over a comrade's death and a desire to rid himself of its effects, Pyle is merely concerned about his shoes looking messy, telling Fowler that he 'must get a shine before [he] see[s] the minister' (162).

Although Pyle is 'quiet', in contrast to Kurtz's loquaciousness, he also constructs a theoretical defence of imperialist terrorism from 'phrases in the style of York Harding' (62), an American political scientist who writes on Vietnam. Although not outwardly so extreme as Kurtz's scrawled recommendation to the Society for the Suppression of Savage Customs that they 'exterminate all the brutes' (51), Pyle is likewise 'impregnably armoured by his good intentions and his ignorance' (163). These lead him to the conclusion that the victims of his terrorist attack were 'only war casualties [who] died in the right cause' (179). Just as Kurtz sets himself up as a god of Western civilisation, Pyle establishes himself as a prophet of democracy at gunpoint. Although Kurtz's savagery is hedonistic and Pyle's ideological and moralistic, both characters ironically represent the savagery Western culture rationalises from a distorted interpretation of 'primitive' culture. Both figures are 'extremists', as the journalist who visits Marlow describes Kurtz (71). Kurtz shoots natives who refuse to obey his orders, while Pyle, as well as organising bomb attacks, will make no bones about killing the two Vietnamese soldiers in the guard-tower for their intentions to hand Fowler and him over to the Vietcong. Both Kurtz and Pyle personify the insidious refusal of Western imperialism to understand that concepts such as 'rebellion' or 'treachery' may have very different meanings within the cultures they exploit.

The observer–narrators, Fowler and Marlow, however, present themselves as enjoying superior insight to that of Pyle and Kurtz, in so far as they realise the 'otherness' of native culture. Fowler, for example, wonders why the soldiers shouldn't hand Pyle and him over, commenting, 'We've no business here [because] it's their country' (*Quiet American* 107), while Marlow pronounces ironically on the French ship firing with absurd impotence 'into a continent' (*Heart of Darkness* 17) and reflects upon the ludicrousness of a hypothetical reversal of British colonialism, 'if a lot of mysterious niggers armed with all kinds of fearful weapons suddenly took to travelling on the road between Deal and Gravesend' (23). Although this might reasonably be interpreted as validating a sympathy for native cultures in opposition to their imperialist antagonists, I would suggest that Fowler and Marlow in fact 'tempt' the reader towards a facile liberal solution which is finally unacceptable. It is important to realise that their impossible belief of somehow remaining uninvolved with their political environment gives a significantly ironic turn to their commentaries. In spite of their doubts as to colonising the natives, Marlow's and Fowler's inability to remain detached from ideology is shown clearly in their common tendency to 'colonise' the women characters in each novel. Marlow restricts the Intended's access to free information about Kurtz, while Fowler and Pyle treat Phuong as the 'other', both oriental and female, a force to be manipulated and appeased.[5]

Marlow's and Fowler's unreliable narrations reflect their false positions regarding neutrality. Marlow is not quite straightforward about his interest in Kurtz on a number of occasions,[6] while Fowler hides the part he plays in Pyle's assassination. This process of subterfuge culminates in the lies at the conclusion of each novel. Through allowing the Intended to continue in her illusions regarding Kurtz's character, Marlow implicitly buys into the imperialist venture, becoming involved where he believed he was not. Fowler lies to Vigot and to Phuong about his involvement in Pyle's death, thus also denying his enmeshment in the affairs of Indo-China. In this way, the narrators find themselves in an impossible double bind which dramatises their necessary involvement in political affairs. Moreover, as they attempt to remain free from corruption they both become more isolated from humanity in general. Marlow concludes that 'we live as we dream, alone' (30) and Fowler that '[o]ne can never understand another human being' (*Quiet American* 133–4).

Other comparisons of Pyle and Fowler with a variety of Conrad characters further emphasise the interplay of Greene and Conrad at a deeper generic level. While Pyle's endeavours to create spheres of American influence recall those of the capitalist Holroyd in *Nostromo*, as well as Charles Gould's similar blend of idealism with ruthless fanaticism, Fowler bears a more important structural similarity to the narrator of *Lord Jim*. Like Conrad, Greene creates a defamiliarised antagonist whom the observer-narrator attempts to interpret. Marlow's and Fowler's investigations proceed by means of a series of interviews or discussions with other characters which may or may not lead to the solution of their mysterious interiority. Fowler's interview with the French colonel who still 'believed that a newspaper correspondent cared for his country's honour more than for news' (66) and Marlow's with the French lieutenant, who considers that 'honour is real' (*Heart of Darkness* 148), seem to portray characters who belong to a superannuated culture able to provide little help in understanding Jim's problematic circumstances or Pyle's new form of colonialism. Similarly, neither Trouin's nor Heng's insistence upon the necessity of commitment nor Stein's recommendation that Jim be immersed 'in the destructive element' (*Lord Jim* 214) does justice to the complexity of the interlaced political and existential problems represented in these novels.

Both the narrators of *Lord Jim* and of *The Quiet American* feel a vulnerability which is caused by the trust they are tempted to place in the antagonist's innocence. They are unable to come to a clear judgement of the object of their quest, thus motivating the reader to conclude paradoxically that political and personal commitment may be at tragic odds with one another. Fowler feels, as Marlow does for Jim, a similarly bewildered, almost exasperated affection for Pyle – an urge to protect the young, naive, idealistic quiet American who '[boats] down the river into Phat Diem, with the caution of a hero in a boy's adventure story' (*Quiet American* 113); however, later he thinks there was a greater need to protect himself from Pyle (37). The dramatic development of Fowler's attitude prevents the reader from attaining a completed view of Pyle's character; rather the narrative account of Fowler's perplexity forces us to develop our own conclusions regarding political and personal engagement.

The generic reflexivity of *The Quiet American* metatextually embodies this necessity for the reader's active participation in the interpretive process. Like *The Third Man*, the novel constantly defines itself through references to literature. By invoking masterworks of the European tradition and (often satirically) more popular genres, Greene creates a narrative that mediates between the two, forming a self-conscious adventure story of the kind Conrad writes in *Lord Jim*. Fowler constantly needles Pyle about his naive aspirations to be a hero, telling him as they are hiding from the Vietcong that Pyle has 'been seeing too many war films', that they 'aren't a couple of marines and [Pyle] can't win a war-medal' (110). On the other hand, Fowler characterises his possible abandonment of Phuong on being summoned back to England as 'a turn in the screw for [Dante's] condemned lovers', for 'Paolo was never promoted to Purgatory' (67). The constant intertwining of the two generic poles of the consolatory thriller and the tragedy or epic emphasises Fowler's continual movement between evasion and commitment. We see this again with especial poignancy the night Pyle dies, in the 'film for boys' which Fowler goes to see. Fowler reports that 'Erroll Flynn or it may have been Tyrone Power . . . swung on ropes and leapt from balconies and rode bareback into technicolour dawns' (182); with transparent self-reference, however, he thinks that 'the sight of Oedipus emerging with his bleeding eyeballs from the palace at Thebes would surely give a better training for life today' (182).

The mixed genre of *The Quiet American* – partly adventure story and partly tragedy – suggests that Fowler, like a low-mimetic version of Oedipus, sets himself up as a detective, only to discover his own political implication at the novel's conclusion.[7] A further irony is that Fowler is punished by being confined to a kind of narrative hell made up of the popular film plots recounted by Phuong; Fowler can be interested, however, only in the narrative he has just told, which he can relate to no other character except the reader. His story does not rely metonymically upon what happened next, as thrillers do, but upon the metaphorical totality of 'what happened'.

After betraying Pyle, nothing else significant can happen to Fowler. The circular form of his narrative implies that he will live in it forever, a situation described by Georg Gaston as the correlation between the growing 'panic of the narrator' and the increasing 'division of the scenes into smaller and more confined units, as if to reflect the narrower bounds of escape' (Gaston 81). This circular narrative has much in common with Conrad's structural technique. Tzvetan Todorov identifies 'the crime' and its 'investigation' as 'the first and second stories' of detective narrative;[8] similarly, *The Quiet American*, like *Nostromo*, *The Secret Agent* and *Under Western Eyes*, presents a series of effects before showing their causes. Just as the bomb explosion in *The Secret Agent* comes before the revelation of Verloc's perfidious adoption of Stevie as his acolyte, Pyle's death precedes the account of Fowler's growing exasperation at his callousness.

However, the reader's motivation is not so much to discover the murderer as to investigate Fowler's interior motivations. This becomes clear from a brief comparison of *The Quiet American* with Agatha Christie's murder mystery *The Murder of Roger Ackroyd* (1926), in which the murderer also turns out to be the narrator himself. In Christie's novel, the effect is mainly that of a brilliant gimmick, a masterly variation on the conventional expectations that the narrator will be the least likely culprit; by contrast, *The Quiet American*'s revelation of criminal identity has the tragic intensity of Fowler's image of Oedipus 'emerging with his bleeding eyeballs from the palace at Thebes' (162). Fowler reluctantly accepts his kinship with Pyle, even though he betrays him to his death, intimating that human beings are ineluctably involved with their world and their past. It is this narrative of discovery which Greene develops in his other political novels of this period.

III

Although Catholicism plays a somewhat minor role in the interior narrative of *The Quiet American*, *The Comedians* (1966) and *The Honorary Consul* (1973) continue to develop the religious interior narrative in the way defined by *A Burnt-Out Case* (1960), treating faith in terms of a wider range of social commitment. These novels bring the Catholic and political narratives together without jettisoning either. As Greene told Marie-Françoise Allain in the early 1980s, he had not 'undergone some evolution from religion to politics'; although during recent years there had been 'a preponderance of novels with a political flavour . . . religion still interest[ed him] as much as ever' (Allain 87–8). In *The Comedians*, the Marxist Dr Magiot illustrates this in his posthumous letter to the protagonist Brown, telling him: 'if you have abandoned one faith, do not abandon all faith. There is always an alternative to the faith we lose. Or is it the same faith under another mask?' (*Comedians* 286).

Latin America, as Greene realised in his Mexican books, *The Lawless Roads* (1939) and *The Power and the Glory* (1940), is an environment in which the spheres of religion and politics are intimately and intensely connected. Ideologically speaking, Greene's Latin American fiction has much in common with Conrad's one novel set in that continent, *Nostromo*, which sympathises with the suffering caused by tyranny and lawlessness in post-colonial South America, yet displays a similar scepticism of attempts to redeem the situation either by revolution or by imperialistic economic development. Like Conrad, Greene dramatises a 'weary desire' for peace similar to Costaguana's 'dread of officialdom with its nightmarish parody of administration without law, without security, and without justice' (*Nostromo* 84). Both are also critical of the United States' interest in Latin America. Mr Holroyd's evangelical imperialism calls attention to the development of the subcontinent by North American capitalism, while many of Greene's characters speak out against unwelcome interference, such as support for Papa Doc's Haiti and General Stroessner's Paraguay.

Perhaps because of his greater emphasis on the religious

dimensions of the interior narrative, Greene tends to be more sympathetic than Conrad to the idealist who wishes to remedy the situation. Conrad presents Don José Avellanos's and Mrs Gould's visions as based on illusion at best, while Charles Gould's Utopian plans derive from his obsession with control. Greene's novels, however, more optimistically represent a continued religious and political faith in the protagonists of *The Comedians* and *The Honorary Consul*, who eventually acquire a self-knowledge which transfigures their initial stances of non-commitment. Although this affirmation falls short of the celebratory comedy which characterises another group of Greene's later novels,[9] *The Comedians* exhaustively explores the connections between comedy and faith in a way that takes up the story from Querry's 'last laugh' in *A Burnt-Out Case*. Michael Routh sees *The Comedians* as 'a *parody* of two genres, farce and comedy', going on to argue that Brown, the narrator, establishes 'an essentially farcical pattern through which the serious elements of the story eventually penetrate to transform the farce into a grim comment on Brown's life' (Routh 139–40).

In this way, comedy complicates the issue of commitment. Political or personal involvement are first conceived of as antithetical to comedy, for if one is 'a comedian', then one is uncommitted; this echoes a similar equation from Conrad's *Chance* and *The Arrow of Gold*, seen in the denials that the heroines, Flora and Rita, are 'comedians' (*Chance* 177–8; *Arrow* 338). Brown, the narrator–protagonist of *The Comedians*, and Jones, the quixotic con-man masquerading as an army officer, apparently both approximate this type of uncommitted comedian. However, the husband of Marta, who happens to be Brown's mistress, suggests that the issue may be more complicated. Being a comedian, he argues, is 'an honourable profession', for 'If only we could be good ones the world might gain at least a sense of style' (*Comedians* 134). Deriving an extra ironic twist from the speaker's own status as the stock comic figure of the cuckold, this indicates the possibility of a higher level of comedy in a double vision of the world as both comic and serious. As Erdinast-Vulcan comments, 'Brown fails to understand . . . that when one accepts his part in the comedy with a total commitment, the word "comédien" becomes a title of honour' (Erdinast-Vulcan, *Childless* 76). Brown's mother, whose combination of raffishness and courage marks her as a prototype of Aunt Augusta in *Travels with My Aunt* (1969), demonstrates this: '"Fun" for her', comments Dr Magiot, 'included almost everything. Even death' (*Travels with My Aunt* 234).

Comedy becomes more intricate as the novel progresses. Even Brown is not finally the 'bad comedian' he believes himself to be, precisely because he sees his own faults and has a degree of self-awareness behind his outwardly frivolous attitude to the world. C. S. Ferns notes that 'he frequently acts, as do most of the other 'comedians', from better motives than habit or self-interest' (64), while Michael Larson suggests that although Brown 'denies an active faith, he is clearly haunted by a religious sensibility' (178). Brown seems at first to be a direct descendant of Conrad's reluctantly involved protagonist. He is isolated from the community of mankind, indulging a cosmopolitan rootlessness ascribed partly to lacking a father. Just as Kurtz in Conrad's *Heart of Darkness* has 'kicked himself loose of the earth' (65), for Brown, 'no region of the earth had taken the place of home' (*Comedians* 223). Like Kurtz also, 'all Europe contributed' to his making (*Heart of Darkness* 50); although his father is perhaps English, his mother was possibly French or 'a rare Monegasque' (*Comedians* 59). To be born in Monaco as he was, Brown thinks, 'is almost the same as being a citizen of nowhere' (234).

Nevertheless, a remote source of salvation seems available to Brown, which stems from his upbringing by the Jesuits, who have 'taught [him] to reason', thus making it possible for him to become aware that he is playing the role of a non-committed comedian (163). In Erdinast-Vulcan's words, he 'cannot remain an indifferent spectator to the drama' (84). His self-knowledge qualifies his description of himself as one of 'the faithless', a group of people who 'admire the dedicated . . . for their fidelity to a cause but through timidity, or through lack of sufficient zest . . . find [them]selves the only ones truly committed . . . to the whole world of evil and of good' (*Comedians* 279). Brown is partially absolved from belonging to this category through his knowledge that he does belong to it and by the incapacity for self-deception he shares with many Conradian protagonists. Indeed, he immediately refutes his own specious theorising about 'the faithless', by admitting that the argument probably 'eased the never quiet conscience which had been injected into [him] . . . by the Fathers of the Visitation' (279).

Brown's mistress, Marta, suggests that he is in fact a 'prêtre manqué' (286), like Querry in *A Burnt-Out Case*. Ruefully conscious of himself as a man haunted by bad faith, Brown ironically transforms Greene's character of the 'sanctified sinner' into an unsanctified one. As with Querry, we must read Brown's redemption between the lines from his self-deprecating confession at the end of the novel that he had felt himself 'not merely incapable of love . . . but even of guilt' (286). In his world, he thinks, 'There were no heights or abysses'; he sees himself 'on a great plain, walking and walking on the interminable flats' (286). This image of the desert recalls Bendrix's position, just one step away from faith at the conclusion of *The End of the Affair*. However, the terms which dramatise this transformation are as much secular and political as they are religious, leaving the reader freer to interpret Brown's development from his actions. Braver than he makes out, Brown courageously stands up to the Tontons Macoutes on at least one occasion and 'can find no reason to mock the modest stone that commemorates Jones' (9). It is this ironic heroism which demonstrates his 'salvation' more clearly than the false ambivalence of *The End of the Affair* or *The Heart of the Matter*.

This quality is carried over into the figure of Jones, another 'good comedian'. Jones, a beachcomber con-man on the run from his past, is a low-life version of Conrad's Quixotic figure Lord Jim. Roger Sharrock implicitly brings Jones very close to Jim in his suggestion that, 'like all romantic myth-makers, he secretly desires a test that would enable him to convert dream into reality' (Sharrock 232). Similarly, Brown's observation that he and Jones 'had both been thrown into the water to sink or swim and swim [they] had' (*Comedians* 266) echoes Stein's recommendation that Jim be immersed in 'the destructive element' (*Lord Jim* 214). Like Jim in Patusan, Jones is driven relentlessly to a strange land and a violent death by the threat of disgrace in the outside world; he can find 'no room . . . outside of Haiti' (*Comedians* 282). Describing himself in the dangerous Conradian terms of 'a man of imagination' (41), Jones has fantasies similar to Jim's of becoming a hero in a boy's adventure story: 'Give me back my old company,' he says, 'and I'd go through the police station like a dose of salts' (240). Ironically, he achieves this heroism when he joins the guerrillas and dies providing covering fire for his companions because his flat feet prevent him escaping (282).[10]

The comedians, then, may finally be the heroes, qualifying what initially seems a simplistic opposition between political commitment and egotistic detachment. In this way, Ray Snape's conclusion that 'Magiot remains an idea dressed up' (Snape, 'Political Novels' 79) misses the double irony of what he identifies as Greene's 'browbeat[ing] us with a sense of Magiot's superiority' (79). While the novel validates Magiot's and Philipot's heroic roles of men prepared to die for their beliefs, it does not stop short of occasionally gently poking fun, for example at the incongruity between Dr Magiot's old-fashioned bourgeois manners and his ideological leanings. In Routh's view, Magiot appears, 'upon second look . . . to be less a model of right thought and action' than 'a man out of his own time and place [who] for all his espoused commitment' is 'detached from current realities' (Routh 147–8). Through playing a 'serious' political narrative of autocracy and revolution against a farce consisting of apparent buffoons such as Brown, Jones and the American vegetarian Smith, *The Comedians* portrays political responsibility as deriving from imperfect, reluctantly committed human beings. This begins a trend towards the 'religious laughter' which in later novels most individualises Greene's treatment of the Conradian masterplot.

IV

The Honorary Consul (1973) continues to develop this mixed genre of interior revelation and political plot to an extent not seen since *The Power and the Glory* (1940). Miriam Allott draws attention to the similarity between the opening scenes of the two novels, in which both Tench and Plarr, a dentist and a doctor 'daily engaged with human pain', walk alone by the river, going on to suggest that the later novel 'complements and replies' to the earlier one, for both are 'intensely concerned with pain and loneliness, with spiritual deprivation and social injustice' (Allott, 'Surviving' 240). Dr Plarr is a non-committed protagonist who is set against Father Rivas, a priest turned revolutionary who is tormented by conflicting allegiances to faith and politics. To complicate this interior thriller further, Greene adds two 'criterion' figures – the elderly drunkard Fortnum and his wife, the ex-prostitute Clara.

Like Conrad's Razumov, Plarr is an apolitical bystander reluctantly enlisted in the revolutionary cause. Although he perceives Rivas as a misguided idealist, finally he does not betray him or Fortnum's other kidnappers to the police, instead becoming 'caught up' (*Honorary Consul* 267), almost by accident, because 'he hadn't believed in their plans and to listen to them was only a mark of friendship' (26). With the *sangfroid* of Charles Gould, Plarr is also a failure in emotional relationships, partly through an unsatisfactory relationship with his father. While Gould feels that he has to compensate for his father's failure to work the mine, Plarr feels abandoned by his father, who stayed behind in Paraguay, eventually to die while escaping from a political prison. Again, like Heyst in Conrad's *Victory*, Plarr 'cannot form a tie', reacting against his mother's excessive demands for love, combined with his father's undemonstrativeness. His incapacity for intimacy with his mistress, Clara, also dramatises his detachment from others. While Heyst cannot get 'accustomed' to Lena, nor 'know[s] how to live' with her (*Victory* 200), Plarr can 'no more imagine [Clara's] thoughts than he could imagine the thoughts of a strange animal' (*Honorary Consul* 238). The feeling is mutual, it seems, for Clara also watches Plarr, 'puzzled, as though his actions were too complicated for any girl from the establishment of Señora Sanchez to understand' (180).

As in *Victory*, the Conradian representation of 'woman as other' – particularly as foreign or native 'other' – ironically reflects back upon the male protagonist. Although Plarr thinks of Clara as a kind of mirror who is all things to all men, her support for her aged and abandoned father qualifies the unreflective compliance which so annoys him. Finally, Plarr's refusal to accept her love, because it was 'a claim . . . a responsibility . . . a demand' (172), identifies *him* as the foreigner and *Clara* as a member of the community. Plarr's isolation is also dramatised by the issue of fatherhood. Linking him through Clara's child to the past and the future, it also brings into conjunction the various cultural discontinuities within the novel, as when he thinks of 'the tangle of its ancestry, and for the first time in the complexity of that tangle the child bec[omes] real to him' (212).

Greene complicates this theme further through the introduction of surrogate fathers. Even though Plarr has displaced him as the father of what he thinks to be his own child, Fortnum becomes a father-figure to Plarr; his face, as he lies on the coffin, seems to Plarr to merge with that of his own father (216). Plarr begins fully to identify with Fortnum in the final climactic stages of the novel, when he fully realises that Clara loves him, a fact which he has hitherto repressed. Ironically, at this point he himself becomes a 'father' to Fortnum and sacrifices his life for him in a gesture which identifies with his real father's political commitment.[11]

The Catholic interior narrative also complicates the theme of fatherhood. The revolutionary priest, Father Rivas, has himself relinquished its synonym, 'priesthood'; in him, the plots of religious interiority and political activism are constantly at war, intimating the larger thematic and generic struggle within the novel as a whole.

Plarr attempts to trivialise Rivas's dilemma by teasing him about the inconsistency of his beliefs with revolutionary action, asking, 'Isn't it better not to believe in that horror up there sitting in the clouds of heaven than pretend to love him?' (226). Rivas answers this implication that religious faith will lead to a revelation as hostile to humankind as the Conradian heart of darkness, by declaring that he has 'always wanted to understand what [Plarr] call[s] the horror and why [he] cannot stop loving it' (226). Rivas attempts to resolve his desperate interior conflict between the demands of faith and those of revolutionary action by a resort to Manichaean theology, which includes both 'the evil of God [and] his goodness too' (227). God, he explains, 'made us in His image - and so our evil is His Evil' (227); he asks: 'How could I love God if He were not like me? Divided like me. Tempted like me' (227), concluding this humanist reflection of Greene's larger generic programme in the belief that his God 'has to be . . . made in our image with a night-side as well as a day-side' (227).

However, it is Fortnum, the drunken honorary consul, who in a final irony becomes a father both to Plarr and to Rivas. Rivas has rebelled against his own rich bourgeois father by becoming a priest, and has then rejected the fatherhood of the church by becoming a revolutionary. Subsequently abandoned by another surrogate 'father', the revolutionary El Tigre, Rivas eventually makes his confession to Fortnum, the hostage he intends to kill, in an ironic reversal of roles. In the novel's final scene, Fortnum as father-figure modulates into a blend of husband, father and priest, as he comforts his wife Clara over the death of Plarr, her former lover. This episode reverses Marlow's deception of Kurtz's Intended in *Heart of Darkness*, in a closure which affirms the possibility of a human love which is at once social, personal and religious. While Dr Saavedra's funeral oration perpetuates the official lie that Plarr was killed by the revolutionaries rather than by Colonel Perez, the personal deception of *Heart of Darkness* (as well as the mendacious complaisance of *The Ministry of Fear*) is refused. By comforting Clara over Plarr's death as well as for Plarr's inability to love her, Fortnum succeeds in breaking down 'the wall of silence which was growing up between them' (265), pleading Plarr's cause in an ironic adaptation of Marlow's defence of Kurtz. Clara lies that she 'never loved [Plarr]' (268), but in contrast to *Heart of Darkness*, no deception results: 'Her lie meant nothing to [Fortnum] now at all. It was contradicted too plainly by her tears. In an affair of this kind it was the right thing to lie. He felt an immense sense of relief' (270). In *The Honorary Consul*, Greene finds a Christian, though not narrowly Christian, way in which to resolve Conrad's deadlocked triangle.

V

Returning to a more secular mode, one of Greene's most Conradian works, *The Human Factor* (1978), develops further the narrative of political commitment in the form of an espionage thriller. Many studies compare *The Human Factor* with Conrad, especially with *The Secret Agent*, yet most fail to draw out the full significance of the parallels they adduce. Both Gary P. Storhoff and Andrew Wright compare the two novels in thematic terms; Storhoff points to 'the vast discrepancy between our romanticised conception of the secret agent and dull reality' (Storhoff 59),[12] while Wright discusses the 'dehumanisation . . . in the necessarily corrupt societies of the twentieth century' (Wright 87). However, these critics do not place *The Human Factor* in the full context of Greene's developing relationship with Conrad. The greater degree of resonance is due more to *The Human Factor*'s integration of multiple Conradian intertexts. The novel creates a generic gestalt from the political espionage narratives of *The Secret Agent* and *Under Western Eyes*, as well as from the dramatisation of global politics in *Nostromo*, to make the wide-ranging 'prediction', as Greene terms it, of America's and West Germany's intervention in South Africa (*Ways of Escape* 299). Against this far-reaching political narrative, the novel sets an interracial version of the Conradian love narrative of *Victory*.

Narrative structure loosely follows Conrad's tendency to reverse cause and effect, with the reader not discovering until almost halfway through the novel that Castle is the mole MI5 has been seeking. As in *Under Western Eyes*, we come to understand the motivations behind Castle's actions after reading of those actions themselves. Like Razumov with Prince K. and Councillor Mikulin, Castle is also a reluctant spy who comes to feel repugnance for his employers, discovering that his camaraderie with the KGB agent Boris is finally exploitative and self-serving. In *Under Western Eyes*, Councillor Mikulin, despite being 'a good-natured man [who] wishe[s] no harm to anyone' (291), is promoted to the direction of the general police supervision over Europe and comes to see 'the great possibilities of special usefulness in that uncommon young man on whom he had a hold already' (292). In *The Human Factor*, even Boris, whom Castle had thought of in terms of a father-confessor (117), finally reminds him that 'gratitude like love needs to be renewed daily' (269).

Castle's and Razumov's roles of double agent show their increasing isolation from humanity. Like Razumov, Castle too is 'a conspirator everlastingly on his guard against self-betrayal in a world of secret spies' (*Under Western Eyes* 199), rigorously accounting to himself for his most trivial actions, even as to why he lunches at a certain pub. Although Castle betrays the Western Alliance for the unselfish motives of friendship and gratitude, he ironically ends up as isolated from humanity as Razumov, separated from Sarah and Sam, the two people he values most.

Castle is a tragic figure, unable to integrate the demands of the political and interior narratives in which he is involved. While his heart is in the right place, he does not look into things deeply enough to see that his conspiracy will end up harming Sarah herself. As in Winnie Verloc's scheme for Stevie's advancement in *The Secret Agent*, Castle imagines he is furthering the interests of Sarah's people by passing on secrets to the Russians; both characters, however, unintentionally advance the destruction or abandonment of loved ones. Despite Sarah's protest to the contrary, Castle does in fact betray her through his failure to foresee the consequences of his actions. This takes a final ironic form in his disguise as a blind man in order to escape to the Soviet Union, bereft like Oedipus of wife and child.

If Castle suffers from partial vision, the characters who wield power in the political narrative embody world views which are either nihilistic or nefarious. Developing the ideological dimensions of *Nostromo, The Secret Agent* and *Under Western Eyes*, Greene's vision of world politics reaches its most pessimistic point in this novel. The ideological standoff between Soviet autocracy and the Western oppression of black South Africa replaces the deadlock of Tzarist autocracy and socialist revolution in *Under Western Eyes*. Again, while *The Secret Agent* finally validates Britain as a haven of legality, Dr Percival's erroneous 'elimination' of Davis shows autocratic atrocities within the British Establishment itself. Dr Percival is a sinisterly updated Buchan character, with his surface persona of the genial family doctor thinly protecting a ruthlessness worthy of Conrad's Professor. Faced with his icy threats to separate her from her son, Sarah has to resist Winnie Verloc's temptation to seize a sharp knife from the restaurant table and stab him.

While *The Secret Agent* intimates the ineptness and nepotism in the higher echelons of the British government, *The Human Factor* reveals the cover-ups and mismanagement in the Secret Service during the seventies which would later be confirmed in Peter Wright's memoir, *Spycatcher* (1987). Both writers trace the problem to the monopoly of political power by inherited wealth and position. Sir John Hargreaves, the ineffectual section chief who is unable to control his unscrupulous underling Percival, is a superannuated colonialist with a taste for nostalgia, a reincarnation of Conrad's Assistant Commissioner in *The Secret Agent*. More passive than Conrad's official, who at least prevents Heat from erroneously arresting Michaelis, Sir John reads Trollope in order to forget the unpleasant details of Dr Percival's mistaken murder of Davis.

Altogether, *The Human Factor* is a passionate indictment of what Greene later called 'the hypocrisy of our relations with South Africa' (*Ways of Escape* 299). While Conrad warns in *Nostromo* that England's and North America's concern with material interests and spheres of influence will motivate interference with third world countries to an unprecedented degree, Greene asserts in *Ways of Escape* (1983) that Uncle Remus – the plot to use the nuclear bomb on the black population of South Africa in the event of a revolution – is 'less an invention than a prediction', going on to explain that 'however much opposed the governments of the Western Alliance might pretend to be to apartheid . . . they simply could not let South Africa succumb to black power and Communism' (299).

Yet what makes *The Human Factor* so Conradian a novel is primarily its reworking of a plot which shows how impoverished interiority leads to mistaken forms of public commitment. Greene's 'married love story of an elderly man', as he describes it (*Ways of Escape* 299), develops a variation upon the Heyst–Lena relationship in *Victory*. Although Castle is committed to Sarah and her son Sam in a way unknown to Heyst, rescuing them and taking them to Britain, he also is 'terrible once the desire to act gets hold of [him]' (*Victory* 77). Both are motivated by impulses devoid of circumspection, Castle from an overdeveloped sense of gratitude and Heyst by his courteous pity. This impulsive tendency is exacerbated by their isolation; like *Victory*, *The Human Factor* shows personal and emotional disaster arising from the protagonist's inability to commit himself to any public form of solidarity, whether political or religious. Like Lena with Ricardo, Sarah, alone and friendless, has to duel with Castle's antagonist Dr Percival. Castle can commit himself only to individual human beings such as Carson or Sarah, but is unable to align himself exclusively with the Soviets or against them. Nor can he make any specific religious commitment, as his attempt to use a Roman Catholic priest merely as a psychoanalyst demonstrates (*Human Factor* 184). Although his downfall is clearly due to a confused perception of the interior and political plots in which he is involved, finally *The Human Factor* cannot provide any easy answers. Rather, the novel tragically celebrates a protagonist who is destroyed by the all-too-human inability to mediate between the private and the public.

At first, Greene was reluctant to publish the novel, writing in *Ways of Escape* that he had 'betrayed [his] purpose' (*Ways of Escape* 299), which had been 'to write a novel free from . . . conventional violence' (296). Having 'assumed . . . that [his] writing days were finished' with *A Burnt-Out Case* (1960), he reports feeling 'the same again now' (300). It is significant that both these novels represent landmarks in Greene's developing relationship with Conrad. While I would not wish to argue that Greene's sole motivation in writing was to individualise the Conradian masterplot, the synthetic blueprint of genres I have outlined nevertheless remains an infrastructure of his work. The epigraph of *The Human Factor*, drawn from Conrad's *Victory*, makes this explicit: 'I only know that he who forms a tie is lost. The germ of corruption has entered into his soul.' At a superficial level, this perhaps shows that Greene has transcended the 'anxiety of influence';[13] more specifically, it paradoxically celebrates the self-knowledge and laments the personal disaster which results from Castle's (and Heyst's) flawed personalities. In this way, it may indicate a similarly paradoxical assessment of Greene's relation to Conrad, ruefully admitting the struggle against his influence, yet also celebrating the 'seeding' qualities of the Conradian 'germ' planted in his own fiction.

5

'Dissolving into Laughter': Comedy and Carnival in the Final Chapter

I

While *The Quiet American* (1955) signals the beginning of Greene's mature political era, the same year also marks the publication of a very different work, *Loser Takes All*, which displaces the Catholic interior narrative into the genre of romantic comedy. Declaring that '[a] reputation is like a death mask', which he 'wanted to smash' (*Ways of Escape* 216), Greene describes the book as 'an amusing, agreeably sentimental *novella*, something which neither [his] friends nor [his] enemies would expect' (216). In spite of its apparent lightness, however, the story dramatises a more serious religious and moral theme, initiating a series of comic novels which bring the religious, political and psychological narratives into yet another relation.

Gradually, the inherent seriousness of Greene's late comedies becomes increasingly apparent in the return of the repressed Conradian political thriller and interior narrative. Even the 'amusing' and 'agreeably sentimental' *Loser Takes All* comically transforms a marriage, which is threatened by material interests like the Goulds' in Conrad's *Nostromo*, into an allegory of the biblical creation, fall and redemption. These allegorical leanings take on a darker form towards the end of the cycle in *Doctor Fischer of Geneva or the Bomb Party* (1980).

The movement towards a serious, even tragic form of comedy results from specifically reinvoking the political and interior dimensions of the Conradian masterplot. While the fusion between interior revelation and political thriller of Conrad's *Under Western Eyes* becomes a disturbing farce in *Our Man in Havana* (1958), *Travels with My Aunt* (1969) introduces a Rabelaisian tone to the interior narrative, developing a carnivalesque celebration of the body and the instincts. Finally, *Monsignor Quixote* (1982) deepens these connections between Catholicism and comedy, synthesising laughter and prayer in its interrogation of Catholicism and Marxism.

II

Loser Takes All (1955) creates a variation upon the typical plot of New Comedy, which depicts 'an intrigue between a young man and a young woman . . . blocked by some kind of opposition, usually paternal' (Frye 44). Greene's young man, Bertram, however, is in fact a middle-aged accountant who also plays the role of the paternal 'blocker' figure and proves himself to be the most threatening obstacle to the successful outcome of his love affair. Greene uses the comic love narrative to create a version of Charles and Emilia Gould's gradual emotional alienation from each other in Conrad's *Nostromo* due to Gould's 'hard, determined service of the material interests to which he had pinned his faith' (*Nostromo* 427). However, while Emilia merely pities Gould's 'colossal and lasting success', pathetically concluding that love represents 'only a short moment of forgetfulness' (*Nostromo* 427), in *Loser Takes All*, Cary protests vigorously against Bertram's obsession with his gambling system: 'I married a man I met in the bar of the Volunteer . . . He hadn't had a very good life . . . I wanted – oh, enormously – to give him fun. Now suddenly I've woken up in bed with a man who can buy all the fun he wants' (*Loser Takes All* 101).

While, in the spirit of romantic comedy, Bertram eventually gives up his 'material interests' and wins Cary back in a final scene of reconciliation, a religious dimension complicates the novel's genre. Gwen Boardman notes that 'behind all these jokes, behind the apparent parody of his religious symbols, there lies Greene's familiar territory' in the form of 'Bertram's choice' between Good and Evil' (Boardman 123). Although Greene parodies religious symbols, however, there is also a serious intent behind the myth of creation, fall and redemption which underpins the novel and is reflected in its three-part structure. Bertram and Cary are in a sense 'created' by Dreuther, whose nickname of 'the Gom' represents the almost divine acronym of 'Grand Old Man'. Having arranged their wedding and honeymoon, the Gom withdraws from his 'creation' and apparently abandons them in Monte Carlo; it is then that Bertram falls into the temptation to devise a gambling system, the success of which tempts him to become if not 'a god' himself, then at least a major shareholder in the Gom's firm. Disgusted by his greed and cruel inclination for revenge, Cary is on the point of leaving Bertram when the Gom reappears and reintroduces order into his 'creation'.

This light-hearted burlesque signals the beginning of Greene's movement away from the tortuous problems of individual faith which had so engaged him in earlier novels such as *The End of the Affair* (1951). Descriptions of the Gom as 'like the weather – unpredictable' (*Loser Takes All* 15) deliberately inflate the analogies between him and the divine. When he apparently forgets his appointment, Bertram expostulates: 'He makes the world and then he goes and rests on the seventh day and his creation can go to pot that day for all he cares' (61). In this way, the novel negotiates carefully between Christian mythology and farce. There are other powers vying for Bertram's soul, such as the Gom's rival and other principal shareholder, Sir Walter Blixon. 'Small, spotty, undistinguished, and consumed with jealousy' (16) like Milton's Satan disguised as a toad, Blixon is described in suitably Manichaean terms as 'the other power at No. 45' (16).

Unlike the romantic love fictions of Conrad, which Greene imitates in his early writing, *Loser Takes All* brings the story of Bertram and Cary into relation with a narrative which reveals a wider sense of character. While young love 'wins through' against the forces of age and greed, the novel does not idealise Cary as an elusive and mysterious 'other' like many Conrad heroines. Cary is both comic and romantic; while her face carries 'permanently the sign of Original Innocence' (49), her 'flashes of disquieting wisdom' (42) humanise her, as does her penchant for satire when she orders coffee and rolls as a rebuke to Bertram's caviare (74–6).

Cary's larger function, however, is implicitly to chastise Greene's theological narratives, which are satirically portrayed as being like Bertram's games of chance. Players who use systems, Bertram thinks, are 'like theologians, patiently trying to rationalise a mystery' (51). These 'veterans', he later notes, 'never lost faith in their own calculations [nor] abandoned [their] elaborate schemes' (72). Cary uses a more improvisational and playful method of divining the future from random occurrences which provides a direct contrast with Bertram's rigidly mathematical system for playing the tables; indeed her light-hearted superstitions imply an apology for the vilification of Ida Arnold in *Brighton Rock*. As if to confirm the validity of Cary's intuitive form of faith against Bertram's 'theological' rationalism,

Cary's 'prediction' on the way to their wedding ironically turns out to be correct – she and Bertram are due for bad luck in their relationship. *Loser Takes All* 'completes', as it were, the Conradian love story by bringing romantic comedy into a generic relationship with the interior religious narrative.

III

Written in a similarly minimalist style and sharing its allegorical, fairytale quality, *Doctor Fischer of Geneva or the Bomb Party* (1980) can be seen as a kind of companion piece to *Loser Takes All.* There is, however, a greater emphasis upon the corrupt society which threatens the lovers. The novel pushes comedy almost to the borderline of tragedy,[1] deliberately manipulating the 'anxiety' without which, Christopher Herbert reminds us, few comic writers are able to 'glorify the life of pleasure' (Herbert 415). Greene first establishes a comic plot in which Jones, a poor translator, marries Anna-Luise, the wealthy Doctor Fischer's daughter, resisting the corrupting temptations held out by her father. However, Anna-Luise's death in a shocking and tragic skiing accident ruptures this plot, introducing a Conradian narrative of personal versus public commitment.

This interior narrative dramatises the danger of trusting wholly in private human relationships. The fact that Jones's highest emotional and spiritual commitment is to another isolated individual, Anna-Luise, may make him a 'materialist' in human relationships; he is certain that he has got Anna-Luise 'for life' and that he will die first (*Doctor Fischer* 66). However, after her death he is left in a spiritual wasteland, without 'hope of ever seeing her in any future' (142). Like Castle in *The Human Factor* and Razumov in *Under Western Eyes,* his despair arises from a rejection of anything beyond the private and personal.

Dr Fischer of Geneva represents, then, a love story in search of an interior narrative. This quest takes the form of Jones's interrogation of Dr Fischer, which finally turns back to reveal himself. Dr Fischer's evil, unlike Pinkie's in *Brighton Rock,* is not romanticised, but is portrayed both realistically and transcendentally. It is fully realised on a social and political as well as an allegorical level; like Conrad's professor in *The Secret Agent,* Fischer is a 'mad doctor' with an immense contempt for mankind (54). Together with his sycophantic cronies, the 'Toads', he has succumbed to extreme greed and moral corruption, the political dimensions of which appear in his confidential commission of Jones to translate a letter arranging a shady international arms deal. Fischer's greedy misuse of power is implicitly a force behind political terrorism.

Fischer also takes the form of a more transcendent allegory of evil, although as with Conrad's villains the evil effects of his power stem finally from vanity and lack of vision. He is gradually demoted from his quasi-metaphysical position in a demise similar to Conrad's Professor's descent to 'a pest' (*Secret Agent* 269). Initially established as an allegory of 'Jehovah or Satan', Fischer is described by Anna-Luise both as 'hell' (*Doctor Fischer* 18), and as equivalent to 'Our Father in Heaven' (24). Apparently able to buy over people with ease, he finds a sense of self-identification with a god who is greedy 'for our humiliation' (62) and has hopes of 'creating' Jones, that is corrupting him into greed, 'as God created Adam' (134). It transpires, however, that Fischer's status as an embodiment of the transcendent is primarily in Jones's mind. Casting Fischer as a metaphysically evil 'other' similar to Marlow's Kurtz in *Heart of Darkness*, Jones too eventually finds emptiness rather than evil. After Doctor Fischer's death, Jones feels as though his own 'small half-belief' in a god, 'had somehow shrivelled with the sight of Doctor Fischer's body' (142), which he now thinks of as 'the piece of rubbish which [he] had once compared with Jehovah and Satan' (141).

Unlike Conrad's *The Secret Agent*, which seems to stop short with the ironic, scornful stance of its narrator, Greene offers an implicit critique of Jones's point of view. In fact, Jones's contemptuous view that Fischer's dead body has 'no more significance than a dead dog' (141) mirrors Fischer's own cynicism. Although Jones has 'the impression', just before Fischer's suicide, that Fischer was 'looking to [him] for help' (139), he never learns that the real *senex iratus* of the novel is not Fischer but the unpredictable nature of reality itself. Only in the dream in which Jones simultaneously mocks Fischer weeping 'beside an open grave' and yet feels 'the deep reproach of his tears' (67), does he come near to realising that he is neither a metaphysical entity nor a 'piece of rubbish' but a weak, perhaps pitiable, human being. Significantly, Jones dreams this soon after his smug supposition that he and Anna-Luise 'were going to be together for ever and a day – *le jour le plus long*' (66–7). Through rejecting the religious dimension of the interior narrative, Jones remains caught up within a vicious circle of domination and subjugation similar to Fischer's own sado-masochistic pattern with the Toads.

Jones never grasps that he and Doctor Fischer are 'secret sharers' in unhappiness. Unable to rise above his hatred and frustrated despair, he remains perplexed, enmeshed in a story he does not fully understand. To further the reader's insight into Jones's tortuous interiority, Greene introduces a moral foil in the form of Steiner, who has lost everything at Dr Fischer's hands – Anna-Luise's mother, livelihood and health. In spite of this, Steiner gives up his plan for violent revenge, telling Jones: 'Poor man . . . when you begin to despise like Doctor Fischer, you end up by despising all the world . . . when it came to the point – I pitied him' (140–1). Jones, however, is still unable to understand and only thinks how he 'wished Fischer had been there to hear how he was pitied by Steiner' (141).

Dr Fischer of Geneva, then, substitutes quasi-Christian forms of love and pity for Winnie Verloc's revenge and suicide in *The Secret Agent*, Marlow's perplexity at the end of *Heart of Darkness* and Linda Viola's despairing cry in *Nostromo*. Even in the darkest of Greene's late novels, the teleological optimism of comedy remains to ironise the ironic narrator himself.

IV

Our Man in Havana (1958) combines romantic comedy with a farcical political thriller in which the protagonist, Wormold, adapts Razumov's role of a spy pretending to be a revolutionary to one of a vacuum cleaner salesman pretending to be a spy. Despite this tendency to parody the espionage formula, however, the novel moves towards a more serious political dramatisation than is at first apparent. The comic reversals and discoveries resulting from Wormold's deception of MI5 initially disguise the closeness of *Our Man in Havana* to Conrad's *Under Western Eyes*. As a result of his entanglement with the MI5 control, Hawthorne, Wormold is drawn into the Secret Service with the inevitability of Razumov's recruitment as a Tzarist agent. Caught up in circumstances beyond their control, Razumov and Wormold both become involved in an ironic charade in which each pretends to be something he really is. Razumov plays the part of friend to Victor Haldin and potential lover of his sister Natalia, while Wormold never abandons his original identity of a down-at-heel vacuum cleaner salesman who can only reply to Hawthorne's observation that his profession 'has quite a natural air' with the weak protest that 'it *is* natural' (*Our Man in Havana* 42).

Like Razumov, Wormold is an isolated protagonist who becomes reluctantly involved with the community of mankind. Encouraged by his friend Dr Hasselbacher to fabricate secrets rather than provide British intelligence with real ones, Wormold finds himself standing 'on the frontier of violence, a strange land he had never visited before' (184). Like Razumov before meeting Natalia, Wormold feels increasing fear at the arrival of Beatrice on the scene, an assistant sent to him from London who he believes has penetrated his ruse. Beatrice, however, reads Wormold as the protagonist of a less formulaic narrative than espionage, which she calls 'a *Boy's Own Paper* game' (109). She suspects him not of fabricating Raul, but of being indifferent to human life, asking him: 'Aren't you ever tired of other people taking risks?' (109).

Ironically, Wormold is in fact playing a *Boy's Own Paper* game, in the sense that he literally writes an imaginative spy story for MI5. Fantasy and reality may have sinister points of interpenetration, however. Just as the Russian revolutionaries in *Under Western Eyes* find an illusory validation of Razumov in Ziemianitch's suicide, so it emerges that there is in fact a Raul, an engineer Cifuentes, as well as other people whose identities correspond to the characters Wormold has created as his 'agents'. When Raul is murdered in a self-fulfilment of Wormold's prophecy, then Wormold is 'safe' from the danger of his fabrications being discovered. With his frantic effort to track down the other 'agents' who really exist, the stripper Teresa and Professor Sanchez, Wormold becomes immersed in a terrifying farce similar to Razumov's, in which he experiences the fervent desire 'to tell Beatrice everything' (132).

Our Man in Havana dramatises the conflicting desires to escape from and to engage with *Realpolitik*. 'You should dream more,' his friend Dr Hasselbacher tells Wormold, 'Reality in our century is not be faced' (10). Later Hasselbacher suggests that all Wormold needs is 'a little imagination', for if the information 'is secret enough' then only Wormold knows it (57). As a direct result of Wormold's taking his advice, however, Dr Hasselbacher develops from a buffoon figure whose attitude to politics is to wish 'a plague' on the houses of both East and West (32) into a tragic victim. Threatened with deportation after the destruction of his scientific experiment, he loses 'his will to live' and agrees to betray Wormold's fictional character, Raul, to the authorities. His initial attempt at political transcendence, his subsequent betrayal of Raul, and his courageous attempt to make amends suggest that in many ways Hasselbacher corresponds more authentically than Wormold to the Razumov prototype.

The novel's alternation between the romantic comedy of the Wormold and Beatrice plot and the ironically pathetic narrative concerning Dr Hasselbacher enacts at a generic level the dilemma between escape and engagement. In Northrop Frye's definition of ironic comedy, 'the demonic world', which is 'never far away', moves 'towards a deliverance from something which, if absurd, is by no means invariably harmless' (Frye 178). Contrastingly, the Wormold–Beatrice plot emphasises romantic comedy in the manner of *Loser Takes All*, with the union of not quite 'young lovers' blocked by a *senex iratus* in the guise of MI5. The narrative manoeuvres constantly between one genre and another, invoking at a level of reader expectation the uneasy dilemma between public and private loyalty. While seeming to validate personal loyalty in Wormold's and Beatrice's romantic apotheosis, the grim farce finally shows all too clearly the tragic results of Wormold's meddling.

Our Man in Havana, then, moves between two irreconcilable modes of interpretation. In this way it approximates Frye's second phase of comedy – between ironic and romantic – 'in which the hero does not transform a humorous society but simply escapes or runs away from it, leaving its structure as it was before' (180). Although Beatrice and Wormold represent the 'happy ending' of comedy in what Frye calls 'the victory of a [real] society controlled by . . . pragmatic freedom' over 'a[n illusory] society controlled by habit, ritual bondage, arbitrary law', this 'escape' is also based upon illusion itself, for the tragic memory of Dr Hasselbacher darkens the fantasy transformation of MI5. In this way, Greene encourages a perpetual interplay between the different narrative demands on the reader. Read carefully, *Our Man in Havana* is a far from comforting novel.

V

In *Travels with My Aunt* (1969), the tension between the interior and comic narratives greatly increases. The plot centres on the opposition between Henry Pulling and his Aunt Augusta; Henry, with his dahlias and regular, suburban life, is like Razumov, 'as lonely in the world as a man swimming in the deep sea' (*Under Western Eyes* 61), while Augusta embodies what Mikhail Bakhtin terms the 'carnivalesque', the 'peculiar culture of the marketplace and of folk laughter with all its wealth of manifestations' (Bakhtin, *Rabelais* 4). Augusta stands for everything that is in conflict with Henry's English middle-class suburban culture, just as the carnivalesque 'opposed the official and serious tone of medieval ecclesiastical and feudal culture' (*Rabelais* 4).

Bakhtin goes on to argue that the 'carnivalesque' is fundamentally a religious impulse, in that 'the serious and the comic aspects of the world and of the deity were equally sacred' (*Rabelais* 6). In these terms, Greene now brings his preference for the primitive and the vulgar[2] together with the Catholic interior narrative to create a comic version of Razumov's story of psychological isolation. Bakhtin describes the Renaissance view of the body as 'a ... finished product ... isolated, alone, fenced off from all other bodies' (*Rabelais* 29), a view towards which carnival is 'hostile' (*Rabelais* 11). In the same way, Henry feels himself to be completed and self-contained. Augusta, on the other hand, embodies what Bakhtin describes as the 'material bodily principle in grotesque realism ... in its all-popular festive and utopian aspect' (*Rabelais* 19). She dramatises the idea that 'all that is bodily becomes grandiose, exaggerated, immeasurable ... [an] exaggeration [which] has a primitive, assertive character' (*Rabelais* 19). Augusta's function is that of Bakhtin's 'carnival-grotesque' form, 'to consecrate inventive freedom ... to liberate from the prevailing point of view of the world, from conventions and established truths, from clichés, from all that is humdrum and universally accepted' (*Rabelais* 34). A carnivalesque guide for Henry, she embodies both age and fertility, recalling W. B. Yeats's Crazy Jane character as well as one of the 'figurines of [laughing] pregnant hags' described by Bakhtin (*Rabelais* 25).

Henry's re-joining the ranks of humanity depends on his fully realising an identity with Augusta's carnivalesque world and discovering 'for the first time in [himself] a streak of anarchy' (*Travels with My Aunt* 52). At Brighton, he feels 'a sense of fear and exhilaration too' at finding himself, like Razumov, on the frontier of a phantasmagoric psychic landscape which 'was not the simple life which [he] had known at the bank, where [he] could judge a client's character by his credits and debits' (49). His process of identification culminates in an interesting variation on the hermeneutic detection motif frequently used by Conrad and Greene, in his deduction from her photograph as a younger woman that she is pregnant with him – that she is not in fact his aunt but his mother.

In this way, Greene plays a comic drama far more exuberant than anything by Conrad against the prototypical interior narrative of faith and betrayal drawn from the masterplot. Henry is the 'haunted' figure; abandoned in the spiritually bankrupt surroundings of suburban London after quarrelling with Augusta, he cannot settle back into his prior 'completed' mode of existence. It seems to him that his aunt 'had come into [his] life only to disturb it' (163); having 'lost the taste for dahlias' (163), he finds himself looking at his old life 'with an ironic eye, as though [he] had borrowed [her] vision' (167). Subsequently, Henry falls into a quieter, more 'English' version of Razumov's despair, feeling 'the sad impression that [his] aunt might be dead and the most interesting part of [his] life might be over' (182).

In the background of this psychological detective story, the Catholic interior narrative reappears in a greatly altered form. Augusta is a Catholic agnostic who 'just [doesn't] believe in all the things [Catholics] believe in' (151); however, the fundamental thrust of her hedonism is paradoxically religious in its nature – a *memento mori* rather than an urge towards *carpe diem*. The shadow of death throughout *Travels with My Aunt* emphasises that Bakhtin's 'grotesque image' includes 'both poles of transformation, the old and the new, the dying and the procreating, the beginning and the end of metamorphosis' (*Rabelais* 24). For Augusta, this constant threat of death paradoxically makes life worth living; as she tells Henry, 'if you live with us, you won't be edging day by day across to any last wall. The wall will find you of its own accord without your help, and every day will seem to you a kind of victory' (*Travels with My Aunt* 225). Of Sophia Antonovna's alternatives between burning and rotting in *Under Western Eyes* (248), Augusta chooses for herself the former and saves Henry from the latter.

Travels with My Aunt embodies contrasting and conflicting qualities which it barely attempts to reconcile. The picaresque structure of the fiction conveys a celebration of the unformed and unfinished, creating an episodic series of adventures along which are strung the journeys Henry makes with his aunt, as well as the narratives she relates to him. In this way, the apparently fragmented narrative structure embodies the carnivalesque urges of the novel's theme. Greene corroborates this in his declaration that, writing the novel, he 'had no idea what was going to happen to Henry or Augusta next' and felt 'like a rider who has dropped the reins and left the direction to his horse or like a dreamer who watches his dream unfold without power to alter its course' (*Ways of Escape* 287).

In this spirit, Greene playfully inscribes self-referential allusions to genre within the fiction itself. Henry's and Augusta's conflicting aesthetic tastes dramatise a conflict between the 'popular' and 'great' traditions. Rejecting his aunt's taste for detective stories, Henry thinks that 'it was in the Victorian age that English poetry and fiction reached the highest level' (141). Confining himself to Thackeray and the Waverley novels, he believes that 'Too many books by too many authors can be confusing, like too many shirts and suits' (43). He prefers what Bakhtin describes as the 'completed' form of art, popular since the Renaissance, the 'classic canon [which] we still live according to' (*Rabelais* 29). Augusta, however, has a taste for something that 'moves a great deal quicker and [with] fewer descriptions [than *Rob Roy*]' (130); she thinks that 'there were occasions when Shakespeare was a very bad author indeed', with his 'meaningless generations' (109). In the realm of the fine arts too, her room is full of Venetian glassware which Henry thinks 'exaggerated and not in the best of taste' (19). In a vein of macabre humour, she rejects the classical sculpture of the Louvre, explaining that she doesn't like '[a]ll those naked women with bits missing', because she 'once knew a girl who was chopped up that way between the Gare du Nord and Calais Maritime' (89). Aesthetically illiterate in terms of accepted authority, Greene's raffish muse, as one critic has called Augusta,[3] deliberately flouts the conventions of taste in order to open them up to a wider, more humanitarian view. In both content and form, the novel's iconoclasm embodies the tendency towards 'opening up' at work in Greene's later fiction, a tendency he quite consciously cultivated, writing the novel on 'blank sheets of foolscap', having 'abandoned the single-lined variety' as 'a symbol of [his] newfound-freedom' (*Ways of Escape* 287).

At the level of genre and theme, then, *Travels with My Aunt* introduces an exuberantly carnivalesque quality into the Conradian masterplot. Henry's first-person narrative approximates the Conradian search for the 'other' or 'secret sharer', while Augusta's embrace of the primitive and vital comically reverses the 'horror' usually associated with the 'heart of darkness'. With her pot-smoking black lover as a foil to Kurtz's exotic savage woman, she transforms Conrad's 'abomination' into her own celebratory figure of carnival. Although like Kurtz she is 'cosmopolitan' (*Travels with*

My Aunt 12), she retains her ties with humanity, unlike Greene's earlier, sanctified sinners; Greene in fact celebrates her anarchic urge to '[kick herself] loose of the earth' (*Heart of Darkness* 65). However, there is an implicit qualification here, a final suggestion of doubt introduced to the novel, recalling the way Conrad makes us read between the lines to discover the 'truth' about Marlow. It is an uncomfortable moment when Visconti's henchman's murder of Augusta's rejected lover shows how destructive her passions can eventually prove. The comic and religious demands of the narrative make dangerous demands upon interiority in this novel, forcing us to re-evaluate Henry's closing Browningesque affirmation that 'God's in his heaven – / All's right with the world!' (265).

VI

In his later fiction, Greene introduces so many different variations on the masterplot that the explicit presence of Conrad becomes increasingly less discernible. In spite of this, the concept of a generic infrastructure still provides a useful perspective through which to examine the variations upon Conrad which he introduces in his last novels. An important development in this respect takes place in the many 'post-modernist' or 'magic–realist' novels he read during the sixties, fictions with a marked quality of self-conscious gamesmanship which fuse the mythical with the realistic. In a monthly list of books he kept during 1961, Greene recorded Muriel Spark's *Voices at Play* and *The Prime of Miss Jean Brodie*, followed in 1962 by Gunter Grass's *The Tin Drum*, and in 1963 by Beckett's *Malone Dies* and Kurt Vonnegut's *Cat's Cradle*. In 1967, he read Flann O'Brien's *At Swim-Two-Birds*, and in 1969 Nabokov's *Speak Memory* and Kundera's *The Joker* ('Appointment Books' 1961–9).

It is not surprising, then, that Greene's fictions during this period increasingly foreground comic fable and allegory. *Loser Takes All* (1955) adapts the monological hagiography of *The End of the Affair* into a self-consciously ludic fable to become a version of Samuel Beckett's recently produced *Waiting for Godot* (*Waiting for the Gom* perhaps?). Similarly, *Our Man in Havana* and *Travels with My Aunt* share a post-modernist tendency self-referentially to manipulate the fact that they are fictions, through making the act of storytelling part of the story itself. This culminates in *Monsignor Quixote* (1982), which John F. Desmond argues 'challenges the distinctions between fact and fiction', in order '[to explore] the theological meaning of the real' (Desmond 67), converging 'towards a mystery . . . rooted in the belief in Christ's Incarnation and the Resurrection of the body' (70). From this, Desmond concludes, 'the evolutionary vision of love in the world becomes the very substance – in theme, form, and dynamic development – of the novel's meaning' (61).

The tension between fact and fiction provides a major structuring device in *Monsignor Quixote*. In *The Dialogic Imagination* (1981), Mikhail Bakhtin describes the openness of the novel form as an 'endless multitude of dialogic confrontations, which do not and cannot resolve [novelistic dialogue]' (Bakhtin, *Dialogic* 365). These dialogic confrontations function in *Monsignor Quixote* at the levels of character, plot and genre. A continuing conversation between the communist ex-mayor Sancho's Marxist materialism and Father Quixote's Catholicism structures the novel; this provides a cross-fertilisation of ideas between the two ideologies, in the course of which each character comes to doubt the literal form of his own belief, yet begins to grasp the sense of an interplay, a possible common ground where both can meet.

Robert M. Polhemus's study of 'the underlying, original ties between religious and comic celebration' (Polhemus 3) argues for 'the validity of equating prayer and laughter' in fiction, which 'perform[s], in secular and hypothetical fashion, many of the conventional religious functions of the old 'divine comedy'; these are 'to defend culture by authoritative moral sanction against selfish and destructive behaviour', to 'let loose wrathful indignation and hostility in good conscience' and 'to lift [people] out of themselves and free the spirit' (4–5). In the context of Victorian fiction, Polhemus argues that consciously or not, 'comic novelists are trying by means of wit, humor, and satire to fulfil at one time or another all these missions of religious faith' (5). The comic sense 'can cause a sensation of wholeness and integrity of being', he concludes, for 'when we are in a festive mood and laughing, we seem to go out of our normally anxious reflective selves into a different phase of being'; in this way, 'the act of laughter . . . could be seen and felt as a natural intrusion of the miraculous into the self – as, that is, a religious experience' (7–8).

The comic thematic and generic dialogues embody this festive mood of religious mirth in *Monsignor Quixote*. Ever since Querry learnt to laugh in *A Burnt-Out Case* (1960), Greene's treatment of Catholicism has emphasised comic modes of celebration, as opposed to the more romantic admiration of the 'sanctified sinner'. Where Greene once used Catholicism in order to deviate from the Conradian protagonist caught up in a dilemma of faith and betrayal, he now creates comic variations upon this haunted figure. The tensions between these genres celebrate the Bakhtinian qualities of openness and doubt, rather than dramatising a Conradian deadlock between individual and social values.

Quixote's and Sancho's debates, which cover topics as diverse as Torquemada, Stalin, Marx's *Das Kapital* and the Books of *Numbers* and *Deuteronomy*, emphasise the positive and benevolent qualities of doubt. Father Quixote thinks that 'It's odd . . . how sharing a sense of doubt can bring men together perhaps even more than sharing a faith' (59), later telling Sancho: 'Doubt is not treachery as you Communists seem to think. Doubt is human' (205). The dramatisation of scepticism – Quixote's feeling of 'a shadow, the shadow of disbelief haunting [his] belief' (197) – develops the Catholic interior narrative of the man haunted by God into a comic pursuit whereby Father Quixote and Sancho 'hound' each other with their conflicting philosophies and end by interchanging some qualities. Father Quixote concedes that *The Communist Manifesto* is 'the work of a . . . man as good as [the Mayor is] – and just as mistaken' (126), while Sancho, having submitted to receiving communion from the delirious Father Quixote in the final surreal episode in the Trappist monastery, learns that 'the hate of . . . even a man like Franco . . . dies with his death and yet love . . . seemed now to live and grow in spite of the final separation and the final silence' (256).

A major factor behind Greene's increasing sense of the connections between faith and doubt is his growing 'distrust of theology', which he thinks was encouraged by his reading of Unamuno's book *A Tragic Sense of Life* (1931) (*Ways of Escape* 258). The incongruity between Father Quixote's radical simplicity and the church's overbearing and repressive insistence on dogma is comically intensified by Quixote's insouciant yet earnest curiosity. Recalling the account of Curran, 'the doggies' preacher' in *Travels with My Aunt* (1969), Father Quixote delicately questions the Bishop of Motopo regarding the souls of animals in order to discover if his car, Rocinante, might have one too, for he is rather worried as to whether it is heretical to pray to God for it (19). This '[revelation of] the perplexing mystery of spirit within animate and inanimate creation', as Desmond puts it (70), both affirms and satirises Greene's theological plot. In a similar fashion, Quixote demonstrates the concept of the

Trinity to Sancho with three bottles of wine: 'There you have God the Father and God the Son and there in the half bottle, God the Holy Ghost. Same substance, same birth. They're inseparable. Whoever partakes of one partakes of all three' (52).

The union of interior and comic narratives is radically open-ended; the only constant in the novel is the continual questioning. Even the comic spirit itself is comically called into question by Quixote's mortification when he realises that he has disrespectfully represented the Holy Ghost with only half a bottle: 'I have been guilty of heresy . . . I think – perhaps – I am unworthy to be a priest' (53). Forever denying us a point of rest, the fiction embodies the 'hopping', by which, in Quixote's extemporisation upon St Francis de Sales, we may 'recognise love' (246). Love is constant only because of its intrinsically dynamic and unpredictable quality, which is expressed in Sancho's final questions: 'for how long, he wondered with a kind of fear, was it possible for that love of his to continue? And to what end?' (256).

Mark A. Wollaeger comments that 'Rather than simply offering commentary on skepticism . . . the narrative, descriptive, and generic modes of Conrad's fiction *enact* the operations of skepticism as a perpetual assessment of our constructions of the world' (xvii). In *Monsignor Quixote*, Greene too has arrived at a form of 'embodied scepticism' through his own deviating comic and Catholic routes. *Monsignor Quixote* embodies a radical scepticism regarding the institutional forms of both Marxism and Catholicism, which are allowed to battle it out in the form of Father Quixote's and Sancho's arguments. By the end of *Monsignor Quixote*, both faiths in their official, dogmatic form have been subverted and exposed to doubt, allowing the radical core of each system of belief to engage with the other in the friendship of the two men, a friendship which enacts continuity rather than closural stasis.

The conflict between the serious and the absurd and the tension between fact and fiction in *Monsignor Quixote* find an explicit intertext in Cervantes's *Don Quixote*, which was also an important source for Conrad himself. Discussing Conrad's relation to *Don Quixote* in the autobiographies, *A Personal Record* and *The Mirror of the Sea*, Daphna Erdinast-Vulcan suggests that Conrad's invocation of Cervantes is 'ambiguous', in that *Don Quixote* 'can be viewed either as a celebration of Romanticism, an assertion of the power of imagination and of inward vision over external reality, or as a corrosive attack on the futile idealism of the chivalric tradition' (226). Greene, on the other hand, comes to Cervantes largely through his reading of Miguel de Unamuno. Although he testifies to having read Unamuno's *The Life and Death of Don Quixote* (1927) in his early career 'with no particular interest' (*Ways of Escape* 258), he thinks that 'perhaps [it] had continued to work its way through the cellars of the unconscious', for 'at the end of a long journey [he] found [him]self . . . in that tragi-comic region of La Mancha', where in 1983 he 'expect[ed] to stay' (*Ways* 258–9). It seems likely that Greene reached this Christian embodiment of Cervantes's novel through Unamuno's identification in *The Life and Death of Don Quixote* of Cervantes's latent Christian subtexts. Unamuno portrays Don Quixote as having 'lost [his wits], to leave us an eternal example of spiritual generosity', while 'on the altar of his people he made the greatest of sacrifices, that of his reason', believing 'to be truth what is only beauty . . . so that he decided to put into effect what his folly revealed to him' (Unamuno, *Life* 9).

What Greene does in *Monsignor Quixote* is to combine the sense of ambiguity which Conrad finds in Cervantes's novel with the latent Christianity identified by Unamuno. *Monsignor Quixote* paradoxically celebrates faith, while simultaneously satirising its institutionalised forms; however, it also mocks the romantic expressions of idealism which seek to do battle with the establishment, in this way consciously celebrating the ongoing and dynamic quality of a doubting faith. This is especially clear towards the end of the novel, when the narrative begins to modulate into heroic romance. Treading a very thin line between this genre and farce, Quixote's confrontation of the Mexicans and their mercenary travesty of the religious procession implicitly invokes Christ's expulsion of the moneychangers from the Temple, yet also has the ludicrous qualities of Cervantes's burlesque on knightly idealism. The fusion between the sublime and the ridiculous is brought to light by Father Quixote himself, who tells Sancho: 'We are going into battle . . . I need my armour. Even if it is as absurd as Mambrino's helmet' (227).

In *Monsignor Quixote*, then, Conrad and Greene find a final meeting point in one of Europe's earliest 'dialogical' novels, *Don Quixote*. Bakhtin sees Cervantes's work as centrally important in the development of the novel as a genre. In this and 'other great seminal works', he argues, the 'authentic double-voiced novelistic images fully ripen . . . and become the unique thing they ultimately are' (*Dialogic* 409). Polhemus thinks that Cervantes's *Don Quixote* 'makes us respect the pluralism of life and the shifting nature of appearance and reality' (Polhemus 15); the same is true of Greene's *Monsignor Quixote,* where doubt and belief work together in a dynamic interchange. This last major novel adapts Greene's earlier, more abstractly theological vision into a version of Polhemus's 'comic faith', the 'tacit belief that the world is both funny and potentially good' (3), leaving us to contemplate a 'heart of darkness' which is not the spiritual nihilism of modern civilisation, as in Conrad, but what Greene called the profound '*mystery* . . . which can't be destroyed even by the Church' ('Confessions' 34). After Quixote's death, the mayor is denied his attempt to flee from his partial belief 'in a God' into his 'prefer[ence for] Marx to mystery' (254); we leave him in a state of disturbance which has grown out of his friendship and conversations with Father Quixote. This 'disturbance' affirms Greene's vision of the regenerating possibilities of faith through doubt, reflecting the larger interchange between the interior and political narratives in *Monsignor Quixote* which embodies his hope for a mutual *rapprochement* between Catholicism and Marxism.

Epilogue

If *Monsignor Quixote* represents an 'open' conclusion to Greene's long dialogue with Conrad, his final novel, *The Captain and the Enemy* (1988), returns to a kind of narrative quiescence, a coming to rest in a more or less unmodified version of the Conradian masterplot which recapitulates the secular interior narrative of *Under Western Eyes*. The book begins as a comic, quasi-religious allegory, with the Captain winning the narrator–protagonist Jim from his father, nicknamed 'the Devil', in a game of Backgammon; later, however, it abandons this potential dialogue between a religious interior plot and a political one to become a more purely Conradian version of the narrative of political commitment and betrayal.

The Captain and the Enemy also attempts to emulate *Under Western Eyes* in accounting for its narrative origins, with Jim continuing the autobiography he had begun in the first part of the book as 'a journal' in the second and third parts. The hermeneutic search seems all too familiar. Like Marlow, Jim seems to tell his tale in a frustrated attempt to understand his 'exact position in life' through his mysterious counterpart the Captain (*Captain* 36). '[Continuing] to write in order to turn the question [of the Captain] over and over without any hope of an answer' (109), he attempts to understand a committed person who has *not* kicked himself loose of the earth.

At first, the Captain appears as a kind of creator figure who, like Christ with his disciples, gives Jim a 'free choice' of whether to accompany him or return to school. Taking up a central theme of *Monsignor Quixote* (1982), he provides an essential element of mystery in Jim's childhood. Jim characterises him as 'an eternal question mark never to be answered, like the existence of God' (109); with him, '[t]he word "wonder" seemed to come only too often into [his] mind' (92). However, Jim's failure to understand 'the complexity of human love' (38), which the Captain apparently embodies, dooms his narrative quest to understand his past. Jim sees human affection in terms of the Conradian image of disease; the Captain's and his foster-mother Lisa's 'small timorous kiss on either cheek' suggests to him that 'even that gesture was something which could be dangerous to the loved one, like an infection' (59).

Jim constantly questions the nature of love from the day when, puzzled by the film *King Kong*, he asks the Captain why the ape doesn't drop the girl; he cannot, however, understand the Captain's answer: 'He loves her, boy. Can't you understand that – he loves her?' (44). While there is 'no lack of the word in [his] own love letters', he finds, on reading the Captain's correspondence with Lisa, that he is 'entering a foreign land where the language was totally strange' (90). He himself feels no grief over Lisa's death (132) and is 'astonished' to find in the end that 'there had been, after all, some kind of love between [her and the Captain]' (168).

What detracts from the narrative impetus, however, is that the 'mystery' of love constructed around the Captain is never fully realised within this novel, as it is in *Monsignor Quixote*. We are never told enough about the Captain to appreciate the weightiness of his role, which is stated rather than demonstrated; his character is drawn only in outline and his status as a committed person emerges only towards the end in his undercover political work for the Sandinistas. In this way, the political narrative seems to become detached once more from interiority at the end of Greene's career. Beginning with his concealment from the Captain that Lisa is dead, Jim grows increasingly enmeshed in a network of deception which takes on more and more a political dimension. To establish himself safely 'in this strange world' (127), he becomes involved with Quigley, a CIA agent who would like to use the scandal of the Captain's missions for the Sandinistas to 'kill the Canal Treaty' (164). Jim's exasperated betrayal of the Captain to Quigley is very like Razumov's of Haldin. Aware that he 'wasn't trusted' and 'infuriated . . . all the more because [he knew] very well that [he] wasn't trustworthy' (150), he projects his guilt onto the Captain; later, however, he comes to feel remorse and realises that he has 'never understood the nature of love' (179). However, the novel fails to make clear why Jim *should* in fact love this very distant father-figure. What had seemed to promise a complex generic fusion, a 'mysterious' interplay between romantic and religious interiority and politics, becomes whittled down to a more familiar narrative of commitment and betrayal within the context of revolution.

The Captain and the Enemy, however, is an exception in Greene's later works, which, as we have seen, succeed in integrating the sub-genres of the Conradian masterplot in terms of a complex series of original variations. In the other novels of his mature phase, the more Conradian Greene becomes, the more Greenean he paradoxically seems. In the eighteenth century, Richard Steele suggested that originality is analogous to 'that kind of double delight' we have in looking at 'the children of a beautiful couple, where the eye is not more charmed with the symmetry of the parts than the mind by observing the resemblance' (Bate 40). In this way, Greene's relation to Conrad is similar to the mature offspring's to his parent, a connection characterised by both affinity and mutual independence.

It is above all the contrasting, polyphonic interaction of the different narrative genres which energises Greene's interrogation of individual and political problems of commitment. This dialogical interplay of genres, which we have discussed in terms of Mikhail Bakhtin's theory of the novel, is pertinent to the study of literature and critical theory today, as well as to the larger questions of culture which these fields have come to embody. Gary Saul Morson argues that contemporary literary theory manifests an unfortunate monological tendency, while the work of Bakhtin, by contrast, suggests the need for openness and the acceptance of an 'unfinished' epistemological mode. Greene's and Conrad's fiction enacts this openness and dynamic interplay, especially between narratives of individual, private experience and plots which situate the subject within a larger political context. Their major work avoids exclusive insistence upon a rigid conception of one generic component, instead dramatising the interaction of contrasting literary forms and different spheres of human endeavour. At a time when the practice of criticism is becoming excessively historicised and ideologised, Greene's and Conrad's narrative counterpointing of private interiority with political exteriority serves to remind us that the engagement with ideology cannot make sense unless it stems from individual lives, while at the same time individual modes of experience cannot become meaningful unless viewed within a wider critique of culture.

Greene's and Conrad's developing intertextuality itself embodies this dynamic interplay. Greene's Conradian epigraph to *The Human Factor* points to the necessary process of thematic and generic 'rupture': 'He who forms a tie is lost. The germ of corruption has already entered into his soul.' Embodying the proposition that corruption and integrity are intrinsically interdependent, this 'germ of corruption' may stand as a metaphor for Greene's and Conrad's intertextuality, as well as for their common themes of faith and betrayal. A paradoxical Latin epitaph reads: 'Baths, wines, love corrupt our bodies / But baths, wines, love make life worth living' (Kinchin Smith 55); similarly, the 'germ of corruption' which takes root in Greene's early fiction as Conrad's 'disastrous influence' produces a complex affinity between two writers engaged in similar generic and thematic endeavours. This affinity flourishes, not in anxiety, but in Greene's inspired, lifelong development of the Conradian masterplot.

Notes

Notes to the Introduction

1. Quoted in Norman Sherry, *The Life of Graham Greene*, vol. 1 (London: Cape, 1989). Greene's poem was published in *Weekly Westminster*, 30 September 1922, and the letter to Vivien Dayrell is dated January 1926.
2. Ford Madox Ford was one of the earliest commentators to identify Conrad's use of popular genres, noting in 1937 that *The Secret Agent* 'is one of the best – and certainly the most significant – detective stories ever written' (Ford, *Portraits* 89). Similarly, Philip Stratford notes that 'Clearly it is the adventure story that is in [Greene's] blood, and Conrad and Stevenson are, at the least, his literary godparents. The exotic setting, the taste for the grotesque which borders sometimes on the absurd, the heightened coloring, the loose-ranging action, the high density of incident – all these are shared characteristics' (Stratford 15). Greene, however, was conceived of preponderantly as a 'Catholic' writer for many years until such critics as David Lodge began to defend his use of melodrama as 'handled with a sophisticated and very personal sense of values in order to displace the usual distribution of sympathy and empathy' (Lodge 13).
3. Frederick Benjamin Korn argues in his 1973 dissertation, 'Condemned to Consequences', that Conrad's and Greene's 'shared technique and world view suggest . . . a prototype novel' which depicts 'any moral action' as leading 'to disparate consequences'; this prototype offers 'certain moral constants [which] elevate the main character to an heroic stature even though the effects of his heroism are often deleterious' (Korn 2–5). Similarly, Ronald Bryden, in his article 'Graham Greene, Alas', suggests that Greene's 'notion of duty is Conradian'; both authors, he thinks, depict mostly in a stoic form 'the idea of serving without vanity earthly ends which prove vain' (Bryden, 'Alas' 442). Finally, Jeffrey Meyers contributes a brief discussion in 'Conrad's Influence on Modern Writers' (1990), suggesting that 'the genre and themes of *The Secret Agent* were continued in . . . *It's a Battlefield* (1934), *A Gun For Sale* (1936), and *The Confidential Agent* (1939)' (Meyers 195). Meyers also discusses *Journey without Maps* as 'both an exorcism and a journey into self', like *Heart of Darkness* and compares *Victory* and *A Burnt-Out Case* (Meyers 195–6).
4. Popular literature, Rabinowitz continues, demands different 'rules of notice' from serious literature, the 'implicit rules, shared by readers and writers alike, that give priority to certain kinds of details, and that thus help us to sort out the figure from the ground by making a hierarchy of importance' (Rabinowitz 44). In popular literature, 'attention to textual nuances is greatly influenced by the speed with which

we read' (185). Because 'popular tales are more plot-oriented, psychological novels more character-oriented, in reading psychological novels, we tend to stress rules of signification' (185), those rules 'that tell us how to recast or symbolise or draw significance from the elements that the first set of rules has brought to our attention' (44). In popular literature, he concludes, 'we expect less complex, less ironic plot patterns, whereas in serious art we look for more elaborate forms of coherence and tend to interpret inconsistencies as ironies rather than flaws' (186).

5. In his article 'Modernism and What Happened to It' (1987), Kenner suggests that T. S. Eliot's 'taking a popular form and making of it something rich and strange' can illuminate 'the great Modernist enterprise as a whole' (Kenner 109).
6. Bloom summarises his six stages of influences as follows: in '*Clinamen*', which he identifies as 'poetic misreading or misprision', a poet 'swerves away from his precursor.... This appears as a corrective movement in his own poem, which implies that the precursor poem went accurately up to a certain point, but then should have swerved, precisely in the direction that the new poem moves ...'. In '*Tessera*', which means 'completion and antithesis', he 'antithetically "completes" his precursor, by so reading the parent poem as to retain its terms but to mean them in another sense, as though the precursor had failed to go far enough'. Bloom defines '*Kenosis*' as 'a movement towards discontinuity with the precursor', while in '*Daemonisation*', the later poet 'opens himself to what he believes to be a power in the parent-poem that does not belong to the parent proper, but to a range of being just beyond that precursor'. In '*Askesis*', which is 'a movement of self-purgation', the 'later poet ... yields up part of his own human and imaginative endowment, so as to separate himself from others, including the precursor', and in the final stage of '*Apophrades*', which Bloom translates as 'the return of the dead', the poet 'holds his own poem so open again to the precursor's work that at first we might believe that the wheel has come full circle, and that we are back in the later author's flooded apprenticeship'. The difference here is that 'the poem is now *held* open to the precursor, where once it *was* open, and the uncanny effect is that the new poem's achievement makes it seem to us, not as though the precursor were writing it, but as though the later poet had written the precursor's characteristic work' (Bloom 15–16).

Notes to Chapter 1: 'The Proper Formula'

1. For a discussion of Fluck and Rabinowitz, see pp. 2–3.
2. The uneasy conflict within Conrad between the exterior emphasis of adventure fiction and the interior scrutiny of character in the psychological novel can perhaps be traced biographically and culturally to his Polish heritage. Cedric Watts thinks that 'One of Conrad's great motives in his fiction was a resolution of the quarrel between the

Korzeniowski and the Bobrowski temperaments', the impulsive, externally orientated adventurer against the more inward-looking, sceptical personality (Watts, *Life* 33). Andrzej Busza translates this into the terms of Conrad's Polish literary background, suggesting that Apollo Korzeniowski's 'romanticism' and Tadeusz Bobrowski's 'profound wisdom' correspond closely with the two dominant literary movements in nineteenth-century Polish literature: romanticism and positivism' (Busza 161).

3. The theme of betrayal in Conrad is thoroughly discussed by Jackson W. Heimer, who suggests that 'betrayal and its aftermath fall into two definite, yet related patterns: the major . . . pattern – act, confession, attempted redemption and punishment – and the minor pattern – isolation, involvement, and isolation' (Heimer 30–1). Similarly, Stephen Land describes the typical Conrad plot as one where the hero initially exerts his will, but then, 'unable to achieve his aims through his initial efforts, accepts a *compromise* frequently entailing some form of betrayal or dereliction of duty' (Land 2). Bernard Meyer relates the 'numerous and varied patterns of those themes of rescue and betrayal' (Meyer 85) in psychoanalytic terms to Conrad's early childhood, while Andrzej Busza notes that 'the word *sdrada* ("betrayal") haunts the pages of Polish Romantic literature'. Because of its emergence 'at a time when Poland was under foreign domination . . . subversive action . . . must of necessity take the form of underground activity. The basis of all secret organisations is mutual trust. Hence, the most dreaded enemy is the traitor' (Busza 205).
4. For a discussion of *The Third Man* see pp. 82–7.
5. For a brief discussion of Brooks's narrative theory, in so far as it relates to the present study, see pp. 7–8.
6. See p. 12.
7. Conrad wrote this in a letter to Garnett which is cited in Thorburn (171n3).
8. In his study of *Nostromo*, Cedric Watts decisively refutes Fredric Jameson's claim that the novel embodies 'the classic "Anglo" picture of a Latin "race," lazy, shiftless, and the like, to which political order and economic progress must be "brought" from the outside' (Jameson 270). Watts comments that Jameson overlooks one consistent feature of Conrad's novels and tales: 'outsiders who seek to impose order on a foreign area usually make matters worse rather than better' (Nostromo, ed. Watts, 101). Watts also successfully discredits Edward Said's view that Conrad 'writes as a man in whom a *Western* view of the non-Western world is so deeply ingrained that it blinds him to other histories, other cultures, other aspirations' ('Under Gringo Eyes' 70). Watts counters: 'Far from suggesting that Costaguana could never have had "a meaningful existence of its own," the novel emphasises that the known history of Costaguana is one of recurrent invasion, conquest and exploitation; it is the victors, not the victims, who tend to be the historians of any region. Conrad emphasises that the reign of the new imperialists is just one phase in that long process of imposition' (102).

9. In his article 'Imperialism, Marxism, Conrad: A Political Reading of *Victory*' (1989), Terry Collits notes the political dimensions of *Victory*, in contrast to earlier, archetypal readings in terms of the Eden myth.
10. I am grateful to Eloise Hay for suggesting this method of reading the end of *Victory*.
11. Collits goes on to argue that *Victory* 'marks the end of the old colonial novel and, in those intriguing glimpses into that "other" world of Wang, anticipates the new grounds for English-language fiction in a "post-colonial" world' (Collits 320).

Notes to Chapter 2: 'Writing off the Elaborate Scaffolding'

1. Jerome Buckley, in *Season of Youth* (1974), notes that the typical hero of a bildungsroman undergoes 'at least two love affairs or sexual encounters, one debasing, one exalting [demanding] that . . . [he] re-appraise his values' (Buckley 17).
2. Cedric Watts has suggested to me that Greene often quite self-consciously and mischievously slips Conrad's names into his text; there is Conrad Drover in *It's a Battlefield*; Kurtz in *The Name of Action* and *The Third Man*. One thinks also of Carleon Anthony in *Chance* and Carlyon in *The Man Within* – both poets. Again, Greene gives the names of Conrad's villains Brown and Jones to two central figures in *The Comedians*, displacing melodrama into non-committal banality, on the one hand, and into quixotic chivalry, on the other.
3. The running down of Conrad by a car, Higdon thinks, together with the reprieve of his brother Jim for the killing of a policeman, seems 'to dramatise Greene's renunciation of a style, an interpretative intelligence, and a detached way of looking at life, while retaining the trapped, betrayed, suffering character isolated in a world either operating irrationally or intentionally according to a design beyond the individual's comprehension' (Higdon 33).
4. I am grateful to the Harry Ransom Humanities Research Center at the University of Austin, Texas, for allowing me to inspect Greene's 'Diaries', which he kept between 1932 and 1933.
5. Ivan Melada, in his article 'Graham Greene and the Munitions Makers: The Historical Context of *A Gun for Sale*', investigates the contemporary atmosphere of conspiracy theories regarding the armaments industry, in which 'the public was exposed . . . to a plethora of information revealing that the munitions maker would willingly play the midwife to calamity at the expense not only of his fellow man but also of his fellow countryman. . . . Publishing *A Gun for Sale* the year after the enquiry of a royal commission into the armaments industry, Greene out-Herods Herod. . . . [Sir Marcus's] deed surpasses anything that the critics of the private armaments firms could come up with in the way of evidence against the merchant of death in the flesh' (Melader 311).

6. For a brief discussion of Brooks's narrative theory in so far as it relates to the present study, see pp. 7–8.
7. W. H. Auden writes in 'The Guilty Vicarage' that murder in a detective story occurs in a society where there is no need for the law, no contradiction between the aesthetic individual and the ethical universal, and where murder, therefore, is the unheard-of act which precipitates a crisis. . . . The law becomes a reality and for a time all must live in its shadow, till the fallen one is identified. With his arrest, innocence is restored, and the law retires forever' (Auden 150).
8. For a discussion of Rabinowitz's narrative theory, see p. 3.
9. John Atkins misses the point when he suggests that 'the reflection [of the epigraphs] is dream, not reality, and it is in keeping with the story's character that it should be associated with the innocent work of a Victorian lady-novelist' (Atkins 128).
10. In 'The Typology of Detective Fiction', Todorov applies the Russian Formalists' distinction between the fable (story) and the subject (plot) of a narrative to detective fiction: 'At the base of the whodunnit we find a duality . . . not one but two stories: the story of the crime and the story of the investigation. In their purest form, these stories have no point in common' (Todorov 44).
11. Greene writes in his introduction to *The Third Man* that the novel, 'though never intended for publication, had to start as a story before those apparently interminable transformations from one treatment to another . . . these treatments Carol Reed and I worked closely together. . . . The film . . . is better than the story because it is in this case the finished state of the story' (*Third Man* 9–10).
12. Bruffee excludes Calloway, the narrator of *The Third Man* novella, from the category of 'observer–hero' because unlike Marlow he 'is not affected by the telling of the tale [and] is not a victim of the obsessive relationship of hero-worshipper to hero that is essential to elegiac romance' (Bruffee 29). However, this does not apply to his substitute, Holly, in the film version.
13. The sequence recalls a similar one in Fritz Lang's *Spies*, where we see two fingerprints and a photograph of the suspects, with a magnifying glass being brought down over the prints.
14. In the preface of *The Third Man*, Greene relates that he jettisoned this character from the screenplay because he bore 'certain echoes of the gentle genius of Mr E. M. Forster' (10).
15. In his review of *Fury*, Greene writes that it 'is . . . the only film I know to which I have wanted to attach the epithet of "great". . . . [It] has allowed no value to slip [and] has conveyed completely by sound and image better than by any other medium the pity and terror of the story' (Greene, *Pleasure* 84).
16. In the introduction to *The Tenth Man*, Greene writes: 'In 1983 a stranger wrote to me from the United States telling me that a story of mine called *The Tenth Man* was being offered for sale by MGM to an American publisher. I didn't take the matter seriously. I thought that I remembered – incorrectly, as it proved – an outline which I had

written towards the end of the war [which] perhaps had covered two pages of typescript' (9).

Notes to Chapter 3: 'A Distant Memory of the Sanctus Bell'

1. Nehrung argues that 'The weight of the secular indignation in *Brighton Rock* makes it more a political novel than an exercise in Jansenism, as many have considered it. . . . Both Pinkie and Rose define themselves against conventional society through their Catholicism, virtually making their religion a subcultural emblem – they wear their conviction of evil like a safety pin in the nose' (Nehrung 239). In this brilliant piece of distortion, Nehrung forces the political dimensions of punk onto a novel with social implications which are heavily obscured by its theological content; a more appropriate text to argue such a case for would have been *A Gun for Sale*. Maria Couto similarly overemphasises the social implications of *Brighton Rock*: 'Greene is less interested in the development of character than in determining in all their complexity the forces that shape life and motivate action. The social sin of injustice and exploitation underlie the "evil" actions of Pinkie. Nowhere does the power of these forces, both socio-economic and spiritual, come alive more vividly' (Couto 58).
2. This is corroborated by Greene's own remarks in Paris in 1950 for the Catholic journal *Dieu Vivant*. Richard Johnstone reports that 'Greene [assured] his interlocutors . . . that . . . Pinkie is indeed saved at the end' (Johnstone 77).
3. Philip Stratford's book *Faith and Fiction: Creative Process in Greene and Mauriac* (1964), provides the seminal comparison of these two writers. Stratford argues that their 'general moral outlook . . . and purpose . . . is so close that their assessment of each other is reflexive and equally well describes what they set out to do in their own novels. . . . Greene perhaps encouraged by Mauriac's example, set out in 1938 to give his characters a supernatural dimension and to do what he could to restore the lost religious sense to the English novel' (Stratford 3).
4. Desmond also notes that 'the Gnostic roots of the lieutenant's materialist philosophy [which overlook ambiguities] are underscored ironically by the asceticism he practices as if to truly involve himself in the physical world would be to risk contamination' (Desmond 62).
5. Marlow says, referring to his encounter with Kurtz: 'It seemed somehow to throw a kind of light on everything about me' (*Heart of Darkness* 11).
6. Urs Bitterli notes that 'A Chance for Mr Lever' is 'reminiscent of Conrad's *Heart of Darkness*, not only in theme, but also in the way the high-flown projects of European overseas traders are portrayed as amazingly unrealistic' (116).
7. Surprisingly, Gwen Boardman finds that 'In *A Burnt-Out Case* the shadow of Conrad is reduced to one detail in Greene's mocking

characterisation of the cynical and "corrupt" newspaperman Montagu Parkinson' (Boardman 137). More substantially, Philip Stratford devotes a long paragraph to *Heart of Darkness* as a 'logical choice' for 'a source-book' for *A Burnt-Out Case*: 'The battered "tin-pot steamboat" ... is Conrad's. Descriptions of the oppressive massive beauty of vegetation are similar. The same kind of mystery hangs about Querry and Kurtz. ... The Congo itself represents much the same thing to both authors – for Conrad, too, it is more "a region of the mind". ... Like Greene, Conrad was interested in recording "the mental changes of individuals on the spot" (Stratford 14). *Heart of Darkness*, Stratford concludes, like *A Burnt-Out Case* 'describes the universal fascination of the savage and the incomprehensible – "the fascination of the abomination." There can be no doubt that Greene read this interpretation with fraternal feeling' (15). Leon Higdon finds Querry to be 'obviously cut from the same material ... as Axel Heyst' in *Victory*. 'It is easy', Higdon argues, 'to discern shadows of Samburan, the unholy trio of Ricardo, Jones, and Pedro, Lena, Wang, and the melodramatic ending in the leper colony, the trio of Father Thomas, Parkinson, and Rycker, Marie, Deo Gratias, and the melodramatic shooting of Querry during a tropical thunderstorm' (Higdon 34). Jeffrey Meyers also compares the novel with *Victory*, finding that 'Greene follows Conrad's ironic plot rather precisely, for both novels concern the flight to a remote tropical retreat by a lonely man who attempts to extinguish all human emotions' (Meyers 195). 'As the outside world breaks into their isolation', Meyers continues, these protagonists 'meet their death and achieve their victory or their cure' (295). Surprisingly, however, he concludes that '*A Burnt-Out Case* is virtually a diluted and derivative version of the greater novel' (196), apparently failing to grasp the totally different texture of Querry's character in the light of the religious theme and the overt response to *Heart of Darkness*.

8. Enrique Riveros-Schaffer points out the differences between Conrad's 'Congo Diary' and Greene's *Congo Journal*: while Conrad represents the 'apprentice-observations of a sailor', Greene deliberately writes a 'source book' for his fiction (86).
9. Towards the end of his life, Greene often described himself as a Catholic agnostic, for example in a 1989 *Observer* interview with John Cornwell (Cornwell 33).
10. For example, in the preface of *The Comedians*: 'Many readers assume ... that an "I" is always the author. So in my time I have been considered the murderer of a friend, the jealous lover of a civil servant's wife, and an obsessive player at roulette' (5).
11. Kermode writes: 'Querry, the famous Catholic architect is a famous Catholic writer thinly disguised. ... Querry more than any other of the heroes is a *poseur*' (Kermode 130–1).

Notes to Chapter 4: 'He Who Forms a Tie'

1. Graham Smith suggests that 'Political currents run in [Greene's] work from an early stage; it is fascinating that they should resurface at the point in his career marked by *The Quiet American*. . . . [Greene] brought the entertainment to its highest level in *The Ministry of Fear* and crowned this stage of his achievement with three novels – *The Power and the Glory*, *The Heart of the Matter* and *The End of the Affair*. It seems reasonable to suggest that something had been worked through during these years' (Graham Smith 129). Ray Snape similarly notes that '[i]n the years which intervened between *England Made Me* and *The Quiet American* (1955) Greene had articulated his religious apprehension of man's condition and he had also found a distinctive voice and a stylistic identity. So he could return to political themes without apeing Conrad or, say, Eliot' ('Political' 73).
2. Inspection of Greene's library, which apparently contains many annotated works, may well lead to the need to revise these conclusions regarding Greene's literary tastes; sadly, however, the collection is not available to scholars at the time of this book going to press.
3. Many critics have noted that Greene's political and religious interests are brought together in this novel. Philip Stratford comments: '*The Quiet American* must be seen as the story of how Fowler is forced out of his initial position of non-commitment, and in this sense the novel closely parallels Bendrix's story in *The End of the Affair*, though the terms of the narrative are political and not "explicitly" religious' (Stratford 310), Miriam Allott examines the novel 'in the context of sophisticated moral analyses of the kind associated with some later nineteenth-century English and American fiction', suggesting that 'it reminds us particularly of James and Conrad [and] gives a fresh focus to themes which Greene explores in his "Catholic" novels' (Allott, 'Moral' 65). Similarly, Georg Gaston comments that 'although war and politics are prominent issues in the novel, they serve to poise the ultimate concern of personal salvation' (Gaston 55).
4. Brian Thomas comments that 'as Fowler's shadow or secret sharer, Pyle ceases to be the phantom embodiment of the protagonist's sense of his own lost innocence and becomes instead the embodiment of his own sense of guilt' (Thomas 48).
5. Maria Couto sees Phuong as accentuating 'the nature of the relationship between the subject-race and the outsider. When they come together as human beings the level of the relationship expresses the political situation: entertainer and entertained, service loyally rendered and affection protectively disposed' (Conto 170).
6. Compare, for example, two comments of Marlow's. He tells us: 'I had plenty of time for meditation and now and then I would give some thought to Kurtz. I wasn't very interested in him. No. Still I was interested to see whether this man who had come out . . . would climb to the top after all' (Heart of Darkness 33). Later he becomes aware that 'exactly what [he] had been looking forward to [was] a talk with Kurtz' (48). He is constantly shifting ground.

7. Erdinast-Vulcan in her *Graham Greene's Childless Fathers* takes the theme of Oedipus further: 'Fowler's complicity in the murder of Pyle – a complicity which is born out of the need to protect the innocents from further bloodshed – is an inversion of the archetypal – biblical – sacrifice of the son . . . which is the ultimate act of submission to God. In the biblical event, however, the actual sacrifice is rejected by Divine intervention . . . Fowler, too, sacrifices the son-figure. He tries to pray for some miracle, some Divine intervention which should prevent Pyle's death. . . . But the miracle does not occur . . . and Fowler is condemned to remain lonely and sterile in the spiritual desert he inhabits' (64).
8. See Chapter 2, note 10.
9. See Chapter 5.
10. Michael Routh notes that this parodically echoes another post-Conradian hero, Hemingway's Robert Jordan (Routh 146), while Erdinast-Vulcan suggests that Jones is a *'miles gloriosus'*, to whose typical comic role of 'be[ing] exposed . . . ridiculed' and 'trapped by his own boasting', Greene 'contrives to give . . . a heroic turn' (*Graham Greene's Childless Fathers* 78).
11. Erdinast-Vulcan comments: 'even . . . when [Plarr] knows that his father cannot be saved, he risks his own life . . . [because h]e is motivated by his father's idealism rather than the personal wish to save his father' (ibid. 94).
12. Storhoff also comments that the description of Castle as a 'man in love [who] walks through the world like an anarchist, carrying a time-bomb' is an explicit allusion to Conrad's mad professor' (59). Erdinast-Vulcan notes another Conradian echo of the nickname of 'the firm' for the British Intelligence Service in *The Human Factor* by 'The Great Trading Company' in Conrad's 'An Outpost of Progress', likewise, 'an anonymous overpowering system' whose people 'exploit and dehumanise the natives and themselves' (100).
13. In these terms, Greene perhaps arrives here at one of Bloom's more useful categories – the sixth and last stage of his scheme of influence, '*Apophrades*', or 'The Return of the Dead', where, Bloom suggests, 'the poem is now *held* open to the precursor, where once it *was* open, and the uncanny effect is that the new poem's achievement makes it seem to us, not as though the precursor were writing it, but as though the later poet himself had written the precursor's characteristic work' (Bloom 16).

Notes to Chapter 5: 'Dissolving into Laughter'

1. Northrop Frye remarks in *The Anatomy of Criticism* (1957) that 'An extraordinary number of comic stories . . . seem to approach a potentially tragic crisis near the end . . . a point at which the tone suddenly becomes serious, sentimental, or ominous of potential catastrophe' (179).

2. Greene extols the primitive and vulgar throughout his film reviews, which are collected in *The Pleasure Dome*.
3. The anonymous author of 'Graham Greene: The Man Within' remarks on 'the comical résumé of [Greene's] entire career, revisited in the company of his muse, a raffish old Catholic lady in *Travels With My Aunt*' (13).

Bibliography

Adamson, Judith, *The Dangerous Edge: Where Art and Politics Meet* (Basingstoke: Macmillan, 1990).

Allain, Marie-Françoise, *The Other Man: Conversations with Graham Greene*, trans. Guido Waldman (New York: Simon and Schuster, 1983).

Allott, Miriam, 'The Moral Situation in *The Quiet American*', in *Graham Greene*, ed. Harold Bloom (New York: Chelsea House, 1987) pp. 65–78.

——, 'Surviving the Course, Or a Novelist for All Seasons: Graham Greene's *The Honorary Consul*', in Douglas Jefferson and Graham Martin (eds), *The Uses of Fiction* (Milton Keynes: Open University Press, 1982) pp. 237–48.

Allott, Kenneth and Miriam Farris, *The Art of Graham Greene* (New York: Russell and Russell, 1963).

Atkins, John, *Graham Greene* (1957; London: Calder and Boyars, 1966).

Auden, W. H., 'The Guilty Vicarage', in *The Dyer's Hand and Other Essays* (New York: Random House, 1956, 1962) pp. 146–58.

Baines, Jocelyn, *Joseph Conrad: A Critical Biography* (New York: McGraw-Hill, 1960).

Bakhtin, Mikhail, *The Dialogic Imagination*, ed. Michael Holquist, trans. Caryl Emerson and Michael Holquist (Austin: University of Texas, 1981).

——, *Rabelais and His World*, trans. Hélène Iswolsky (1965; Bloomington: Indiana University Press, 1984).

Ballantyne, R. M., *The Coral Island* (1856), ed. J. S. Bratton (1856; Oxford: Oxford University Press, 1990).

Bate, Walter Jackson, *The Burden of the Past and the English Poet* (Cambridge, Mass.: Belknap, 1970).

Bitterli, Urs, *Conrad, Malraux, Greene: Schriftsteller und Kolonialismus* (Zurich: Bensiger, 1973).

Bloom, Harold, *The Anxiety of Influence* (New York: Oxford University Press, 1973).

Boardman, Gwen, *Graham Greene: The Aesthetics of Exploration* (Gainesville: University Press of Florida, 1971).

Bonney, William, 'Politics, Perception, and Gender in Conrad's *Lord Jim* and Greene's *The Quiet American*', *Conradiana* **23** (1991) pp. 99–123.

Brooks, Peter, *Reading for the Plot* (New York: Random House, 1984).

Bruffee, Kenneth, *Elegiac Romance: Cultural Change and the Loss of the Hero in Modern Fiction* (Ithaca: Cornell University Press, 1983).

Bryden, Ronald, 'Graham Greene, Alas', *Spectator*, 28 September 1962, pp. 441–2.

——, 'Graham Greene Discusses with Ronald Bryden the Collected Edition of his Novels which was Published Not Long Ago', *Listener*, 23 April 1970, p. 544.

Buchan, John, *The Thirty-Nine Steps* (1915; San Diego, University of California Extension, 1978).

Buckley, J. H., *Season of Youth* (Cambridge, Mass.: Harvard University Press, 1974).

Busza, Andrzej, *Conrad's Polish Literary Background* (Rome: Institutum Historicum Polonicum Romae, 1966).

Butts, Dennis, 'Introduction', Rider H. Haggad, *King Solomon's Mines* (Oxford: Oxford University Press, 1989).

Cawelti, John G., *Adventure, Mystery, Romance* (Chicago: University of Chicago Press, 1976).

Cheney, Lynne, 'Joseph Conrad's *The Secret Agent* and Graham Greene's *It's a Battlefield*: A Study in Structural Meaning', *Modern Fiction Studies* **16** (1970) pp. 117–31.

Childers, Erskine, *The Riddle of the Sands* (London: Smith, Elder, 1903).

Christie, Agatha, *The Murder of Roger Ackroyd* (1926; New York: Pocket Books, 1929).

Collits, Terry, 'Imperialism, Marxism, Conrad: A Political Reading of *Victory*', *Textual Practice* **3** (1989) pp. 303–32.

Conrad, Joseph, *Almayer's Folly* (1895; Harmondsworth: Penguin, 1986).

——, *The Arrow of Gold* (1919; Garden City, NY: Doubleday, Page, 1924).

——, 'Autocracy and War' (1905), in *Notes on Life and Letters* (1921; Garden City, NY: Doubleday, Page, 1924) pp. 83–114.

——, *Chance* (1913; Garden City, NY: Doubleday, Page, 1924).

——, 'The Congo Diary' (1899), in *Heart of Darkness* (New York: W.W. Norton, 1988) pp. 159–66.

——, 'The End of the Tether' (1903), in *Youth* (Garden City, NY: Doubleday, Page, 1924).

——, *Heart of Darkness* (1899; New York: W. W. Norton, 1988).

——, 'Henry James: An Appreciation' (1905), in *Joseph Conrad on Fiction*, ed. Walter F. Wright (Lincoln: University of Nebraska Press, 1964) pp. 82–8.

——, *Lord Jim* (1900; Oxford: Oxford University Press, 1983).

——, *The Nigger of the Narcissus* (1897; Garden City, NY: Doubleday, Page, 1924).

——, *Nostromo* (1904; Harmondsworth: Penguin, 1963).

——, *An Outcast of the Islands* (1896; Garden City, NY: Doubleday, Page, 1924).

——, 'An Outpost of Progress' (1898), in *Selected Tales from Conrad*, ed. Nigel Stewart (London: Faber & Faber, 1977) pp. 14–42.

——, *A Personal Record* (1912; Garden City, NY: Doubleday, Page, 1924).

——, *The Rescue* (1919; Garden City, NY: Doubleday, Page, 1924).

——, *The Rover* (1923; Garden City, NY: Doubleday, Page, 1924).

——, *The Secret Agent* (1907; Harmondsworth: Penguin, 1986).

——, *The Shadow-Line* (1915; Oxford: Oxford University Press, 1985).

——, *Suspense* (Garden City, NY: Doubleday, Page, 1925).

——, *Typhoon and Other Stories* (1903; Garden City, NY: Doubleday, Page, 1924).

——, *Under Western Eyes* (1911; Harmondsworth: Penguin, 1985).

——, *Victory* (1915; Garden City, NY: Doubleday, Page, 1924).

——, *Youth* (1902; Garden City, NY: Doubleday, Page, 1924).

—— and Ford Madox Hueffer, *Romance* (1903; Garden City, NY: Doubleday, Page, 1924).

Coppola, Francis Ford (dir.), *Apocalypse Now*, with Marlon Brando and Martin Sheen, 1979.

Cornwell, John, 'The Confessions of Graham Greene', *Observer*, 24 September 1989, pp. 33–4.

Couto, Maria, *Graham Greene: On the Frontier* (New York: St Martin's Press, 1988).

Defoe, Daniel, *Robinson Crusoe* (1719–20), ed. Harry Shefter (New York: Pocket Books, c.1974).

Desmond, John F., 'The Heart of the Matter: The Mystery of the Real in *Monsignor Quixote*', *Religion and Literature* **22** (1990) pp. 59–78.

Devereux, James A., S.J., 'Catholic Matters in the Correspondence of Evelyn Waugh and Graham Greene', *Journal of Modern Literature* **14** (1987) pp. 111–26.

Dickens, Charles, *Bleak House* (1853), ed. Norman Page (Harmondsworth: Penguin Classics, 1985).

——, *Little Dorrit* (1857), ed. John Holloway (Harmondsworth: Penguin, 1967).

Dostoevsky, Fyodor, *Crime and Punishment* (1866), trans. David Mararshack (Harmondsworth: Penguin, c.1966).

——, *The Possessed* (1871–2), trans. Constance Garnett (New York: Macmillan, 1948).

Doyle, Sir Arthur Conan, 'The Adventure of the Bruce Partingdon Plans' (1917), in *Sherlock Holmes: The Complete Novels and Stories*, 2 vols (New York: Bantam Books, 1986) vol. 2.

Eliot, T. S., *Complete Poems and Plays: 1909–1950* (New York: Harcourt, Brace, 1952).

——, 'Hamlet', in *Elizabethan Essays* (New York: Haskell House, 1964).

Erdinast-Vulcan, Daphna, 'Conrad's Double-Edged Arrow', *Conradiana* **20** (1988) pp. 215–28.

——, *Graham Greene's Childless Fathers* (London: Macmillan, 1988).

Ferns, C. S., '"Brown is not Greene": Narrative Role in *The Comedians*', *College Literature* **12** (1985) pp. 60–67.

Fluck, Winifred, 'Fiction and Fictionality in Popular Culture: Some Observations on the Aesthetics of Popular Culture', *Popular Culture* **21**: 4 (1988) pp. 49–62.

Fögel, Aaron, *Coercion to Speak* (Cambridge, Mass.: Harvard University Press, 1985).

Ford, Ford Madox, 'Joseph Conrad: A Remembrance', in *Portraits from Life* (Chicago: H. Regneny, 1937).

Friedman, Alan Warren, 'Conrad's Picaresque Narrator: Marlow's Journey From "Youth" Through *Chance*', in W. T. Zyla and W. M. Aycock, *Joseph Conrad: Theory and World Fiction* (Lubbock: Texas Technical University Press, 1974) pp. 17–39.

Frye, Northrop, *The Anatomy of Criticism* (London: Oxford University Press, 1957).

Gaston, Georg M. A., *The Pursuit of Salvation* (Troy, NY: Whitson, 1984).

Gilbert, Sandra and Susan Gubar, *The War of the Words*, vol. 1 of *No Man's Land*, 2 vols (Binghamton, NY: Ballou Press, 1989).

'Graham Greene: The Man Within', in Samuel Hynes (ed.), *Graham Greene: A Collection of Critical Essays* (Englewood Cliffs, NJ: Prentice Hall, 1972).
Green, Martin, *Dreams of Adventure, Deeds of Empire* (New York: Basic Books, 1979).
Greene, Graham, 'Appointment Books', 1957–77 (Harry Ransom Humanities Research Center, Austin, Texas).
——, *Brighton Rock* (1938; New York: Viking Penguin, 1977).
——, *A Burnt-Out Case* (1960; New York: Viking Penguin, 1977).
——, 'A Burnt-Out Case', Composite T and Tccms (ii. 182 pp.) (Harry Ransom Humanities Research Center, Austin, Texas).
——, *The Captain and the Enemy* (London: Reinhardt, 1988).
——, 'A Chance for Mr Lever', in *Collected Stories* (New York: Viking, 1955–72) pp. 490–509.
——, *Collected Essays* (New York: Viking, 1969).
——, *Collected Stories* (New York: Viking, 1955–72).
——, *The Comedians* (1966; Harmondsworth: Penguin, 1980).
——, 'Diaries', 1932–33 (Harry Ransom Humanities Research Center, Austin, Texas).
——, *Dr Fischer of Geneva or the Bomb Party* (Harmondsworth: Penguin, 1980).
——, *The End of the Affair* (New York: Viking, 1951).
——, *England Made Me* (1935; Harmondsworth: Penguin, 1970).
——, *A Gun For Sale* (1936; Harmondsworth: Penguin, 1974).
——, *The Heart of the Matter* (1948; Harmondsworth: Penguin, 1971).
——, *The Honorary Consul* (1973; Harmondsworth: Penguin, 1974).
——, *The Human Factor* (Harmondsworth: Penguin, 1978).
——, *In Search of a Character* (New York: Viking, 1961).
——, *It's a Battlefield* (1933; New York: Viking, 1977).
——, *Journey without Maps* (1936; Harmondsworth: Penguin, 1980).
——, *The Lawless Roads* (1939; Harmondsworth: Penguin, 1981).
——, 'The Last Buchan', in *Collected Essays* (New York: Viking, 1969) pp. 223–5.
——, *Loser Takes All* (1955; Harmondsworth: Penguin, 1977).
——, *The Man Within* (1929; Harmondsworth: Penguin, 1977).
——, *The Ministry of Fear* (1943; Harmondsworth: Penguin, 1974).
——, *Monsignor Quixote* (1982; Harmondsworth: Penguin, 1983).
——, *The Name of Action* (Garden City, NY: Doubleday, Doran, 1931).
——, *Our Man in Havana* (1958; Harmondsworth: Penguin, 1971).
——, *The Pleasure Dome* (Oxford: Oxford University Press, 1980).
——, *The Power and the Glory* (1940; Harmondsworth: Penguin, 1971).
——, *The Quiet American* (1955; Harmondsworth: Penguin, 1977).
——, 'Remembering Mr Jones' (1937), in *Collected Essays* (New York: Viking, 1969) pp. 182–84.
——, *Rumour at Nightfall* (Garden City, NY: Doubleday, Doran, 1932).
——, *A Sort of Life* (New York: Simon and Schuster, 1971).
——, *Stamboul Train* (1932; Harmondsworth: Penguin, 1975).
——, *The Tenth Man* (London: Bodley Head, 1985).
——, *The Third Man* (1947), in *The Third Man/The Fallen Idol* (Harmondsworth: Penguin, 1976).

——, *Travels with My Aunt* (1969; Harmondsworth: Penguin, 1971).
——, *Ways of Escape* (London: Bodley Head, 1980).
—— and Carol Reed, *The Third Man* (New York: Simon and Schuster, 1968).
Gregor, Ian, '*The End of the Affair*', in Samuel Hynes (ed.), *Graham Greene: A Collection of Critical Essays* (Englewood Cliffs, NJ: Prentice Hall, 1972).
Guerard, Albert, *Conrad the Novelist* (1958; Cambridge: Atheneum, 1967).
Haggard, Rider H., *King Solomon's Mines* (1885), ed. Dennis Butts (Oxford: Oxford University Press, 1989).
——, *She* (1887), ed. Daniel Karlin (Oxford: Oxford University Press, 1991).
Harkness, Bruce, 'Conrad, Graham Greene, and Film', *Joseph Conrad: Theory and World Fiction*, ed. T. Zyla Wolodymyr and Wendell M. Agcock, *Proceedings of the Comparative Literature Symposium* (Lubbock: Texas Technical University Press, 1974).
Hay, Eloise Knapp, *The Political Novels of Joseph Conrad* (1963; Chicago: Univesity Press of Chicago Press, 1981).
Heimer, Jackson W., 'Patterns of Betrayal in the Works of Joseph Conrad', *Ball State University Forum* **8** (1967) pp. 30–9.
Herbert, Christopher, 'Comedy: The World of Pleasure', *Genre* **17** (1984) pp. 401–16.
Hernadi, Paul, 'Entertaining Commitments: A Reception Theory of Literary Genres', *Poetics: International Review for the Theory of Literature* **10** (1981) pp. 195–211.
Higdon, David Leon, 'Joseph Conrad and Graham Greene', *L'Epoque Conradienne*, May 1979, pp. 29–44.
Hirsch, E. D., Jr, *Validity in Interpretation* (New York: Yale University Press, 1967).
Hyland, Peter, 'The Little Woman in the *Heart of Darkness*', *Conradiana* **20** (1988) pp. 3–11.
Hynes, Joseph, 'Two Affairs Revisited', *Twentieth Century Literature: A Scholarly and Critical Journal* **33** (1987) pp. 234–53.
Hynes, Samuel (ed.), *Graham Greene: A Collection of Critical Essays* (Englewood Cliffs, NJ: Prentice Hall, 1972).
Jacobson, Roman, 'Two Aspects of Language and Two Types of Aphasic Disturbance', in *Fundamentals of Language* ('S-Gravenhage: Mouton, 1956).
James, Henry, *The Princess Casamassimma* (1886), ed. Derek Brewer (Harmondsworth: Penguin, 1986).
——, *The Turn of the Screw* (1898; New York: Airmont, c.1967).
Jameson, Fredric, *The Political Unconscious* (Ithaca, NY: Cornell University Press, 1981).
Jensen, Paul M., *The Cinema of Fritz Lang* (New York: A. S. Barnes, 1969).
Johnstone, Richard, *The Will to Believe* (Oxford: Oxford University Press, 1982).
Karl, Frederick, *Joseph Conrad: The Three Lives* (New York: Farrar, Strauss & Giroux, 1979).
——, *A Reader's Guide to Joseph Conrad* (New York: Farrar, Strauss & Giroux, 1969).
—— and Laurence Davies (eds), *The Collected Letters of Joseph Conrad*, vols I–VI (Cambridge: Cambridge University Press, 1983–).

Kenner, Hugh, 'Modernism and What Happened to It', essays in *Criticism: A Quarterly Journal of Literary Criticism* **37** (1987) pp. 97–109.

Kermode, Frank, 'Graham Greene's Eggs and Crosses', in Samuel Hynes (ed.), *Graham Greene: A Collection of Critical Essays* (Englewood Cliffs, NJ: Prentice Hall, 1972).

Korn, Frederick Benjamin, 'Condemned to Consequences: A Study of the Tragic Processes in Three Works by Joseph Conrad and Graham Greene' (Diss., University of Illinois at Urbana-Champaign, 1973).

Land, Stephen K., *Conrad and the Paradox of Plot* (London: Macmillan, 1984).

Lang, Fritz (dir.), *M.*, with Peter Lorre and Gustav Grungens, 1931.

——, *Spies*, with Rudolph Klein-Rogge and Gerda Maurus, 1928.

Larson, Michael, 'Laughing Till the Tears Come: Greene's Failed Comedian', *Renascence* **41** (1989) pp. 177–87.

Leavis, Q. D., *Fiction and the Reading Public* (London: Chatto and Windus, 1932).

Lodge, David, *Graham Greene* (New York: Columbia University Press, 1966).

McConnell, Frank D., *The Spoken Seen* (Baltimore: Johns Hopkins University Press, 1975).

Melada, Ivan, 'Graham Greene and the Munitions Makers: The Historical Context of *A Gun For Sale*', *Studies in the Novel* **13** (1981) pp. 303–21.

Meyer, Bernard, *Joseph Conrad: A Psychoanalytic Biography* (Princeton: Princeton University Press, 1967).

Meyers, Jeffrey, 'Conrad's Influence on Modern Writers', *Twentieth-Century Literature* **36** (1990) pp. 186–206.

Morson, Gary Saul, 'Bakhtin's Prosaics: The Surplus of Humaneness', Div. on Narrative, MLA Convention, Chicago, 29 December 1990.

Moser, Thomas, *Joseph Conrad: Achievement and Decline* (Hamden, CT: Archon, 1957).

Moss, Robert F., *The Films of Carol Reed* (Basingstoke: Macmillan, 1987).

Murray, Robert Davis, 'The Struggle with Genre in *The End of the Affair*', *Genre* **XVIII** (Winter 1985) pp. 397–411.

Najder, Zdzislaw, 'Joseph Conrad's *The Secret Agent* or the Melodrama of Reality', in *Melodrama*, ed. Daniel Gerould (New York: Literary Forum, 1980) pp. 159–66.

Nehrung, Neil, 'Revolt into Style: Graham Greene Meets the Sex Pistols', *PMLA* **106** (1991) pp. 222–37.

Nelson, Bill, 'Evil as Illusion in the Detective Story', *Clues: A Journal of Detection* **1** (1980) pp. 9–14.

Nettels, Elsa, *James and Conrad* (Athens: University of Georgia Press, 1977).

Orwell, George, 'The Sanctified Sinner', in Samuel Hynes (ed.), *Graham Greene: A Collection of Critical Essays* (Englewood Cliffs, NJ: Prentice Hall, 1972).

Palmer, Jerry, *Thrillers* (New York: St Martin's Press, 1987).

Phelan, James (ed.), *Reading Narrative: Form, Ethics, Ideology* (Columbus: Ohio State University Press, 1989).

Phillips, Gene D., 'Graham Greene on the Screen', in Samuel Hynes (ed.), *Graham Greene: A Collection of Critical Essays* (Englewood Cliffs, NJ: Prentice Hall, 1972).

Pittock, Murray, 'Rider Haggard and *Heart of Darkness*', *Conradiana* **19** (1987) pp. 206–8.
Polhemus, Robert, *Comic Faith* (Chicago: University of Chicago Press, 1980).
Rabinowitz, Peter J., *Before Reading* (Ithaca: Cornell University Press, 1987).
Radell, Karen Marguerite, *Affirmation in a Moral Wasteland: A Comparison of Ford Madox Ford and Graham Greene* (New York: Peter Lang, 1987).
Rader, Ralph, '*Lord Jim* and the Formal Development of the English Novel', in James Phelan (ed.), *Reading Narrative* (Columbus: Ohio State University Press, 1989).
Reed, Sir Carol (dir.), *Outcast of the Islands*, with Trevor Howard, Sir Robert Morley, and Ralph Richardson, London Films, 1952.
——, *The Third Man*, with Joseph Cotton, Trevor Howard, and Orson Welles, London Films, 1949.
Riveros-Schaffer, Enrique, 'Flights from the Polis' (Diss., University of California, San Diego, 1982).
Routh, Michael, 'Greene's Parody of Farce and Comedy in *The Comedians*', *Renascence* **26** (1974) pp. 139–51.
Ruppel, Richard, '*Heart of Darkness* and the Popular Exotic Stories of the 1890s', *Conradiana* **21** (1989) pp. 3–14.
Said, Edward, 'Under Gringo Eyes', *Harper's Magazine*, April 1981, pp. 70–72.
Scholes, Robert, 'Stillborn Literature', in Paul Hernadi (ed.), *The Horizon of Literature* (Lincoln: University of Nebraska Press, 1982) pp. 53–69.
Sharrock, Roger, *Saints, Sinners and Comedians* (Notre Dame: University of Notre Dame Press, 1984).
Sherry, Norman, *Conrad and his World* (London: Thames and Hudson, 1972).
——, *Conrad's Eastern World* (London: Cambridge University Press, 1966).
——, *Conrad's Western World* (London: Cambridge University Press, 1971).
—— (ed.), *Joseph Conrad: The Critical Heritage* (London: Routledge Kegan Paul, 1973).
——, *The Life of Graham Greene*, vol. 1 (London: Cape, 1989).
Shires, Linda M., 'The "Privileged" Reader and Narrative Methodology in *Lord Jim*', *Conradiana* **17** (1985) pp. 19–30.
Shuttleworth, Martin and Simon Raven, 'The Art of Fiction: Graham Greene', in Samuel Hynes (ed.), *Graham Greene: A Collection of Critical Essays* (Englewood Cliffs, NJ: Prentice Hall, 1972).
Silverstein, Marc, 'After the Fall: The World of Graham Greene's Thrillers', *Novel: A Forum on Fiction* **22** (1988) pp. 24–44.
Simmons, Allan H., 'Ambiguity as Meaning: The Subversion of Suspense in *Almayer's Folly*', *The Conradian* **14** (1989) pp. 1–18.
Smith, F. Kinchin, *Teach Yourself Latin*, ed. Leonard Cutts (London: English Universities Press, 1986).
Smith, Graham, *The Achievement of Graham Greene* (Sussex: Harvester, 1986).
Snape, Ray, 'Plaster Saints and Flesh and Blood Sinners', *Durham University Journal* **74** (1982) pp. 241–50.
——, 'The Political Novels of Graham Greene', *Durham University Journal* **75** (1982) pp. 73–81.
Stevenson, Robert Louis, *Catriona* (1893; Edinburgh: Chambers, 1980).
——, *Treasure Island* (1883; Philadelphia: Courage Books, 1989).

—— and Fanny de Grift Stevenson, *The Dynamiter* (London: Longmans, Green, 1885).
Stewart, David H., 'Kipling, Conrad and the Dark Heart', *Conradiana* **19** (1987) pp. 195–205.
Storhoff, Gary P., 'To Choose a Different Loyalty: Greene's Politics in *The Human Factor*', *Literature* **11** (1984) pp. 59–66.
Stratford, Philip, *Faith and Fiction: Creative Process in Greene and Mauriac* (Indiana: University of Notre Dame, 1964).
Thomas, Brian, *An Underground Fate: The Idiom of Romance in the Later Novels of Graham Greene* (Athens: University Press of Georgia, 1989).
Thorburn, David, *Conrad's Romanticism* (New Haven: Yale University Press, 1974).
Todorov, Tzvetan, 'The Typology of Detective Fiction', in *The Poetics of Prose*, trans. Richard Howard (Oxford: Blackwell, 1977) pp. 42–52.
Turgenev, Ivan, *Virgin Soil* (1877; New York: Grove Press, 1956).
Unamuno, Miguel de, *The Life of Don Quixote and Sancho*, trans. Homer P. Earle (New York: Alfred A. Knopf, 1927).
——, *The Tragic Sense of Life*, trans. J. E. Crawford Fitch (London: Macmillan, 1931).
Walker, Ronald. G., 'World without End: An Approach to Narrative Structure in Greene's *The End of the Affair*', *Texas Studies in Literature and Language* **26** (1984) pp. 218–41.
Walton, James, 'Conrad, Dickens, and the Detective Novel', *Nineteenth-Century Fiction* **23** (1969) pp. 446–62.
Watts, C. T., *The Deceptive Text* (Sussex: Harvester, 1984).
——, *Joseph Conrad: A Literary Life* (Basingstoke: Macmillan, 1984).
——, (ed.), *Joseph Conrad's Letters to R. B. Cunninghame Graham* (Cambridge: Cambridge University Press, 1969).
——, *Nostromo* (New York: Penguin, 1990).
West, Richard, 'Note on Graham Greene and Conrad', *Spectator* **240** (20 May 1978) p. 5.
Wollaeger, Mark A., *Joseph Conrad and the Fictions of Skepticism* (Stanford: Stanford University Press, 1990).
Wright, Andrew, *Fictional Discourse and Historical Space* (San Diego: University of California Press, 1988).
Wright, Peter, *Spycatcher* (New York: Dell, 1987).
Yeats, W. B., *The Poems of W. B. Yeats* (London: Macmillan, 1979).
Yonge, Charlotte, *The Little Duke, Richard the Fearless* (London: Macmillan, 1898).
Zyla, Wolodymyr T. and Wendell M. Aycock (eds), *Joseph Conrad: Theory and World Fiction*, Proceedings of the Comparative Literature Symposium (Lubbock: Texas Technical University Press, 1974).

Index